# Our Northern Shrubs

AND HOW TO IDENTIFY THEM

Panicled Dogwood, *Cornus candidissima*.

# Our Northern Shrubs

AND HOW TO IDENTIFY THEM

BY HARRIET L. KEELER

with a new Appendix of Nomenclatural Changes by
EDWARD G. VOSS
*Curator and Associate Professor*
*University of Michigan Herbarium*

Dover Publications, Inc., New York

Published in Canada by General Publishing Company, Ltd.,
30 Lesmill Road, Don Mills, Toronto, Ontario.
Published in the United Kingdom by Constable and Company,
Ltd., 10 Orange Street, London WC2.


This Dover edition, first published in 1969, is an unabridged republication of the work originally published
by Charles Scribner's Sons in 1903. A new Appendix
of Nomenclatural Changes has been prepared for this
edition by Dr. Edward G. Voss. The Glossary of Latin
Specific Epithets has been revised and corrected.


*Standard Book Number: 486-21989-5*
*Library of Congress Catalog Card Number: 68–9484*

Manufactured in the United States of America

DOVER PUBLICATIONS, INC.
180 Varick Street
New York, N.Y. 10014

# PREFACE

THE shrubs described in this volume are those which find their most congenial home in the region extending from the Atlantic Ocean to the Mississippi River, and from Canada to the northern boundaries of our Southern States; together with those imported shrubs which have so long adorned our yards and gardens that we have almost forgotten their foreign origin.

The volume is prepared not only for the amateur botanist who seeks a more complete description of plants than the text-books in common use afford; not only for the lover of nature who desires a personal acquaintance with the bushes that grow in the fields and the fence corners; but also to serve those who are engaged in the establishment and decoration of city parks, roadways and boulevards; those who are seeking to beautify country roadsides, school-yards and railway stations, as well as those who, in the decoration of their own home grounds, would gladly use our native shrubs were their habits and character better understood.

It is hoped that this volume may lead to a clearer appreciation of the wonderful variety, the exquisite beauty and the real value of that neglected part of our native flora, the shrub.

The author is glad to acknowledge her indebtedness to the following books of reference: Britton and Brown's "Illustrated Flora of the United States and Canada," Bailey's "Cyclopedia of American Horticulture," Emerson's Report on the Trees and Shrubs of Massachusetts, Gray's "Manual of Botany," Britton's "Manual of the Flora of the Northern States and Canada," Bailey's "Evolution of Our Native Fruits," Card's "Bush Fruits," and the magazine *Garden and Forest*.

The extracts from the works of Lowell, Emerson, Whittier, Torrey, Thoreau, and Higginson are used with the permission of the publishers, Messrs. Houghton, Mifflin & Co.; that from Fred W. Card, with the permission of the Macmillan Co.; that from Joseph Y. Bergen, with the permission of Ginn & Co.

The quotations from the writings of Professor L. H. Bailey, Mr. J. G. Jack and Mr. Jackson Dawson are made by the kind consent of the authors.

Especial acknowledgment is due to Professor Charles S. Sargent, who so generously placed the magnificent resources of the Arnold Arboretum at the service of the author; and also to Mr. Alfred Rehder, whose expert knowledge has been invaluable in deciding every case of doubt.

The full page illustrations are from photographs, many of which were made by Mr. Alfred Rehder of the Arnold Arboretum, the remainder by Decker & Co., and by the Edmondson Studio Co., both of Cleveland, Ohio.

The outline pictures are the work of Miss Mary Keffer of Lake Erie College, Painesville, Ohio.

Thanks for specimens kindly sent upon request are due to Mr. Watson of Plymouth, Mass.; Gen. G. W. Shurtleff, of Oberlin, Ohio, and Mr. Michael H. Hovarth, landscape gardener and forester of the parks of Cleveland, Ohio.

# CONTENTS

# GENERA AND SPECIES

# GENERA AND SPECIES

# GENERA AND SPECIES

## GENERA AND SPECIES

## GENERA AND SPECIES

# ILLUSTRATIONS

# ILLUSTRATIONS

## ILLUSTRATIONS

# ILLUSTRATIONS

# ILLUSTRATIONS

# GUIDE TO THE SHRUBS

Leaves deciduous, compound :

*a.*—Stems with spines or prickles............
- *Raspberries*
- *Blackberries*
- *Roses*
- *Prickly Ash*
- *Rose Acacia*

*b.*—Stems without spines or prickles......
- *Sumachs*
- *Elders*
- *Pea Family*
- *Shrub Yellow-root*
- *Bladder-nut*
- *Dwarf Buckeye*
- *Wafer Ash*
- *Shrubby Cinquefoil*

Leaves deciduous, simple, opposite on the stem..
- *Dogwood Family*
- *Honeysuckle Family*
- *Staff-tree Family*
- *St. John's-worts*
- *Strawberry-shrub*
- *Button-bush*
- *Oleaster Family*

Leaves deciduous, simple, alternate on the stem :

*a.*—Stems prickly ; flowers yellow or greenish....
- *Barberries*
- *Gooseberries*

*b.*—Flowers large, white or purplish, solitary.......
- *Magnolias*
- *Stuartia*
- *Gordonia*

*c.*—Flowers white, clustered, in umbels or corymbs or spikes...........................
- *Plums*
- *Cherries*
- *Choke-berries*
- *Exochorda*
- *Clethra*

*d.*—Flowers white, pale pink or greenish, bell-like or urn-shaped ...........
- *Huckleberry Family*
- *Many genera of the Heath Family*

*e.*—Flowers white, pink or yellow ; each corolla made up of a tube and a spreading border..............................
- *Lilacs*
- *Privet*
- *Azaleas*
- *Rhodora*
- *Mezeron*

*f.*—Flowers yellow:

    Appearing late in autumn.................*Witch Hazel*

    Appearing very early in spring ..............*Spice-bush*

*g.*—Fruit conspicuous, persistent:

    Scarlet....................................*Holly Family*

    Gray, covered with wax ......................*Bayberry*

*h.*—Flowers in catkins.... .............. $\begin{cases} Willows \\ Birches \\ Alders \\ Hazels \\ Chestnut \\ Bayberry\ Family \end{cases}$

Shrubs with alternate leaves not mentioned above: Hudsonia, Tamarisk, Deutzia, Forsythia, Althæa, Japan Quince, Currants.

Leaves evergreen:

*a.*—Very narrow....................... $\begin{cases} Yew\ Family \\ Crowberry\ Family \end{cases}$

*b.*—Large:

    Flower azalea-like......................*Rhododendron*

    Flower saucer-shaped................... *Kalmias*

*c.*—Two to three inches long; woolly beneath....*Labrador Tea*

*d.*—Arctic-alpine plants.................. $\begin{cases} Phyllodoce \\ Cassiope \\ Alpine\ Azalea \end{cases}$

*e.*—Stems creeping or trailing.................... $\begin{cases} Mayflower \\ Snowberry \\ Bearberry \\ Cranberry \end{cases}$

*f.*—Flowers bell-shaped or urn-shaped.....*Several genera of the Heath Family*

Plants with evergreen leaves not mentioned above: Inkberry, Evergreen Thorn, *Daphne cneorum,* Sand Myrtle.

## SIGNS USED IN THIS BOOK.

(´) Acute accent over a vowel marks the short sound.

(`) Grave accent over a vowel marks the long sound.

(°) The sign of degree is used for feet.

(´) When used with figures means inches.

# INTRODUCTION

## THE SHRUB

THE dividing line between tree and shrub is of little importance botanically; it is simply a matter of one stem or many stems. Rising from the ground, the tree uplifts its branches, leaves, flowers and fruit upon its trunk, a massive, single shaft. A shrub rises from its roots with a group of stems whose number forbids to any one of them the attainment of great size. Because of this unity of central structure a tree has an individuality which is denied to a plant that may have five stems one year and ten the next.

The position of the shrub is distinctly secondary; and the burden of the inferior race is upon it. A tree may be valued for what it is, but a shrub is rated for just what it can do. It must render a service to compensate for its cultivation. This service may be one of beauty, through its flowers; or of use, by its fruit; or its foliage or habit of growth may be especially attractive, or of such a nature as will give it value as a shield or a cover for waste and barren places. A shrub which cannot render some such service is held to be a cumberer of the ground.

The economic value of the shrub upon the forest-floor is very great. It holds the fallen leaves in place against the force of the wind; it conserves the water supply; under its protecting and fostering care the wreckage of the forest is transformed into vegetable humus, an almost indispensable constituent of a fertile soil.

Probably because it has not yet been made the subject of careful study, the duration of life, even among those shrubs that have been longest in cultivation and are best known, is not very well understood. The short generation, however, implies a relatively short life period. This short generation tends to the multiplication of species. Seed variations can more easily perpetuate themselves. Bud variations, technically known as sports, in the case of cultivated shrubs, can be readily observed and reproduced within a reasonably limited time. So that the limited life of the shrub serves both as an aid and a reward to the observant gardener in multiplying the variants of the most valued species.

Our northern climate is so favorable to the growth of hardy shrubs that if their value were fully and generally comprehended they would play a much more important part than they now do in lawn and park decoration. Their beauty, unfortunately, is often lessened, if not wholly destroyed, by careless or ignorant pruning. Severe pruning tends to enfeeble both shrub and tree, and the removal of large branches usually interferes with the natural and therefore more graceful lines of either. Shrubs will be in their best form and vigor the year through when no pruning is attempted beyond the thinning out of the weaker and overshadowed branches. Moreover, shrubs have a winter beauty that severe pruning entirely destroys. In the leafless season, a mass of shrubbery is enveloped with a hazy mist of delicate color which comes from the coalescence of the different tints of the barks of the small branches; and this color, together with the fine tracery of the spray, adds much to the winter landscape.

When shrubs are planted for mass effect, the treatment of the group differs from that given to a single bush, but even then the plants should not be cut back so far as to impair their vigor. The proper time for pruning depends upon the habit of the plant. Those which bloom early on wood of the previous year's growth should not be pruned in autumn or in early spring; for this removes all the flower buds, and consequently no flowers are produced. These shrubs should be pruned immediately after the blooming period. On the other hand, shrubs which bloom late, on wood of the current year, should be pruned after the leaves fall in autumn, or in early spring before growth begins.

In view of the great sums expended by towns and cities in the care and decoration of roadways, park lanes and boulevards, in order that they may be shrub-bordered and tree-shaded, it is difficult to comprehend why our country roadsides are so generally forlorn, cheerless, barren, and desolate. Were the wild growth of shrubbery encouraged, cared for and properly controlled, nature would decorate the country roadside with a generosity that no Park Commissioner could emulate. With very little or no expenditure of money, and with a minimum of intelligent care and protection on the part of the owners of the land, the country roadside might be a source of pleasure to all who pass, as well as a most valuable arboretum of its native flora.

# Our Northern Shrubs

AND HOW TO IDENTIFY THEM

Shrub Yellow-root, *Xanthorrhiza apiifolia*.

Leaves 3′ to 6′ long.  Flowers $\frac{5}{16}$′ across.

# RANUNCULACEÆ—CROWFOOT FAMILY

## SHRUB YELLOW-ROOT

*Xanthorrhìza apiifòlia.*

*Xanthorrhiza,* compounded of two Greek words, *xanthos,* yellow, and *rhiza,* a root. *Apiifolia,* leaves like those of celery.

A low shrub of upright stems, two to three feet high, growing along the shady banks of streams in Pennsylvania and New York and in the mountains of the South. Suckers freely; roots long, slender, deep yellow; from their bitter juice the Indians procured a yellow dye.

*Bark.*—Outer bark yellowish brown; the inner bark yellow; branchlets pale greenish gray.

*Winter buds.*—One slender, pointed, terminal bud about an inch long crowns the stem; two or three small, lateral buds appear somewhat below.

*Leaves.*—Alternate, pinnately compound, sometimes bipinnate, three to six inches long; leaflets five, ovate or oblong, incisely cleft or divided, and coarsely toothed, sessile, wedge-shaped at base, one and one-half to three inches long. They come out of the bud involute, pale green, hairy, and shining; when full grown are bright green above, paler beneath. Autumnal tints are either bright yellow, or a glowing reddish purple, melting from dark bronze into paler tints; two plants may stand side by side, one purple, the other yellow. Petioles long, slender, clasping.

3

*Flowers.*—April, May, with or before the leaves. Small, starlike, prune-purple shading to brown ; in compound drooping racemes which are produced, together with the leaves, from the terminal bud.

*Calyx.*—Sepals five, petaloid, ovate, acute, imbricate in bud.

*Corolla.*—Petals five, hypogynous, much smaller than the sepals, dark prune, obscurely two-lobed, slightly concave, raised on a claw.

*Stamens.*—Five to ten, hypogynous, filaments short ; anthers large for the size of the flower.

*Pistil.*—Carpels five to fifteen, entirely distinct, sessile, pointed with curved styles, two-ovuled ; one ovule aborts, making the pod one-seeded.

*Fruit.*—Follicles, borne in small clusters along the axis of the raceme, greenish yellow, inflated, one-seeded, curved at apex, minutely beaked, inconspicuous. August.

This tiny shrub is not very well known, there is so little about it to attract attention. A botanist finds it interesting because it belongs to the *Ranunculaceæ*, whose genera are chiefly herbs. The landscape gardener values it for its hardy, free-growing habit, both in sun and shade; and uses it as a dwarf undershrub to clothe the ground under trees or to carry up the line of green from the grass to the higher plants. In winter, each stem and branchlet bears one terminal bud with two or three small lateral ones. Late in April or in early May, this terminal bud opens and there comes forth, together with the leaves, a cluster of racemes—sometimes single and sometimes compound—of tiny, five-pointed, prune-colored stars, each with a golden centre. The central stem of the flower cluster, and the short stems that bear the blossoms are all of the same rich purple color. Botanically the points of the stars are sepals; the corolla is so small that it must be searched for; and the stamens make the golden centre. The leaves crown the stem, and as they are long and the stem is short the effect is that of full foliage. The autumnal tints vary from deep purple to glowing yellow and the leaves persist until beaten off by the storms of winter.

# MAGNOLIÀCEÆ—MAGNOLIA FAMILY

## MAGNOLIA

*Magnòlia.*

Named after Pierre Magnol, professor of medicine and director of the botanic garden at Montpellier, France, from 1698 to 1715.

The early flowering magnolias must surely be counted among the pleasant sights of the spring-time. Natives of China and Japan, they have readily accepted new conditions and, perhaps, are better known to the general public than are our own species. They appear in the original types, together with a goodly number of hybrids; and, showy and striking, command attention wherever seen.

The Chinese White Magnolia or Yulan, *Magnolia conspicua*, was the first of the Asiatic magnolias to bloom in English gardens. Introduced in 1789, it made its way slowly because it was not considered hardy. It has, however, proved itself hardy both in England and in this country. This is our common white magnolia; often shrub-like in youth, but at maturity becoming a tree. The flowers open as great cups, are produced most abundantly, and at their best quite cover the tree. This magnolia has been

Soulange's Magnolia, *Magnolia Soulangeana*.

Flowers 3' to 5' across

cultivated in China for more than a thousand years and is there considered a symbol of candor and of beauty.

The Purple-flowered Magnolia was the second importation, introduced by Thunberg, who discovered it in Japan and brought it into England in 1790. Relatively this is a small shrub with slightly obovate or acuminate leaves and fragrant flowers. The flowers have small yellowish or yellow-green sepals and large acuminate petals which are deep purple on the exterior and cream-white on the interior face. This is *Magnolia obovata*, also known as *Magnolia purpurea* and *Magnolia discolor*. Although perfectly hardy it is now seldom seen in gardens, having given way to a race of hybrids of which it is one of the parents.

One of the best of these hybrids dates from 1826. It sprang from a seed of *Magnolia conspicua*, in the garden of M. Soulange-Bodin, of Fromont, near Paris, the flowers of which, it is believed, had been accidentally fertilized with the pollen of *Magnolia purpurea*. The plant is known as *Magnolia soulangeana* and is almost intermediate between the two parents except in habit, which is arborescent. It is thoroughly hardy and produces fertile seeds. The flowers are white with a dash of purple, and appear a week or ten days later than those of *Magnolia conspicua*. There are several other hybrids of these species offered by the trade, of which one of the best is *Magnolia lennei*, whose flowers are deep crimson without and cream-white within.

Our gardens were enriched a few years ago by the introduction of the shrubby *Magnolia stellata*, which

8

Two upper, *Magnolia stellata*.   The lower, *Magnolia kobus*.

Flowers of *M. stellata*, 3′ across ; those of *M. kobus*, 4′ to 5′ across.

is indeed most rightly named—a star. Perfectly hardy, it blooms the earliest of all the magnolias, coming into flower with the forsythias. The blossom is pure white, and deliciously fragrant; the petals at first spread into a star but later become reflexed. Extremely beautiful, it needs but to be known to be highly valued.

Other magnolias have come, and others, no doubt, are yet to come, from that great storehouse of the East, China. A recent arrival is *Magnolia kobus*, a small bushy tree which is perfectly hardy but whose flowers are not so fine as those of *Magnolia stellata*.

The family characteristics of all the magnolias are the leathery texture of the petals, and the successive rows of stamens packed around the prolonged receptacle which is crowned with pistils, also packed in rows and closely cohering with each other. The fruit is a fleshy cone containing brilliant scarlet seeds.

In order that a magnolia should do well it ought to stand by itself in the open, so that it may have an abundance of light and air; otherwise the flowering wood does not properly ripen.

The secret of transplanting magnolias is to do it as the leaves are opening; that is, in the case of these Asiatic species, after the flowers have fallen. This seems rather astonishing, but the reason lies in the character of the roots, which are large and fleshy and which decay rapidly when cut or bruised. They consequently do not recover from transplanting unless moved at a time when they are in active growth and so in a condition to make new root growth rapidly.

All the magnolias love moisture, and grow best in

peat soil, or sand and turfy loam, in the full sunlight. It is now well known that the Chinese magnolias grow more rapidly and make better plants for us if they are grafted on some of the strong-growing American species, preferably *Magnolia acuminata* or *Magnolia tripetala*.

# BERBERIDÀCEÆ—BARBERRY FAMILY

## COMMON BARBERRY

*Bérberis vulgàris.*

The derivation of *Berberis* is very greatly in doubt; it has
been referred to the Arabic, to the Greek, and to the
Hindoo, but its origin is lost in the mists of antiquity.

Thorny, three to ten feet high, introduced from Europe, and
hardy throughout our northern range.   It suckers freely; is long-
lived; grows rapidly when young but slowly afterward; prefers
a soil with lime.   Wood is yellow; roots are long and crooked;
berries, leaves, and roots are acid and astringent.

*Leaves.*—On fresh shoots of the season the leaves are scattered,
mostly reduced to sharp, triple or branched, slender spines; from
whose axils, in the next season, proceed rosettes of obovate leaves
of varying sizes.   Finally, by annual growth a short, stout, little
branch is formed in the axil of each bunch of spines and at the
apex of these tiny branches the leaves appear, really alternate, but
so crowded as to look like rosettes.   The thorns are from three-
eighths to one inch long.   Leaves are oval to obovate, one to one
and one-half inches long, pointed at the base, rounded at the
apex, bristly toothed, pinnately veined.   They come out of the
bud yellow-green, glabrous, when full grown are bright green
above, paler beneath; in autumn they become a dull purplish
green, or fall unchanged.

*Flowers.*—May, June.   Perfect, yellow, borne in drooping,
many-flowered racemes.

*Calyx.*—Sepals six, in two rows, hypogynous, imbricate in bud,
roundish, with two to six small bracts beneath.

Common Barberry, *Berberis vulgaris.*

Racemes 2′ to 2½′ long. Leaves 1′ to 1½′ long.

*Corolla.*—Petals six, in two rows, yellow, hypogynous, imbri-cate in bud, obovate, concave, with two glandular spots inside, above the short claw.

*Stamens.*—Six, hypogynous, opposite the petals, irritable; fil-aments short; anthers two-celled, opening by lids hinged at the top.

*Pistil.*—Ovary one, superior; style short; stigma circular, de-pressed.

*Fruit.*—Berry about half an inch long, borne in drooping ra-cemes from the tiny branchlets which bear the rosettes of leaves; scarlet, oblong, crowned with a remnant of the stigma as a black spot, edible, heavily charged with malic acid. Seeds few or one.

The spines of the Barberry are a curious state of leaf in which the leaf texture is displaced and the ribs have become indurated. They, as well as the simple leaves of ordinary appearance, are articulated with the petiole, and are therefore compound leaves reduced to a single foliole.

The Barberry is a graceful bush bearing in the spring from its bending shoots drooping racemes of beautiful yellow flowers. These flowers are especially interest-ing because of the remarkable irritability of the sta-mens. When a filament is touched on the inside with the point of a pin or any other hard instrument the stamen bends forward toward the pistil, touches the stigma with the anther, remains curved for a short time and then partially recovers its erect position.

There is no evidence that the Common Barberry is native to this continent, but it thrives luxuriantly in New England, where it is now well established as a wild shrub. The plant is most satisfactory for yard or lawn; is graceful in habit; most attractive when in flower, and bears its bright red berries long after the leaves fall, and well into the winter.

*Berberis canadensis* is a rare plant of the Alleghanies which grows to the height of five feet. The leaves are

American Barberry, *Berberis canadensis*.
Leaves 1′ to 1½′ long.

repandly toothed, the teeth less bristly-pointed and the racemes bear fewer flowers than those of the Common Barberry. The petals are notched at the apex and the scarlet berries are oval. Its autumnal tints are scarlet and orange.

The other barberries which adorn our gardens are Asiatic in origin. They come from Siberia, Afghanistan, China, Japan, and one, *Berberis concinna*, from the mountain valleys of the higher Himalayas. Their fruit has the well known barberry taste and flavor, and the leaves of many of them turn a beautiful scarlet and orange before they fall.

The old belief that barberries produced rust in wheat has finally been laid to rest by the microscope. The two rusts are entirely different—one has nothing to do with the other. That one should follow the other is mere coincidence.

### MAHONIA. OREGON GRAPE

*Bérberis aquifòlium. Mahònia aquifòlia.*

*Mahonia*, named in honor of Bernard McMahon, a patron of botanical science.

The Mahonia is one of that group of valuable ornamental plants which have come into our gardens from the Pacific coast. It looks like a holly, fruits like a grape and is a barberry. In Oregon it is evergreen, here it is subevergreen; if the bush is protected somewhat the leaves will remain green throughout the winter, but if compelled to face the full severity of our climate, the leaves turn brown and most of them fall.

Mahonia, *Mahonia aquifolia*.
Leaflets 1½′ to 2′ long.

## BARBERRY FAMILY

The plant reaches three to six feet of stature; the
leaves are compounded of five to seven leaflets and
each leaflet looks like the leaf of a holly. It has the
same coarse teeth, each armed with a bristle. The
flowers are yellow, they resemble those of the barberry; are borne in erect, clustered racemes. The fruit
is a blue berry, the size of a large pea, in color and
bloom greatly resembling the berries of the Concord
grape. The plant is hardy, and is a real acquisition
to our flora.

# CISTÀCEÆ—ROCK-ROSE FAMILY

## DOWNY HUDSONIA

*Hudsònia tomentòsa.*

Named in honor of William Hudson, a London apothecary,
the author of *Flora Angelica*, published in 1762.

A small, bushy, hoary-pubescent undershrub, growing in
thick matted patches, rising but a few inches from the ground;
erect or slightly bent. Found oftenest on the sandy plains
along the shore from Maine to Maryland; especially abundant
in New Jersey; also found along the border of the Great Lakes.
It has a creeping underground stem which throws out many
roots, branching with threadlike fibrils.

*Leaves.*—Simple, alternate, stiff, lanceolate or narrowly
oblong, entire, acute, close-pressed and densely imbricated on
the stem. Thickly covered with whitish down, and about one-
twelfth of an inch long.

*Flowers.*—May, June. Perfect, small, bright yellow, sessile·
or short-stalked; crowded along the upper part of the branches.

*Calyx.*—Sepals five, obtuse, small, yellowish within, downy
without; two outer minute, bractlike; the three others larger,
slightly twisted in the bud, persistent.

*Corolla.*—Petals five, yellow, much larger than the sepals,
convolute in bud, fugacious.

*Stamens.*—Nine to eighteen, hypogynous; filaments slender,
anthers short, innate, two-celled.

*Pistil.*—Ovary one, superior, one-celled; style long and
slender; stigma minute.

19

*Fruit.*—Capsule enclosed in the calyx, obovate-oblong, glabrous, slightly three-sided, one-celled, three-valved, one to three-seeded.

The Downy Hudsonia is a little gray bush very common on the sea shore of New England and New Jersey ; also found on the shores of the Great Lakes. Because of its long, slender, delicate root fibres it is enabled to hold its own and flourish despite the hard conditions of changing winds and drifting sands.

Every morning during the blooming season which lasts two or three weeks, the plant is covered with a sheet of golden yellow flowers, from which the petals fall by two o'clock in the afternoon, fresh flowers opening each day.

Mr. J. H. Hill writes in *Garden and Forest* concerning the Downy Hudsonia as follows : " Another plant of the sand hills will lead one to stop and inspect it when met with in winter. It is the smallest shrub of the flora of the lakes. The bush rises but little above the ground, six or eight inches high, its stem usually bending to one side. It branches so excessively as to have a tuft-like crown. The bark is very dark, almost black, and the branches near their ends, and all the twigs are covered with a gray tomentum. When seen in the winter the plant seems dead and uninviting ; the slender twigs break square off as if dry, thus adding to the deception. But under a thick covering of hairy scales are the small green buds, and the wood of the fresh fracture shows a green color when closely examined. These dry shrubs make their home in exposed positions where little else grows, striking their roots firmly in the sand, and the apparently dead

Downy Hudsonia, *Hudsonia tomentosa.*

tufts at which the wind tugs hard to draw them from the ground will be lively in spring or early summer with small but numerous flowers."

The other species, the Heath-like Hudsonia, *Hudsonia ericoides*, is less downy than *Hudsonia tomentosa*. The leaves are slender and awl-shaped; are a little longer, spread a little more, and are covered with longer and thinner hairs than those of the Downy Hudsonia. The old leaves are persistent and the stem often looks dry. It usually blooms the earlier of the two. The flowers of both species are very similar in size and color and equally fleeting. Both plants are difficult to establish in gardens, but once established they grow, spread, and make excellent, dwarf, rock garden shrubs; they can also be used as a carpet about taller plants.

# HYPERICÀCEÆ—ST. JOHN'S-WORT FAMILY

## SHRUBBY ST. JOHN'S-WORT

*Hypéricum prolìficum.*

*Hypericum* is an ancient Greek name of obscure meaning. The name St. John's-wort was given to the family because one member of it, *Hypericum perforatum*, was believed in olden times to have the power of keeping off evil spirits, who were supposed to be particularly busy on St. John's night.

Low, one to three feet high, diffusely branched near the base; branchlets slender, two-edged; stems stout, covered with light reddish brown bark; found in rocky or sandy soil. Ranges from New Jersey to Georgia and west to Michigan and Minnesota. Variable.

*Leaves.*—Opposite, simple, punctuate with small translucent dots, one to three inches long, narrowly oblong, sessile or narrowed at base into a short petiole, entire, mostly obtuse at apex, often mucronate; midvein prominent, secondary veins obscure. Tufts of small leaves frequently occur in the axils of larger ones. Autumnal tint is greenish yellow.

*Flowers.*—July, September. Perfect, bright yellow, three-fourths to an inch and a half across, conspicuous for many stamens, borne in compound few-flowered cymes which are terminal or axillary; bracts leafy. Pedicels three-fourths to an inch long.

*Calyx.*—Sepals five, leaf-like, shorter than the petals, persistent, imbricate in bud.

*Corolla.*—Petals five, hypogynous, brilliant yellow, convolute in bud.

*Stamens.*—Conspicuous, numerous, distinct; filaments slender, bright yellow; anthers yellow, two-celled.

*Pistil.*—Ovary superior, three-celled, styles three.

*Fruit.*—Capsule three-lobed, three-celled, many-seeded.

> Hypericum all bloom, so thick a swarm
> Of flowers, clothing her slender stems,
> That scarce a leaf appears.
>
> —COWPER.

The Shrubby St. John's-wort responds admirably to cultivation, often reaching the height of six feet with a wide spreading head. The flowers are extremely showy, borne as they are in large terminal clusters; and blooming almost continuously from July to September they produce a glow of brilliant color among the prevailing green of midsummer shrubbery.

*Hypericum densiflorum* is closely related to *Hypericum prolificum*, but a much rarer plant. Its leaves are linear-lanceolate, with slightly revolute margins, bristle-pointed. The flowers are small, about half an inch across, and are crowded in broad, compact cymes. The capsules are short, remarkably slender, and with the smaller flowers serve to distinguish it from *Hypericum prolificum*, which it greatly resembles. It is a southern plant, coming naturally no farther north than New Jersey.

Shrubby St. John's-wort, *Hypericum prolificum.*

Leaves 1′ to 3′ long.   Flowers ¾′ to 1½′ across.

## KALM'S ST. JOHN'S-WORT

*Hypéricum kalmiànum.*

Named in honor of Peter Kalm, the Swedish botanist who discovered it, probably at Niagara Falls, in 1750.

Low, one to two feet high, freely branching, very leafy, branches four-angled; twigs flattened and two-edged; bark reddish, exfoliating. Ranges from Ontario and western New York to Wisconsin and Michigan.

*Leaves.*—Opposite, simple, one to two and a half inches long, oblong-linear, or oblanceolate, sessile or narrowed into a short petiole, entire, obtuse or acute at apex, rather thick, dark green above, paler or sometimes glaucous beneath; midvein prominent, secondary veins obscure. Generally with tufts of smaller leaves in the axils of the larger ones. In autumn they turn a greenish yellow.

*Flowers.*—August. Perfect, golden yellow, one-half to one inch across, borne in few-flowered terminal cymes.

*Calyx.*—Sepals five, oblong, acute, leaf-like, persistent, one-half the length of the petals, imbricate in bud.

*Corolla.*—Petals five, golden yellow, convolute in bud.

*Stamens.*—Very numerous, distinct, conspicuous; filaments yellow, slender; anthers orange, two-celled.

*Pistil.*—Ovary superior, five-celled; styles five.

*Fruit.*—Capsule, ovoid, five-lobed, five-celled, many-seeded.

This St. John's-wort was first discovered upon the wet rocks at Niagara Falls and finds its most congenial home in the region about the Great Lakes. It is rather a rare plant. The chief botanical distinction between *Hypericum kalmianum* and *Hypericum prolificum* lies in the five styles and five-celled capsules of the one, and the three styles and three-celled capsules of the other. In cultivated seedlings, however, these distinctions are not constant and sometimes the cells vary from three to six.

Kalm's St. John's-wort, *Hypericum kalmianum.*

Leaves 1′ to 2½′ long. Flowers ½′ to 1′ across.

## ASCYRUM. ST. PETER'S-WORT

*Áscyrum stáns.*

*Ascyrum,* an ancient Greek name of an unknown plant; without special significance here.

A small, stout shrub, one to two feet high, in dry or sandy soil, found frequently in pine-barrens. Ranges from Long Island along the coast to Florida and Texas. Stem smooth, erect and straight, two-edged or slightly winged.

*Leaves.*—Opposite, simple, pinnately veined, oval or oblong, one to one and a half inches long, sessile at base, somewhat clasping, entire, rounded at apex. When full grown, rather thick, pale green, black-dotted.

*Flowers.*—July, August. Perfect, showy, bright yellow, about an inch across, borne in terminal few-flowered cymes. Pedicels half an inch long, two-bracted below the middle.

*Calyx.*—Sepals four; in pairs, the outer round-cordate, the inner lanceolate.

*Corolla.*—Petals four, obovate, very deciduous, convolute in bud.

*Stamens.*—Many, hypogynous, distinct or slightly clustered.

*Pistil.*—Ovary superior, one-celled; styles three or four.

*Fruit.*—Capsule, ovoid, one-celled; seeds many.

## ST. ANDREW'S CROSS

*Áscyrum hypericoides. Áscyrum crux-ándreæ.*

Low, much branched and decumbent, six to ten inches high; found in dry sandy soil; stem smooth, flattened and two-edged. Ranges from Massachusetts to Florida, westward to Illinois and Nebraska and southwest to Indian Territory and Texas.

*Leaves.*—Opposite, simple, pinnately veined, one-half to an inch and a half long, narrow-oblong or obovate, narrowed at

28

base, entire, rounded at apex; when full grown, thin, pale green, black-dotted, usually two glands at base.

*Flowers.*—July, August. Perfect, regular, yellow, terminal and axillary, one-half to three-fourths of an inch across. Pedicels short, two-bracted.

*Calyx.*—Sepals four; the two outer very broad and leaf-like; the inner much smaller, imbricate in bud.

*Corolla.*—Petals four, oblique, bright yellow, hypogynous, convolute in bud, oblong-linear, about the length of the outer sepals, approaching each other in pairs in the form of St. Andrew's cross.

*Stamens.*—Many, hypogynous, scarcely in clusters.

*Pistil.*—Ovary superior, one-celled, styles two.

*Fruit.*—Capsule, one-celled, many-seeded.

Among the different crosses known in the symbolism of the Christian church that of St. Andrew is distinguished by its oblique arms which are arranged in the form of an X. This little shrub gains its specific as well as its common name because its four petals make a very perfect St. Andrew's cross.

The plant is not very generally known, although it is rather common in the pine-barrens of New Jersey, and not rare along the coast.

St. Andrew's Cross, *Ascyrum hypericoides.* Leaves ½′ to 1½′ long. Flowers ½′ to ¾′ across.

Closely related to the St. John's-worts, it differs in having four petals instead of five; in its four unequal sepals, and its numerous

29

distinct, not clustered stamens. The bloom continues through the better part of the summer, and the habit of the plant is to spread into broad mats, no stem rising higher than four or five inches. Although a plant of the sands it does very well in rock gardens.

# THEÀCEÆ—TEA FAMILY

## STUARTIA

*Stuártia pentágyna.*

*Stuartia*, in honor of John Stuart, Marquis of Bute, who was characterized by Linnæus as " a most knowing botanist."

An erect, sturdy shrub six to twelve feet high, native to the mountains of Virginia and southward. The leaves are large, frequently five inches long, rather thick and heavy ; the margins slightly serrulate or entire.

The plant is really one of the most attractive of summer blooming shrubs. It has been cultivated for more than a hundred years ; is fairly hardy at the north, perfectly so at the Arnold Arboretum, yet is virtually unknown in northern gardens.

The flowers are solitary, borne in the axils of the leaves ; the blooming period extends through July and August. The buds are large, round and fully an inch in diameter before they expand.

The flowers are cream-white, three to four inches across and look not unlike a single camellia. Each flower has five petals normally, though sometimes there are more, and each petal is one to one and a half

Stuartia, *Stuartia pentagyna.*

Leaves 3′ to 5′ long.  Flowers 3′ to 4′ across.

Gordonia, *Gordonia pubescens.*

Leaves 5′ to 6′ long.

inches broad and two inches long; the edges are somewhat crimped and scalloped. In the centre of the flower is a cluster of many stamens with large orange-colored anthers. In full bloom the plant is an object of surpassing beauty.

## GORDONIA

*Gordònia pubéscens. Gordònia altamàha.*

Named in honor of James Gordon, a London nurseryman.

*Gordonia pubescens* has a unique history, for so far as known the species at one time consisted of a single individual; and all the plants of the species now existing are the offspring of that ancestor. The original form was discovered in Georgia and planted in the Bartram Gardens near Philadelphia in 1790. Since that time all efforts to rediscover the tree have been futile and it is now believed that no other wild specimen exists. Either by mere chance a species was rescued as it was upon the point of extinction, or the individual discovered was a hybrid of a different species.

The plant is a fairly hardy shrub eight to ten feet high in the Arnold Arboretum; at the south it becomes a small tree. The bright shining foliage is very handsome, and ere the leaves fall they assume a rich crimson tint. The blossoms are pure white, deliciously fragrant, three inches across, with a cluster of bright yellow stamens within. The petals do not continue very long, falling usually upon the second day.

The high personal value of the shrub rests upon the fact that it is an autumn bloomer. The flowers appear early in September and continue throughout October. Severe early frosts will blast the buds, but usually the bloom is sufficiently abundant to repay for all care that has been expended.

The original tree in the Bartram Gardens has recently died, but it lives in the persons of hundreds of descendants. A fine specimen is reported as growing in Lafayette Square, Washington.

# MALVÀCEÆ—MALLOW FAMILY

## ROSE-OF-SHARON. SHRUBBY ALTHÆA

### *Hibíscus syriàcus.*

*Hibiscus*, a classical name of unknown meaning. Althæa, given in allusion to the supposed healing properties of the species.

An erect shrub, ten to twenty feet high, received from Europe, but a native of Asia ; thoroughly acclimated in northern gardens.

*Leaves.*—Alternate, simple, palmately three-nerved, two to three and a half inches long, obovate or rhomboidal, almost three-lobed, wedge-shaped at base, coarsely and irregularly serrate, entire from middle to base ; when full grown bright green, and glabrous above, paler green beneath. In autumn they turn a clear yellow, or fall without change, remaining on the branches until late.

*Flowers.*—August, September. Showy, abundant, looking like hollyhocks, in color ranging through rose, scarlet and magenta to white, perfect, solitary or two or three together, odorless, nectar-bearing.

*Calyx.*—Five-lobed, surrounded by a whorl of slender, linear, pointed bractlets, persistent, valvate in bud.

*Corolla.*—Petals five, veiny, short-clawed, rose, scarlet, magenta, white, often with an eye of different color from that of the petal, convolute in bud.

*Stamens.*—Many, monadelphous in a column formed by the union of the filaments, united at base with the claws of the

Shrubby Althæa, *Hibiscus syriacus.*

Leaves 2′ to 3½′ long.  Flowers 2′ to 3′ across.

petals; anthers kidney-shaped, one-celled; cells opening along the top.

*Pistil.*—Ovaries several, united in a ring, forming a five-celled pod.

*Fruit.*—Capsule, ovoid, five-lobed, five-celled, many-seeded. Seeds kidney-shaped.

A stranger from a far-off land, the Althæa has bloomed in English gardens for three hundred years and has been in America at least one hundred. It is here proving itself an excellent city plant; flourishing even where soft coal is burned and where the atmosphere is laden with gas and smoke. Its habit of midsummer bloom makes it a favorite, together with its remarkable freedom from insects' attacks and fungus enemies.

One characteristic of the bush is very noticeable. The stem and larger branches of a thrifty individual are apparently directly clothed with leaves; really the little groups of leaves are borne at the summit of dwarfed branchlets, not more than an inch long and frequently shorter. In winter these are very apparent.

The varieties of Althæas offered by the dealers are legion. Plants with green leaves and plants with variegated ones; flowers single and flowers double; light-eyed or dark-eyed, ranging through purple, magenta and rose to white. The plant is a mallow, belonging to the family of which the hollyhock is the type; and the single flowers look like hollyhocks. When the flower doubles, the additional petals spring from the central column of united stamens. Linnæus supposed the plant was a native of Asia Minor; it is now believed to be of Chinese origin.

# TAMARÍSCEÆ—TAMARISK FAMILY

## TAMARISK

*Támarix.*

So called, according to some, from the plants growing on the banks of the river Tamaras, now Tambra, on the borders of the Pyrenees; or according to others, from the Hebrew word *tamaris*, cleansing, on account of their branches being used for brooms.

The Tamarisks are a group of tall shrubs inhabiting a broad continental belt extending from Central Europe to the China Sea. In favoring climates they are subevergreen, with us they are frankly deciduous. We have no native shrub that in any way resembles them. The stems are erect but so slender that the whole plant sways with the wind. The branchlets and spray are so delicate and at the same time so abundant that the effect of the plant is that of a green feathery mass. Moreover, this effect is produced by the spray alone, for although leaves are present in great numbers, they are minute green scales, closely imbricated and scarcely separable from the bark. The flowers are small, usually pink, borne in racemes or in terminal panicles which give a charming effect among the soft foliage. The fruit is a small capsule.

The Tamarisk is especially recommended for seaside planting, as it is perfectly hardy there, will grow and flourish even under the wash of the salt sea spray. The minute leaves and pliant stems enable the plant successfully to withstand a storm that would rend another one in sunder.

The African Tamarisk, *Tamarix parvifolia*, *Tamarix tetrandra*, *Tamarix africana*, is perhaps the earliest species to bloom ; the small pink flowers appearing in great abundance along the slender branches of the previous season's growth in May or early in June.

The French Tamarisk, *Tamarix gallica*, a native of the Mediterranean regions of Europe, has long been in cultivation. It attains the height of eight or ten feet. Its small pink flowers appear in slender spikes at the end of the slender branches. The twigs and branches are conspicuous because of their copper-colored or reddish bark. The plant is very tolerant of the knife and can be trained to almost any desired form.

The late-flowering Tamarisk, commonly known as *Tamarix indica*, unlike those already named, blooms on wood of the same season. Flowering profusely in August and September, it ranks with the Althæa as a desirable autumn plant.

Some form of the Tamarisk has been in cultivation from most ancient times. It seems to have been highly valued among the ancient Arabians for its medicinal qualities. The plant is mentioned by many of the ancient poets ; Homer makes it the tree against which Achilles laid his spear before he plunged into the Xanthus to pursue the flying Trojans ; Theocri-

Tamarisk.

tus in his Pastorals, Virgil in his Eclogues, and Ovid in several of his poems, all refer to this plant. Evelyn speaks of it as a tree accursed; and says that the Romans wove wreaths of it with which they crowned their criminals.

# RUTÀCEÆ—RUE FAMILY

## PRICKLY ASH

*Xanthóxylum americànum.*

Derived from two Greek words, *xanthos*, yellow, and *xylon*,
wood.

Low branching, sometimes becoming a small tree, usually
four to twelve feet high ; growing in rocky woods and on
river banks. Ranges from Quebec to Virginia especially along
the mountains, west to Minnesota, Ne-
braska, and Missouri. Bark, leaves,
and fruit pungent and aromatic ; stems
and often leaf - stalks prickly ; wood
pale, yellowish brown.

*Bark.* — Branchlets pale brown,
downy ; later smooth, light gray ;
finally dark gray.

*Winter buds.* — Round, reddish
brown, with two, short, sharp prickles
just beneath.

*Leaves.*—Alternate, pinnately compound, dotted with oil glands ; leaflets
five to eleven, nearly sessile, one and
one-fourth to two inches long, ovate
or ovate - oblong, wedge - shaped or
rounded at base, entire or crenulate,
acute at apex ; when full grown are
dark green above, pale green and

Leaf of Prickly Ash.  Leaflets
1′ to 2′ long.

43

Prickly Ash, *Xanthoxylum americanum*, in flower.

downy beneath. Autumnal tints are scarlet touched with yellow. Two stout prickles are on the stem just below the clusters of leaves and flowers.

*Flowers.*—April, May, before or with the leaves. Diœcious, small, greenish white, borne in short umbels in the axils of the leaves. Sepals four to five or obsolete; petals five; stamens four to five; pistils two to five, with slender styles slightly united. Capsules ellipsoid, thick and fleshy, on short stalks, two-valved, one to two-seeded; seeds black, smooth, shining.

The common name of Prickly Ash explains itself; the stem of the shrub is prickly and its leaves resemble those of the ashes. There the likeness ceases. The small greenish flowers are inconspicuous and appear early. All parts of the shrub are pungent and aromatic; when the leaves are crushed they yield a strong lemon-like odor.

## WAFER ASH. HOP-TREE

*Ptèlea trifoliàta*

*Ptella,* the Greek name of the elm-tree, transferred to this genus because of the similarity of the fruits. Wafer refers to the size and shape of the fruit. Hop recalls the fact that the leaves have been substituted for hops in the making of beer.

Samaras of the Wafer Ash.

The Wafer Ash, though small, is arborescent in habit and properly described as a tree; but it consorts with the shrubs and is grouped with them for landscape effects. The green flowers, though abundant, are inconspicuous and the plant does not become noticeable before midsummer; then the winged seed vessels mature and form great green-

Wafer Ash, *Ptelea trifoliata.*
Leaflets 2′ to 5′ long.

ish white clusters well scattered among the foliage, sometimes fairly overpowering it. This unusual combination of the pale green of the samaras with the dark green of the leaves gives the plant its decorative value. The name of Wafer seems to refer to the size and form of the fruit; and Hop-tree indicates that the leaves have been used instead of hops in the manufacture of beer.

# ILICÍNEÆ—HOLLY FAMILY

## WINTER-BERRY. BLACK ALDER

*Ìlex verticillàta.*

*Ilex*, an ancient Latin name, here probably misapplied.

A handsome shrub, varying from five to ten feet high, conspicuous for its clusters of bright scarlet berries which cling to the branches well into the winter; found in low grounds, moist woods, and swamps. Ranges from Nova Scotia to Florida, west to Ontario, Wisconsin, and Missouri.

*Bark.*—Dark clouded gray; branchlets at first yellow green, later become grayish brown, finally dark gray; bitter and astringent, medicinal. Winter buds extremely minute.

*Leaves.*—Alternate, simple, pinnately veined, two to three inches long, oval, obovate or oblong-lanceolate, wedge-shaped at base, serrate, acute or acuminate at apex. They come out of the bud involute, yellow green, smooth above, densely hairy beneath; when full grown are bright green, thick, glabrous above, somewhat downy beneath; midvein and primary veins depressed above, prominent beneath. In autumn they darken or fall with little change of color. Petiole one-half an inch long, grooved.

*Flowers.*—May, June. Polygamo-diœcious, greenish white, small. The staminate are in crowded clusters of three to twelve in the axils of the leaves; peduncles short with small brown scales at the base. The pistillate are solitary or clustered. Parts of the pistillate flowers are in fours, fives or sixes; those of the staminate commonly in sixes. Corolla rotate, segments imbricate in bud; stamens inserted on the base of the corolla; anthers large, brown, two-celled.

Black Alder, *Ilex verticillata.*
Flowers $\frac{3}{16}'$ to $\frac{1}{4}'$ across.

*Fruit.*—Berry-like drupe, one-fourth to five-sixteenths of an inch in diameter, globular or slightly depressed, solitary or in clusters of two or three, scarlet, rarely yellow; sits in the persistent calyx and is crowned with the remnants of the stigma. Pulp yellowish, nauseous; seeds three to eight. Remains long after the leaves have fallen. September.

> And I will trust that He who heeds
> The life that hides in mead and wold,
> Who hangs yon alder's crimson beads,
> And stains these mosses green and gold,
> Will still, as He hath done, incline
> His gracious care to me and mine.
> —JOHN G. WHITTIER.

> \* \* \* With coral beads, the prim black alders shine.
> —JAMES RUSSELL LOWELL.

I see where a mouse, which had a hole under a stump, has eaten out clean the inside of the little seeds of the *Prinos verticillata* berries. What pretty fruit for them, these bright berries! They run up the twigs in the night and gather this shining fruit, take out the small seeds and eat these kernels at the entrance to their burrows. The ground is strewn with them.
—HENRY D. THOREAU.

Notes written November 19, 1857.

One often feels that a plant is not without honor save in its own country. Here is a native Holly which equals if it does not surpass in brilliancy and beauty of fruit coloring any imported plant in our garden, and yet it is virtually unknown. Its charm lies in its abundant scarlet berries which cling to the branches in the axil of every leaf and after the leaves fall still cling to the naked stems. At the north they fall by midwinter, in the south they remain until pushed off by the growing buds of spring. The birds, it seems, will have none of them, the thin flesh is too nauseous, and the nutlets are too many; but the field mice are not so particular.

In northern Ohio the Winter-berry adorns the

Black Alder, *Ilex verticillata.*

Leaves 2′ to 3′ long.  Fruit ¼′ to ⁵⁄₁₆′ in diameter.

swamps and lowlands in company with the Carolina rose. In June the rose has the advantage, but when October comes and the Winter-berry stands clothed in scarlet, aflame to the utmost tip of its tiniest twig, it, too, has its day.

In cultivation the bush properly belongs to the group of plants prized for the distinctly effective coloring of their fruit; such as, the snowberries, the barberries and the burning bushes.

### SMOOTH WINTER-BERRY

*Ìlex lævigàta.*

A very pretty shrub, six to ten feet high; found in deep wet swamps, from Maine to Virginia.

*Bark.*—Twigs and branches smooth brownish green; stems grayish, frequently the host of many gray lichens.

*Leaves.*—Alternate, sometimes in tufts, simple, pinnately veined, oval or oblong, two or three inches long, acute at base and apex, obscurely serrate, often slightly revolute; when full grown are thin, light green, shining above and beneath, glabrous, sometimes hairy along the veins beneath. In autumn they turn bright yellow. Petioles short.

*Flowers.*—May, June. Perfect or diœcious, small, white, one-fourth of an inch across, borne in the axils of the leaves. The staminate are scattered or in twos, on very slender pedicels. The pistillate are solitary, sessile or short-stalked.

*Fruit.*—Berry-like drupe, bright red, one-fourth to one-third of an inch in diameter; falls earlier than that of *Ilex verticillata.* September.

The Smooth Winter-berry should be better known; for although native to the swamps it does not disdain a garden home. Often confounded with the Black Alder, it may be distinguished from it; in the spring

Smooth Winter-berry, *Ilex lævigata.*

Leaves 2′ to 3′ long.  Fruit ¼′ to ⁵⁄₁₆′ in diameter.

by the longer stalks of the sterile flowers; in autumn by its leaves which turn bright yellow before they fall. Possibly, the fruit is not quite so abundant as that of *Ilex verticillata;* does not cling to the branches quite so late; and on the average is larger and more scattered.

### INKBERRY. EVERGREEN WINTER-BERRY

*Ilex glàbra.*

Slender, delicate-looking, evergreen, two to six feet high, growing in sandy soil; found mainly near the coast from Nova Scotia to Louisiana.

*Leaves.*— Evergreen, alternate, simple, oblong or oblanceolate, one to two inches long, wedge-shaped at base, serrate with two or three teeth toward the apex, or entire, apex obtuse or acute; when full grown dark green, leathery, shining above, paler and black-dotted beneath. Petioles short.

*Flowers.*—June. Perfect or diœcious, small, white, six-pointed, borne in the axils of the leaves. Staminate in few-flowered cymes; pistillate generally solitary, sometimes two or three together; pedicels slender.

*Fruit.*—Berry-like drupe, black, globose, one-fourth of an inch in diameter; six-seeded; nutlets smooth.

This broad-leaved evergreen of the United States has been cultivated in England for more than a hundred years, but has not yet made its way into our own gardens.

Its natural habit is rather tall and straggling, but under cultivation the bush assumes a more compact form. The leaves remain bright green and glossy throughout the winter, while the shining black berries give an added grace. It is a beautiful plant and should be cultivated both for its summer and for its winter beauty.

Inkberry, *Ilex glabra*.

Leaves 1′ to 2′ long.   Fruit ¼′ in diameter.

## MOUNTAIN-HOLLY

*Ilicioìdes mucronàta. Nemopánthes fasciculàris.*

*Ilicioides*, resembling holly. *Nemopanthes*, flower with a
slender peduncle.

A slender shrub, varying in height from six to twelve feet.
Found in swamps and low wet woods from Nova Scotia to
western Ontario and southward to Virginia, Indiana, and
Wisconsin.

*Bark.*—Greenish gray or ashen gray, often the host of many
lichens ; shoots glabrous, reddish brown.

*Leaves.*—Alternate, sometimes tufted, simple, pinnately
veined, one-half to two inches long, elliptic or obovate, rounded
or acute at base, entire or obscurely serrate, acute or mucronate
at apex ; when full grown are light yellow green, glabrous ;
midvein and primary veins prominent. Petiole grooved, reddish, about one-fourth to one-half an inch long.

*Flowers.*—May, June. Polygamo-diœcious, white, small, on
long slender pedicels in the axils of the leaves ; staminate flowers solitary or two to four together ; pistillate solitary. The
parts of the flowers vary from three to five.

*Fruit.*—Berry-like drupe, sub-globose, bright red, one-fourth
of an inch in diameter; nutlets four to five. September.

The Mountain Holly is the one species of its genus.
The leaves often grow in tufts on short lateral
branches and so give a leafy effect to the tree. Com-
pared with other species of the Holly family it falls
far below them in attractiveness.

Mountain Holly, *Ilicioides mucronata.*
Leaves ½′ to 2′ long.   Fruit ¼′ in diameter.

# CELASTRÀCEÆ—STAFF-TREE FAMILY

## RUNNING STRAWBERRY BUSH. RUNNING EUONYMUS

*Euónymus obovàtus.*

*Euonymus*, of Greek derivation, signifies good repute.

Low, straggling, decumbent, the main stems lying on the ground and rooting at the nodes; upright stems rarely more than one foot high; found in low woods and wet places. Ranges from Ontario to Pennsylvania and westward to Indiana and Kentucky. Branches green, four-angled or slightly winged.

*Leaves.*—Simple, opposite, pinnately veined, one to two inches long, obovate, or oblong, wedge-shaped at base, finely crenulate-serrulate, obtuse at apex, glabrous, thin, dull green above, paler green beneath.

*Flowers.*—April, May. Perfect, purplish green; pedicels solitary, long, slender, one to four-flowered, borne in the axils of the leaves.

*Calyx.*—Four to five-cleft; lobes spreading.

*Corolla.*—Petals five, nearly orbicular, crenulate or erose, with scarcely any claw, inserted beneath the five-lobed disk.

*Stamens.*—Five, inserted on the disk.

*Pistil.*—Ovary sessile, three-celled; stigma three-lobed.

*Fruit.*—Fleshy, dehiscent, two-celled, rough, warty capsule, borne on a long drooping pedicel; when mature is crimson and white, and opens to discharge two to three white oval seeds enclosed in a scarlet aril. Beautiful, persistent. September.

Running Euonymous, *Euonymus obovatus*, in fruit.

Leaves 1′ to 2′ long.

The Running Euonymus was long regarded a variety of *Euonymus americanus*, but is now considered a distinct species. It is an admirable carpet shrub to cover waste places, as it will flourish, both in sun and in shade, and looks bright and fresh and green late into the autumn. It is well placed upon a bank, its scarlet and crimson fruit makes a beautiful combination with the green. It seems to be immune to the attacks of insects, probably because of the acrid character of its juices.

The chief attraction of all the burning bushes is the unique and beautiful fruit which ripens in early autumn and hangs upon the branches long after the leaves have fallen. While there are minor differences which are considered specific characters, the family fruit is a fleshy capsule more or less lobed, sometimes warty and sometimes smooth, becoming crimson when ripe and finally opening to discharge beautiful, bright scarlet seeds, so that the effect is a brilliant scarlet-crimson combination; and as many species fruit abundantly the plants are sought whenever late autumnal effects are desired. The burning bushes rank with the barberries, the snowberries and the winter-berries as decorative shrubs.

The Strawberry Bush, *Euonymus americanus*, is a native of low woods, ranging from southern New York to Florida and westward to Nebraska, and Texas. It certainly is not as abundant in the middle west as *Euonymus obovatus*. It is an erect shrub growing two to six feet high, with four-angled and ash-colored twigs; the branches set upon the stem at wide angles. The leaves are opposite, thick, almost sessile, crenulate, bright green, varying from ovate to oblong-lanceolate, acute at apex. The flowers are green with a suggestion of pinkish purple, borne on peduncles in the axils of the leaves; parts mostly in fives. The fruiting capsule is rough, warty, depressed, crimson when ripe, and opens to disclose its scarlet covered seeds. *Euonymus americanus* and *Euonymus obovatus* are alike in their fruit; the chief specific difference lies in their habits of growth.

Wahoo, Burning Bush, *Euonymus atropurpùreus*, is a shrub at the north, but easily becomes a tree and is described among the trees. The plant is very extensively cultivated and is worthy of all the attention given it. The small flowers are purple, not green, the fruit is deeply three to four-lobed, and smooth, not warty. When ripe the purplish scarlet capsule opens to discharge the crimson covered seeds. Like all its family it holds its fruit late into the autumn.

# RHAMNÀCEÆ—BUCKTHORN FAMILY

## ALDER-LEAVED BUCKTHORN

### *Rhámnus alnifòlia.*

*Rhamnus* is the ancient Greek name, with no obvious sig-
nification.

A stout leafy shrub, two to three feet high, growing in clumps
on moist lands and in swamps.  Ranges from New Brunswick
to British Columbia, south to New Jersey, west to Illinois, Nebraska, and Montana.

*Leaves.*—Alternate, simple, pinnately veined, two to four
inches long, ovate, acute or rounded at base, serrate, acute at
apex ; midvein or primary veins prominent.  They come out
of the bud plicate, yellow green, shining, smooth above, somewhat hairy below, shining and glabrous ; when full grown are
dark green.  Petioles one-fourth to one-half an inch long.

This native of swamps, like so many of its companions, takes kindly to cultivation, and in the garden
makes a clump of erect stems and handsome foliage.
Neither the small yellow flowers nor the black fruit
are conspicuous.  The plant is used by landscape gardeners as a border shrub.

## LANCE-LEAVED BUCKTHORN

### *Rhámnus lanceolàta.*

Tall, erect, growing on hills and on river banks.  Ranges
from Pennsylvania to Alabama, west to Iowa and Nebraska, south

Alder-leaved Buckthorn, *Rhamnus alnifolia.*
Leaves 2′ to 4′ long.

to Texas. Stems thornless, with smooth grayish bark ; branchlets hairy ; juices bitter and astringent.

*Leaves.*—Alternate, simple, one to three and a half inches long, ovate-lanceolate, acute or rounded at base, finely serrate, obtuse or acuminate at apex.

*Flowers.*—May, June, just after the leaves. Polygamo-diœcious, small, yellowish green, axillary, two or three together, fragrant.

*Calyx.*—Tube urn-shaped, four-lobed ; lobes ovate, acute, valvate in bud.

*Corolla.*—Petals four, narrow, deeply notched, inserted on the calyx disk.

*Stamens.*—Four, inserted with the petals and opposite them.

*Pistil.*—Ovary free from calyx, two to four-celled, styles three to four-cleft.

*Fruit.*—Berry-like drupe, globose, black, shining, one-third of an inch in diameter, nauseous.

This shrub bears flowers of two forms on distinct plants, both perfect ; one with short pedicels, clustered in the axils of the leaves and with a short included style; the other with pedicels oftener solitary, the style longer and exserted.

### COMMON BUCKTHORN

*Rhámnus cathártica.*

Tall, upright, six to twenty feet high, bearing leafy thorns ; cultivated for hedges ; naturalized from Europe and sparingly escaped from cultivation. Stems brownish gray with a silver light.

*Leaves.*—Alternate, often seeming to be opposite, simple, one to two and a half inches long, broadly ovate or elliptic, rounded or acute at base, crenate or crenulate, acute or obtuse at apex ; almost five-nerved, midvein and primary veins depressed above,

Common Buckthorn, *Rhamnus cathartica.*

Leaves 1′ to 2½′ long.

very prominent beneath. They come out of the bud involute, bright green, shining, densely covered with white hairs beneath ; when full grown are smooth, dark green above, paler and somewhat downy below. In autumn they fall with little or no change of color.

*Flowers.*—May, with the leaves. Diœcious, yellowish green, borne on short pedicels, in dense umbellate clusters, usually terminal on short branchlets. The terminal bud that produces the flower cluster also produces a growing shoot which comes out of the centre of the cluster.

*Calyx.*—Salver-shaped, four-lobed ; lobes as long as the tube, acute.

*Corolla.*—Petals four, minute, reddish brown, inserted on the calyx-tube, alternate with its lobes.

*Stamens.*—Four, inserted with the petals ; anthers white.

*Pistil.*—Ovary free, three to four-celled.

*Fruit.*—Berry-like drupe, black, shining, nauseous, medicinal ; nutlets two.

The Common Buckthorn is sometimes found growing wild in New England and the Middle States. It is a tall erect shrub, whose lower branches are short and stiff, nearly horizontal and often ending in such sharp points that though leafy they are virtually thorns.

The plant flowers in May, producing abundant clusters of tiny green stars which are followed by shining black berries; these berries were once used medicinally but are now discarded for less violent remedies.

The juices of all the buckthorns are capable of producing dyes. The pigment known as Chinese green is obtained by treating the juice of the ripe berries of *Rhamnus cathartica* and other species with alum and gum arabic. The Avignon berry, which seems to be a name given to the fruit of several species of buck-

Alder Buckthorn, *Rhamnus frangula.*
Leaves 1½′ to 3′ long.

thorn, is used to give the yellow color to leather. Turkey morocco is supposed to be dyed by this pigment.

*Rhamnus cathartica* is an excellent hedge plant. It is perfectly hardy, never suckers; its roots extend but little way, and being fibrous do not interfere with other plants; is free from insects' attacks; the foliage is a rich dark green and held late in autumn.

The Alder Buckthorn, *Rhamnus frangula*, is a handsome lawn shrub, introduced from Europe, which has sparingly escaped in some localities of the Eastern States. It is well formed, compact, and often ten feet high. The flowers are inconspicuous, but its shining foliage and purple black berries give it a certain distinction.

### NEW JERSEY TEA.  RED-ROOT

*Ceanòthus americànus.*

An ancient name of a different plant; of no significance in its present use.

A shrub of upright stems one to three feet high, found in dry open woods.  Ranges from Ontario to Florida and from Manitoba to Texas.  Branchlets downy; root deep red.

*Leaves.*—Alternate, simple, two to three inches long, ovate or oblong-ovate, rounded or slightly heart-shaped at base, serrate, acute or acuminate at apex; three-nerved, ribs and primary veins deeply depressed above, prominent beneath. They come out of the bud involute, clammy, shining, smooth above, densely covered with white hairs beneath.  Petiole short, downy.  Stipules minute, awl-like.

*Flowers.*—June, July.  Small, white, in little umbel-like groups which form dense panicles or corymbs at the summit of naked flower-branches on leafy shoots of the year; calyx and slender pedicels white.

New Jersey Tea, *Ceanothus americanus.*
Leaves 1′ to 3′ long.

*Calyx.*—White ; tube globular ; border five-lobed ; lobes in-curved.

*Corolla.*—Petals five, white, hooded, on slender claws, inserted under the disk.

*Stamens.*—Five ; filaments thread-like.

*Pistil.*—Ovary immersed in the disk, and joined to it at base, three-lobed ; style short, three-cleft.

*Fruit.*—Nearly black, three-lobed, dry, splitting into three carpels when ripe.

The leaves of this plant, according to tradition, were used as a substitute for tea during the tea-less days of the Revolutionary War. There is no tradition, how-ever, that anybody drank the decoction after it ceased to be unpatriotic to drink tea. The red bark of the roots has astringent qualities and has been used me-dicinally; with a proper mordant it will dye wool a cinnamon color.

As a flowering bush the Red-root may very properly claim a place on our lawns. In the blooming season every stem is tipped with clusters of delicate white flowers, which, massed as they are, produce a most charming effect.

Smaller Red-root, *Ceanothus ovatus*, is a western spe-cies with narrow, oval leaves, and denser panicles of flowers. Found on the prairies and in dry, rocky places. Fruit like that of *Ceanothus americanus*.

# HIPPOCASTANÀCEÆ—HORSE-CHESTNUT FAMILY

## DWARF BUCKEYE. DWARF HORSE-CHESTNUT

*Æsculus parviflòra. Æsculus macrostáchya.*

*Æsculus*, derived from *esca*, nourishment.

The Dwarf Buckeye is an effective shrub in midsummer, blossoming profusely in July and August, after the majority of woody plants have passed into the fruiting stage. Its natural habit is to spread broadly; the stems are numerous, the outermost and lowest often becoming horizontal and resting upon the ground, so that a well-grown plant assumes a dome-like form. The branches which rest upon the ground readily form roots, and thus new plants are established which blend with the old ones until the plant is enlarged about its entire circumference.

Crowning the upright stems and borne above the dome of foliage appear the erect panicles of flowers. The flowering axis is eight to sixteen inches long, thickly studded with buds arranged in little groups of which the lowest group is the first to expand, the others following in due order. This arrangement greatly lengthens the flowering period.

The flower has a tubular calyx, four or five white petals, and long thread-like stamens with white filaments, which give the whole a singularly light and feathery aspect. The flowers are slightly fragrant and attractive to many kinds of insects. There is no great production of nuts; each spike produces one or two fruiting balls which are smooth outside, not prickly, and each generally contains a single seed. The leaves borne on long and rather slender petioles are of the typical horse-chestnut form; the five to seven leaflets are oblong-ovate, finely serrate, glabrous above and pubescent beneath. In autumn they become dull yellow before they fall.

The plant is a native of the southern states, but is perfectly hardy throughout the north, and is especially valuable for lawn clumps.

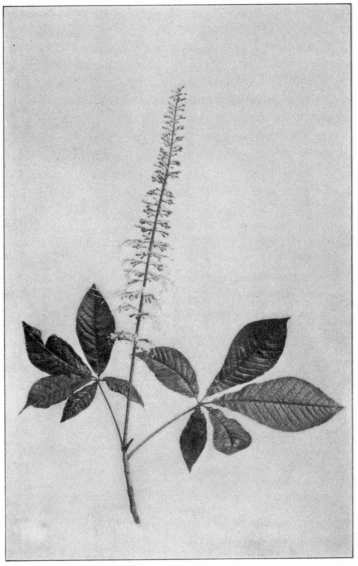

Dwarf Buckeye, *Æsculus parviflora.*
Flower spikes 8′ to 16′ long.

# STAPHYLEÀCEÆ—BLADDER-NUT FAMILY

## AMERICAN BLADDER-NUT

*Staphylèa trifòlia.*

*Staphylea*, cluster, referring to the flowers.

Tall, handsome, quick growing, eight to fifteen feet high, with spreading branches; found on the borders of damp woods. Ranges from Quebec to Minnesota, south to South Carolina, and Missouri. Suckers freely; wood yellowish and close-grained.

*Bark.*—Light, greenish gray with linear white cracks. Branchlets at first pale green with white lenticels, downy; later brownish purple; finally ashen gray.

*Leaves.*—Opposite, pinnately compound, borne on long peti-oles. Leaflets three, terminal leaflet long-petioled; the others short-petioled, ovate or oval, two and one-half to four inches long, wedge-shaped or rounded at base, finely serrate, acuminate at apex; midvein and primary veins depressed above, prominent beneath. They come out of the bud involute, bright green, shining, covered with white hairs beneath; when full grown are pale green, smooth above, slightly downy below. In autumn they turn a pale dull yellow. Stipules and stipels fugacious. Petioles angular and grooved.

*Flowers.*—April, May. Perfect, abundant, bell-shaped, white, borne in terminal or axillary drooping compound racemes, with small bracts at the base of the partial footstalks. Pedicels jointed.

*Calyx.*—Five-lobed; lobes oblong, acute, imbricate in bud, persistent. The calyx, often tinged with rose-color, folds around the petals so as to form an imperfect tube.

American Bladder-nut, *Staphylea trifolia*.
Leaves 2½′ to 4′ long.  Racemes 3′ to 4′ long.

*Corolla.*—Petals five, white, spatulate, inserted on the margin of a disk at the base of the calyx, imbricate in bud.

*Stamens.*—Five, alternate with the petals, filaments thread-like; anthers introrse, two-celled.

*Pistil.*—Ovary of three carpels united in the axis, superior; styles three, slightly cohering; ovules many.

*Fruit.*—An angular, pale green capsule, one and a half inches long and three inches in circumference; made up of three membranous pods grown together, each ending in a sharp point. Seeds two to five, brown, ovoid, flattened. September.

The extraordinarily inflated seed pods are the distinguishing characteristic of the Bladder-nut, and it requires very little imagination to make them look like tiny balloons. Many of the ovules abort, but there are usually one or two that mature in each cell of the capsule. The seeds when ripe break loose from their attachments and rattle about when the pod is shaken. They are brown, shining, and bony; those of a European species are often strung as rosary beads.

While the individual blossom is not very attractive, the full-flowered drooping racemes which cover the bush in the spring give a very pretty effect. The plant improves greatly under cultivation; flowers more abundantly, grows more luxuriantly and in more symmetrical form than its wild relatives.

A late blooming species from Caucasus, *Staphylea colchica*, has lately been introduced. It is a handsome bush with trifoliate leaves and many white flowers which exhale a fragrance suggestive of orange-blossoms.

Fruiting Capsules of American Bladder-nut.

# ANACARDIÀCEÆ--SUMACH FAMILY

## SMOOTH SUMACH. SCARLET SUMACH

*Rhús glàbra.*

*Rhus* is by some referred to a Celtic word meaning red ;
others derive it from the Greek word meaning run, because the roots spread underground to a considerable distance from the trunk ; still others refer it to a Greek word
which indicates its value medicinally.   Sumach is derived
from Simaq, the Arabic name of the plant.

Low growing, spreading, with irregular branches and rather
unshapely form ; rarely becoming a small tree ; the twigs and
branchlets glabrous and more or less glaucous.   Found in dry
soil from Nova Scotia to British Columbia and south to Florida,
Mississippi, and Arizona.   Foliage sometimes used for tanning.

*Leaves.* — Alternate, pinnately compound, eight to fifteen
inches long; leaflets eleven to thirty-one, sessile, lanceolate or
oblong-lanceolate, three to five inches long, on a large smooth
stalk, round and often oblique at base, serrate, acuminate at
apex, rachis not winged; when full grown are dark green
above, whitish beneath ; in autumn they turn a brilliant scarlet
and orange.

*Flowers.* — June to August.   Polygamo - diœcious, small,
green, borne in densely flowered terminal spikes.   Calyx five-
cleft, persistent ; corolla, of five petals, imbricate in the bud ;
stamens five, inserted on a disk ; ovary one, and styles three.

*Fruit.*—Drupe, small, one-seeded, sub-globose, red, covered
with short, crimson, acid hairs ; borne in dense terminal spikes.

Smooth Sumach, *Rhus glabra.*

Leaflets 3' to 5' long.

It often happens that the Smooth Sumach and the Staghorn Sumach, *Rhus hirta*, make thickets together. Both love sandy soil, the gravelly upland, the neglected corners of fields; and by means of their deeply extended roots are able to take possession of and to hold large tracts to the exclusion of other plants. These sumachs cannot be distinguished by the difference in size alone, for the young Staghorn before it completes its growth is often just the height of its smaller brother. But the twigs and petioles of *Rhus hirta* are always clothed in velvet, while similar twigs and petioles of *Rhus glabra* are without hairs and frequently covered with a pale bloom. In autumn the stems are crowned by pyramidal heads made up of velvety red berries; these remain on the bush but slightly changed in color throughout the winter. The autumnal coloring of the leaves is a most brilliant scarlet and crimson, brightened with yellow and orange.

A variety, *Rhus glabra laciniata*, the Fern-leaved Sumach, is believed to be a sport of *Rhus glabra*. It is a very satisfactory shrub for lawn or garden planting. The foliage is finely cut and in autumn as its feathery leaves take on the crimson hues of its type the effect is excellent.

## DWARF SUMACH. MOUNTAIN SUMACH

*Rhus copallina.*

The Mountain Sumach is a tree; but most gardeners think it a shrub, misled no doubt by its name of Dwarf. It is usually planted in lawns and gardens upon the

Mountain Sumach, *Rhus copallina.*

Leaflets 3′ to 5′ long.

supposition that it is a shrub. Whatever form it may have upon mountain tops,—when transferred to the lowlands, given a rich soil and opportunity to grow, it proceeds forthwith to become a tree, and is reduced to a shrub by main force alone.

This beautiful creature, clothed in the summer with foliage of dark glossy green, bearing its great clusters of red fruit throughout the winter, showing in autumn the most superb combination of the hues of crimson and scarlet, pays the price of its beauty and is cut and mutilated out of all semblance of nature in order to make it a shrub.

Long ago Horace told us, " Though you drive out nature with a fork, yet will she always return." And the Dwarf Sumach is and will continue to be a tree, notwithstanding the knife and the pruning shears.

The blooming period is late, sometimes in early August. The panicle of sterile flowers is twelve to eighteen inches long, while that of the fertile ones is three to six. A persistent character is the winged petiole by which it is readily distinguished from other sumachs.

### POISON SUMACH

*Rhus vérnix. Rhus venenàta.*

The Poison Sumach is in its best estate a tree, but it occurs so frequently as a shrub, and is really such a menace where it grows, that the form of its leaves and the general appearance of the plant can not be made too evident to the community at large. It is often confused in the popular mind with the other sumachs of many-foliate leaves, *Rhus hirta, Rhus glabra,* and *Rhus*

Poison Sumach, *Rhus vernix.*

Leaflets 2′ to 4′ long.

*copallina,* and consequently all sumachs are feared. It can, however, be very easily distinguished from them.

The leaflets of the great compound leaves of *Rhus hirta* and *Rhus glabra* have serrate margins; those of the Poison Sumach are entire. The leaves of *Rhus copallina* might perhaps be mistaken for those of the Poison Sumach were it not for the winged petiole which is a never failing character of the Mountain Sumach.

The leaflets of *Rhus vernix* are five to thirteen, nearly sessile, varying from ovate to obovate or oval, entire, acute at apex, a beautiful shining green and the autumnal tints exceedingly brilliant. The petiole is often purple and the veins are frequently purplish.

The fruit is grayish white, about the size of a pea, destitute of hairs, and borne in loose axillary panicles three to eight inches long.

This is the most poisonous woody plant of our flora. Its juices and the effluvium exhaled by it under a hot sun, are extremely poisonous to some persons. There are those who are absolutely immune, others so sensitive that they can not pass the bush with impunity. It is very dangerous to experiment with it recklessly. The poison shows itself in painful and long continued swellings upon the surface of the body, usually the face and hands.

### POISON IVY. CLIMATH

*Rhus radicáns. Rhus toxicodéndron.*

This is a woody vine climbing by numerous aerial rootlets, the stem sometimes two or three inches in diameter. It climbs trees and fence posts and ranges

Poison Ivy, *Rhus radicans.*

Leaflets 1′ to 4′ long.

from Nova Scotia to Florida and westward to Minnesota, Nebraska, and Arkansas. The compound leaves have three leaflets, so that they are very easily distinguished from those of the Virginia Creeper, *Parthenocissus quinquefolia*, which has five palmate leaflets; and from the Bitter Sweet, which has seven to nine pinnate leaflets. These Poison Ivy leaflets are ovate or rhombic, entire or sparingly sinuate, the apex acute or acuminate; the lateral ones almost sessile; the terminal stalked. The flowers are green and borne in loose axillary panicles; the fruit is like that of *Rhus vernix*. The plant is poisonous to the touch, and should be avoided. All the poisonous species of *Rhus* ought to be extirpated root and branch, but instead of that they are increasing. This is largely due to the immunity they enjoy because people are afraid to touch them; but in winter probably they could be easily and safely destroyed; destroyed they certainly should be.

### POISON IVY. NORTHERN POISON OAK

*Rhús microcárpa. Rhus toxicodéndron.*

The two plants now known as *Rhus radicans* and *Rhus microcarpa* were formerly considered as a single species and described under the name *Rhus toxicodendron*, which name is now given to a third species of southern habitat. The plant popularly known as Poison Ivy is the running vine so abundant in fields and by the roadsides throughout the north. The stem often trails upon the ground and sends up erect branchlets six or eight inches high which make a tiny thicket; sometimes the entire plant is erect but low. The leaves are

Poison Ivy, *Rhus microcarpa.*
Leaflets 1½′ to 3′ long.

compound, of three leaflets. These leaflets are pale green, ovate or ovate-rhombic, acute or acuminate, sharply toothed, lobed, or entire. The fruit is similar to that of *Rhus radicans*. The leaves, like those of *Rhus vernix* and *Rhus radicans*, are poisonous to the touch and should be avoided.

## FRAGRANT SUMACH. SWEET-SCENTED SUMACH

### *Rhus aromática. Rhus canadénsis.*

Diffuse or ascending, two to six feet high; found in dry rocky woods from Vermont to Florida, west to Minnesota, Arkansas, and Louisiana. Leaves fragrant when crushed.

*Leaves.*—Alternate, pinnately compound, three-foliate, two to four inches long, aromatic. Leaflets ovate or rhomboid, one to two inches long; lateral leaflets sessile; terminal leaflet short-stalked, wedge-shaped at base, coarsely crenate or crenate-dentate, acute at apex, very downy when young. In autumn they turn a brilliant orange and scarlet. Petioles one-half to an inch long, glabrous or pubescent.

*Flowers.*—March, April. Polygamo-diœcious, yellowish green, small, in clustered spikes, appearing before the leaves. The catkin-like spikes are developed on the branches in late autumn.

*Fruit.*—Drupe, red, globose, downy, borne in short clustered spikes; produced sparingly.

The Fragrant Sumach is often found on sandy banks and knolls, frequently occurring in dense patches. It rarely rises more than four feet, and this habit makes it most valuable to the gardener when he wishes a plant to bring up the line of green from the grass to the taller shrubs; it does not grow away from him, but does just what he expects it to do. The lower branches of a vigorous plant will lie upon the ground.

Fragrant Sumach, *Rhus aromatica*.
Leaflets 1′ to 2′ long.

In the spring the branches are loaded with early yellow flowers; in summer the dark green foliage is clean and bright; in autumn it clothes itself in the red and yellow of its race; and in winter it becomes a little gray bush speckled with small spikes of downy flower buds that look like catkins.

*Rhus trilobata*, the Ill-scented Sumach or Skunk Bush is about the same size as the Fragrant Sumach. The leaves are tri-foliate, leaflets sessile or nearly so, puberulent when young, ovate or oval, obtuse, the terminal one wedge-shaped at base, all crenately few-lobed or toothed or sometimes entire; unpleasantly odorous. The flowers and fruit are very similar to those of *Rhus aromatica*. It is a western species ranging from Illinois westward.

### SMOKE-TREE

*Côtinus côtinus.*

*Cotinus* is an ancient name of obscure meaning, without significance in its present use.

The Smoke-tree of our gardens is one of the most interesting of cultivated plants, and is also one that has been valued from very ancient times. Pliny describes it as an Apennine shrub and Gerard records it as growing in England in 1597.

With us it vibrates between tree and shrub; sometimes reaching the height of twenty feet, again attaining only five or six. The billowy masses of its fruiting panicles attract attention and the plant is well known; in fact it would be difficult for it to remain unknown.

The bloom is polygamo-dioecious; the staminate

Ill-scented Sumach, *Rhus trilobata.*

Leaflets ½′ to 1′ long.

and pistillate flowers are produced upon different individuals and appear in May. These flowers are small, yellowish green, and borne in ample, loose, terminal panicles branching from the axils of linear leaf-like bracts. The petals are small; the stamens are five; the styles are three.

After the blooming season is past the bush begins to show that personal and peculiar character which has made it a garden favorite for two thousand years. A wonderful change comes over the little pedicels or stalks of the fertile flowers. They were at first half or three-quarters of an inch long and now they begin to lengthen and at the same time to develop a thick growth of soft hairs. This is especially the case with the pedicels which bear no fruit. The result is that each fruiting panicle becomes a loose, fluffy aggregation of plumose threads, and takes on a charming range of color,—pale green, dull yellow, lurid red,—and so covers the head and so overpowers the foliage that the bush becomes a billowy mass,—each single spray not improperly likened to a puff of smoke. This "smoke" is in its best condition during June and July.

The plant fruits but sparingly; at the end of some of the feathery pedicels, by searching, a little, greenish brown, one-sided drupe may be discovered almost lost among the clustering threads.

There is an American Smoke-tree, *Cotinus cotinoides*, of southwestern habitat; reaching its best development in Missouri and Indian Territory. As an ornamental plant it is not the equal of our cultivated species.

Stammate Flowers of Smoke-tree, *Cotinus cotinus.*

# PAPILIONÀCEÆ—PEA FAMILY

The pea blossom may, with the aid of a little imagination, be said to resemble a butterfly; it certainly is

Flower of Sweet Pea.

unique in form and so distinctive in character that any plant bearing such a blossom can at once be assigned to its proper place; hence the Latin name of the Pea family,—*Papilionaceæ*, the butterflies.

The petals of this unique blossom differ so greatly in form and size that they have received distinguishing names. The uppermost of the five is very much larger than the others and is called the standard or banner. In

Banner, Wings and Keel Petals of the Sweet Pea.

the bud it is distinctly the protector of the

Stamens and Pistil of Sweet Pea.

others; it surrounds and embraces them; the calyx being unable to do this because of its small size. The two lateral petals are called wings; and the two lowest, which are more or less united, make up

Young Pod of Sweet Pea.

the keel. The keel encloses the stamens and the tiny pod. Stamens usually are ten, with filaments united so as to form one or two groups; some-

94

times nine are together and one is apart; rarely, all are separate. The fruit is a pod called a legume, of which the pea pod is a typical example.

The *Papilionaceæ* are in many respects a wonderful group of plants. One of their greatest and most remarkable qualities has but recently been understood. For ages leguminous seeds have been valued for their nourishing quality, differing from grain in the fact that they contain a large percentage of nitrogen as contrasted with the predominating carbon compounds of the cereals. The question whence came this great quantity of nitrogen long remained a horticultural problem, but recently nature's riddle has been solved. It is now known that the roots of leguminous plants are the hosts of myriads of organisms called bacteroids, some of which possess the power of fixing the free nitrogen of the air, and through them it is acquired by the plant.

### FALSE INDIGO

*Amórpha fruticòsa.*

*Amorpha*, deformed; so named because four petals are wanting.

Tall, five to twenty feet high; prefers the borders of streams; native to the Mississippi valley; frequently cultivated.

*Leaves.*—Alternate, compound, odd-pinnate, six to sixteen inches long; leaflets eleven to twenty-one, short-stalked, one to two inches long, oval or elliptic, rounded or narrowed at base, entire, obtuse, slightly mucronate or emarginate at apex, sparingly punctate with pellucid dots. They come out of the bud pale green, clammy and hairy, when full grown are a bright yellow, green above, paler beneath. In autumn they become pale yellow.

*Flowers.*—May to July. Perfect, violet-purple, borne in dense, terminal, spicate racemes which are three to six inches long.

*Calyx.*—Bell-shaped, five-toothed ; teeth somewhat irregular, green, touched with purple.

*Corolla.*—Deformed papilionaceous ; consisting of one petal only, the standard, which is violet-purple, erect, clawed, emarginate, wrapped around the stamens and the style ; wings and keel wanting.

*Stamens.*—Nine or ten, monadelphous, exserted ; filaments violet-purple ; anthers orange.

*Pistil.*—Ovary one, superior, sessile, two-celled ; style curved, violet-purple.

*Fruit.*—Pod, glandular, short, curved, never opening, usually two-seeded.

The flower of the False Indigo is an interesting example of arrested development. The corolla starts out to be papilionaceous,—a butterfly blossom—but something happens and when the bud opens all that can be seen of the blossom is the broad banner, closely wrapped about the stamens and pistil, trying to do the whole duty of a corolla by protecting the central parts of the flower. The banner, filaments, and style are a deep rich purple ; the protruding anthers a brilliant orange ; and the result is that the terminal spike covered with these flowers glows luridly in the sunlight. The flowering impulse begins at the base and moves spirally around the central axis to the apex, thus prolonging the blooming period for a considerable time. The bush is ornamentally effective. After the blooming period is past it looks not unlike a locust seedling.

False Indigo, *Amorpha fructicosa.*

Leaflets 1′ to 2′ long.   Flower spikes 3′ to 6′ long.

## LEAD PLANT. DOWNY AMORPHA

*Amórpha canéscens.*

A spreading bush one to four feet high; leaves and shoots and flower spikes densely covered with soft, white hairs. Is a plant of the prairies; ranges from Indiana to Minnesota and Manitoba, southward to Louisiana and Texas.

*Leaves.*—Alternate, odd-pinnate, almost sessile, abundant, crowded, two to four inches long; leaflets fifteen to forty-nine, small, crowded, almost sessile, oval or lanceolate, rounded at base, entire, obtuse or acute, and mucronate at apex.

*Flowers.*—July, August. Perfect, bright blue, borne in densely clustered, terminal spikes, two to seven inches long. Flower is conspicuous because of the bright blue of the corolla and the brilliant orange of the anthers.

*Calyx.*—Bell-shaped, hairy, five-toothed; teeth lanceolate.

*Corolla.*—Deformed, papilionaceous, consisting only of the standard which is bright blue, nearly orbicular or obcordate, and wrapped about the stamens and style. Wings and keel wanting.

*Stamens.*—Ten, monadelphous at the very base, otherwise distinct.

*Pistil.*—Ovary superior, sessile, two-celled; style curved.

*Fruit.*—Pod, small, oblong, partly enclosed in the persistent calyx, hairy, one-seeded.

Everything about this shrub seems crowded. The small leaflets fairly push each other to find standing room; the flowers crush each other upon the central axis of the spike; and the spikes themselves are crowded upon the end of the branches.

Curiously enough there has developed concerning this plant of the western prairies a modern reappearance of the ancient doctrine of signatures. In many places it is very generally believed that the presence

Lead Plant, *Amorpha canescens.*

Leaves 2′ to 4′ long.  Leaflets ⅙′ to ¼′ long.  Flower spikes 2′ to 7′ long.

of this gray-hued bush marks the existence of lead ore in the soil; and for no other reason than that the plant being densely covered with silvery hairs has a certain leaden color. It is well known to the medical profession that many plants formerly in high repute for their medicinal properties are absolutely worthless; and that the only reason for this reputation was the resemblance more or less marked between some part of the plant and some part of the human body. In like manner the prophetic value of the Lead Plant is based upon nothing more substantial than the gray color of its leaves.

The Downy Amorpha is a very attractive bush; the fine compound leaves clothed in silken gray contrast well with the deep purple spikes of flowers brightened by their golden stamens. The gardeners report it as hardy, and also as valuable for color combinations. Its blooming season continues several weeks.

Another plant of the genus, *Amorpha nana*, is also found on the western prairies. This is a low bushy shrub, not more than three feet high, with compound leaves of thirteen to nineteen tiny, bright green leaflets and a terminal solitary spike of brilliant fragrant flowers, each with its purple banner and its golden stamens.

### WOAD WAXEN. DYER'S GREENWEED

*Genìsta tinctòria.*

*Genista* is Celtic for small shrub ; the root is *gen*, a bush.

A low branching shrub, one to two feet high, with creeping root-stalks and upright branches. A native of Europe, it has

Woad-waxen, *Genista tinctoria.*
Leaves ½′ to 1½′ long.   Flowers ½′ to ⅝′ long.

escaped from the gardens and is found on dry hills from Maine
to New York, where it becomes a troublesome weed.

*Leaves.*—Alternate, one-foliate, sessile, elliptical or lanceolate,
one-half to one and one-half inches long, narrowed at base, entire, acute at apex, bright shining green ; midvein depressed
above, primary veins obscure.

*Flowers.*—Summer. Papilionaceous, one-half to five-eighths
of an inch long, borne in many short, few-flowered, terminal
racemes. Calyx, two-lipped. Corolla clear bright yellow, without markings.

*Fruit.*—Pod, an inch long, flat, glabrous.

In *Garden and Forest* of August, 1888, is given the
following account of *Genista tinctoria*. " In some parts
of Essex County, Massachusetts, it has become thoroughly naturalized, and has taken possession of thousands of acres of rocky upland, from which it is practically impossible to exterminate it, and which is thus
ruined for pasturage or for tillage. These hills where
the Woad Waxen is in flower, seem to be covered with
a golden carpet and present an appearance quite unlike anything which can be seen in any other part
of the United States. There is a tradition that the
Woad Waxen was introduced into the United States
by Governor John Endicott of Salem, one of the pio-
neers of American horticulture."

The leaf of this plant is a sort of botanical puzzle ;
it is called a compound leaf of a single leaflet, which
seems a contradiction in terms. But if you look at
the petiole under a glass, it is very clear that there is
a joint, and this indicates that the leaf is indeed compound, but that all the leaflets have aborted save one.

In England the Woad Waxen used to be collected
by the poor country people and sold to the dyers.

During the gathering period women could earn about two shillings a day. After a time the industry languished, for the roots were valuable as well as the stem, and eventually the plant was so nearly exterminated that it was no longer profitable to market it. One hears across the pages of the record a familiar echo, for it seems that under the specious purpose of keeping the plants fresh so much water was added to the load that the dealers felt themselves defrauded.

## ROSE ACACIA. MOSS LOCUST

*Robínia híspida.*

*Robinia* commemorates the botanical labors of Jean Robin, herbalist to Henry III., and director of the gardens of the Louvre.

The Rose Acacia is a large shrub of southern range, but hardy at the north and highly prized for its beauty. So thickly beset are twig, petiole, pedicel and fruit pod with bristly hairs that they look mossy. The bush grows vigorously, matures early, and in May and June, also lingering into July, produces the most exquisite rose-colored pea-like blossoms in loose, lax racemes. A native of the woodlands, it requires protection against high winds, for its branches have never learned to defend themselves and are easily broken. It suckers freely and, like the other species of its genus, makes thickets when permitted.

## LABURNUM. GOLDEN CHAIN

*Labúrnum vulgáre.*

The well known tree-like shrub, Laburnum or Golden Chain, is one of the best of our imported

Rose Acacia, *Robina hispida*.

Golden Chain, *Laburnum vulgare.*

plants. It often attains the height of ten to fifteen feet. The leaves are tri-foliate on rather long petioles. Early in May the clear lemon yellow pea blossoms, borne in pendulous racemes six to eight inches long, fairly drip from the branches. The flower is a clear yellow, except that the banner bears a small group of reddish brown lines. The keel, as usual, nearly imprisons the stamens, whose united filaments form a protecting tube for the slender pod within. By the middle of July the pods, one to two inches long, hang in racemes from the branches and later become brown and dry; finally they open, discharging each its quota of small, dark brown beans.

The plant grows freely in any good garden soil, but prefers that with lime in it. Several varieties are in cultivation.

# DRUPÀCEÆ—PLUM FAMILY

## THE PLUM

*Prùnus.*

*Prunus* is the ancient Latin name of the plum-tree.

The genus *Prunus* belongs to the Drupe-bearing family, which is so named because the fruit of every member from highest to lowest is a drupe; that is, a simple stone fruit, of which the plum and the cherry are excellent examples. The individuals are either trees or shrubs.

Within the range covered by this volume are several native and two naturalized *Prunus* shrubs, growing on barrens, sea-beaches, sandy hillsides, or gravelly ridges. The flowers have a marked family resemblance; they suggest tiny roses, white or pink, and are usually borne in clusters. They are produced from separate, lateral, scaly buds which were formed the autumn before, and they either precede the leaves or appear with them. The characters common to the flowers of all members of the genus are: A calyx with an urn-shaped tube and a five-lobed spreading border which falls after flowering; a corolla of five petals which are inserted on the throat of the calyx-tube; many stamens, also inserted on the throat of the calyx-tube; and finally the character that differentiates the genus,—a single long-styled pistil which sits alone at the bottom of the urn-shaped calyx-tube and there remains, continually enlarging as time goes on until it develops into what we know as a stone fruit.

### BEACH PLUM

*Prùnus marìtìma.*

Low, straggling, thornless, one to seven feet high, growing in clumps among the loose stones or in the sand of the sea-shore and in arid sandy places, twenty miles or more from the sea. Ranges from New Brunswick to Delaware and Virginia.

*Stems.*—Shoots stout, brown, pubescent, dotted with orange lenticels. Stems dark, erect, or prostrate; branches stiff.

*Leaves.*—Alternate, simple, pinnately veined, two to three inches long, oval, ovate or obovate, rounded at base, sharply serrate, acute at apex. They come out of the bud convolute, pale green, downy, shining; when full grown are dark green, glabrous above, pale green and pubescent beneath. Often there are one or two glands near the base. In autumn they turn a dull red or orange. Stipules small and early deciduous. Petioles short, pubescent.

*Flowers.*—April, May, before the leaves. White, showy, abundant, one-half to three-fourths of an inch broad, borne in lateral umbels; calyx-lobes rounded, slightly pubescent, petals obovate.

*Fruit.*—Globose drupe, purple or crimson, covered with a bloom, one-half to one inch in diameter, sweet when ripe. Abundant. August, September. Offered for sale in the local markets under the name of Beach Plum.

*Garden and Forest* describes the Beach Plum as " A handsome plant when in flower, and one which is too seldom seen in gardens. A well known coast-plant, it is found from Maine to Virginia, frequently covering sandy dunes adjacent to sea-beaches. It is a low, com-

Beach Plum, *Prunus maritima.*
Flowers $\frac{5}{12}'$ to $\frac{3}{4}'$ across.

pact shrub, rarely more than three or four feet high, in
its blooming period covered with small white flowers,
which in late summer are followed by a profusion of
handsome, globular, purple or scarlet fruit which is
collected in large quantities at some points on the New
England coast and sold in the markets for preserving.

" As a garden plant this shrub covers itself early
in May with innumerable small white flowers which

wreathe the branches from
end to end and have the
merit of lasting for a considerable time."

Graves' Beach Plum, *Prunus
gravesii*, is a rare species, four
feet high, with orbicular serrate leaves. The white flowers, borne in lateral umbels,

Leaves of the Beach Plum, 2′ to 3′ long.    expand with the leaves. Fruit
is globose, nearly black with light blue bloom.

Blackthorn or Buckthorn, *Prunus spinosa*, two to fifteen feet high, is a native of Europe, which has escaped
from gardens and is found along roadsides from Massachusetts to Pennsylvania. It is a much-branched,
thorny shrub, with oblong or ovate leaves, rounded at
base, serrate, and obtuse at apex. The fruit is globose,
half an inch in diameter, nearly black, covered with a
bloom.

### SAND CHERRY. DWARF CHERRY

#### *Prùnus pùmìla.*

A depressed or trailing shrub, sometimes lifting its branches
six inches, sometimes three or four feet. Found on sandy or

Sand Cherry, *Prunus pumila*.

Leaves 1½′ to 2′ long.  Fruit ⅜′ in diameter.

gravelly shores along the sea-coast from New Brunswick to New Jersey, also along the shores of the Great Lakes to Michigan and westward. Suckers freely.

*Stems.*—Shoots reddish; older stems brown with shining, grayish, outer bark.

*Leaves.*—Alternate, simple, pinnately veined, one and a half to two and a half inches long, oblanceolate or spatulate, narrowed at the base, serrate especially toward the apex. They come out of the bud conduplicate, pale green, shining; when full grown are glabrous, deep green above and pale below; midvein and primary veins conspicuous. In autumn they turn a deep blood red. Stipules linear, glandular, serrate at base.

*Flowers.*—April, May, with the leaves. White, one-fourth to three-eighths of an inch broad, borne in lateral few-flowered umbels; calyx-lobes rounded; petals small, obovate; stamens numerous.

*Fruit.*—Drupe, dark red or dark purple, nearly black, without bloom, about half an inch long, three-eighths broad; flesh thin, acid. August.

The Sand Cherry grows on the beach in almost pure sand; in fruiting time the bearing stems are depressed with the burden of the fruit. It suckers freely and forms clumps.

Appalachian Cherry, *Prunus cuneata*, is a form allied to *Prunus pumila*, finding its home among rocks instead of sand. Often four feet high. Leaves oblong or obovate, wedge-shaped at base, more or less serrate, obtuse or acute at apex.

## CHOKE CHERRY

### *Prùnus virginiàna.*

The Choke Cherry is ranked among the trees, but so frequently and so persistently appears as a shrub that it is popularly believed to be one. It produces

Appalachian Cherry, *Prunus cuneata*.

Leaves 1′ to 3′ long.

the choke cherry, that well known fruit, familiar to every country child of New England and the Middle States. These cherries are borne in a full drooping raceme, each one about the size of marrowfat pea, varying in color from dark to bright red and sometimes yellow. There is a peculiar astringent quality about them, that puckers the mouth of the eater and darkens the teeth and the lips. When cooked this quality entirely disappears.

The flowers appear in loose racemes produced upon the leafy branches of the year ; are white, with nearly orbicular petals and exserted stamens.

### FLOWERING ALMOND

*Prùnus japónica. Prùnus nàna. Prùnus amýgdalus.*

> The hope, in dreams of a happier hour,
>   That alights on misery's brow,
> Springs forth like the silvery almond flower
>   That blooms on a leafless bough.
>
> —THOMAS MOORE.

The Flowering Almond was the gem of our grandfathers' gardens. In books and catalogues it possesses a fine collection of Latin names; but when it came into England in the seventeenth century it so surpassed the other almonds known there in the beauty of its flowers that it gained at once the name of Flowering. Through all the changes of changeful science this name it has kept.

This dwarf bush is rarely more than four feet high, and early, before the leaves, the slender branches burst into abundant bloom. The flowers are solitary or in two-flowered umbels, very double, "crimson-

Choke Cherry, *Prunus virginiana*.
Leaves 2′ to 4′ long.   Racemes 3′ to 5′ long.

tipped," and appear so profusely as to transform the branch into a flowery sceptre. Stamens are few, sometimes a perfect one can be found, but usually a few filaments do duty for all. Under a glass the pistil will be seen to have become leaf-like. The leaves are a quarter grown before the petals fall.

This beautiful creature comes into the spring-time with charming grace ; the whole plant is a mass of pinkish bloom ; its surpassing loveliness continues for but one short week ; then scattering its petals to the ground it passes from recollection until another spring calls it to its short-lived service. " Beauty is its own excuse for being."

In its flowering period the little bush is a late companion or an immediate follower of the forsythias ; it blooms with the magnolias and the red-buds ; before its roses have faded the lilacs are in bloom, and the *Spirea prunifolia* is out ; often this last overlaps the other so that one sees two sets of flower buttons side by side. Two varieties of the species are in cultivation, one bearing pinkish flowers, and the other white.

Flowering Almond, *Prunus japonica.*

# ROSÀCEÆ—ROSE FAMILY

## MEADOW SWEET. WILLOW-LEAVED SPIRÆA

*Spiræa salicifòlia.*

*Spiræa*, a Greek name meaning twisted, referring to the twisted pods of some species.

An erect shrub, two to five feet high, simple or branched above, with smooth, yellowish brown bark ; found in swamps or moist ground. Ranges from Newfoundland to Georgia, and west to Missouri ; also native in northern Europe, and in Asia. Roots run for several feet just below the surface ; variable ; often cultivated.

*Leaves.*—Alternate, simple, pinnately veined, two to three inches long, oblong or lanceolate, obovate or oblanceolate, rounded or wedge-shaped at base, serrate especially above the middle, obtuse or acute at apex. They come out of the bud slightly involute, yellow green, tipped with reddish brown ; when full grown smooth, yellow green above, paler green beneath ; when borne on the upper part of a young shoot frequently one or two small leaves appear in the axils of the regular leaf. The autumnal tints are a dull yellow or a dull red. Petioles short ; stipules fugitive or wanting.

*Flowers.*—July to September. White or pinkish, perfect, from one-fourth to five-eighths of an inch across, borne in dense terminal panicles.

*Calyx.*—Tube bell-shaped, five-lobed.

*Corolla.*—Petals five, short-clawed, white, or rose-tinted, obovate ; inserted on the calyx, imbricate in bud.

Meadow Sweet, *Spiræa salicifolia.*

Leaves 2′ to 3′ long.  Flowers ¼′ to ⅜′ across.

*Stamens.*—Numerous, exserted, inserted on the calyx; filaments threadlike.

*Pistil.*—Ovaries five, superior, united at the base; style threadlike, stigma capitate.

*Fruit.*—Dry, consisting of five one-celled, smooth carpels, united at base, encircled by the persistent calyx-cup. September.

The common Meadow Sweet of the eastern states is a variable and widely distributed plant, of which several varieties are in cultivation; all, however, keep fairly true to the type. It suckers freely, so that each little bush, if given time and freedom, will make a thicket of upright stems, each of which, in the flowering season will bear its panicle of white or pinkish flowers. Often this rosy glow comes rather from the calyx disk and the rosy anthers than from the petals. The abundant stamens are characteristic and give the cluster a peculiar " fuzzy " look.

It has gathered to itself several common names, among them, Queen of the Meadow, Quaker Lady, Willow-leaved Spiræa. It differs from *Spiræa tomentosa* in that stem and leaves are glabrous and the flower cluster a little more open.

### HARDHACK. STEEPLE-BUSH

*Spiræa tomentòsa.*

Erect, leafy, two to three feet high; stems usually simple, twigs densely covered with brown tomentum; found in swamps and low grounds. Ranges from Nova Scotia to Georgia and Manitoba to Kansas. Spreads rapidly by underground shoots; worthy of cultivation.

Steeple-bush, *Spiræa tomentosa*.
Leaves 1′ to 3′ long.   Flowers ¼′ to ⅜′ across.

*Leaves.*—Alternate, simple, pinnately veined, one to three inches long, ovate or oval, rounded or wedge-shaped at base, unequally serrate, obtuse or acute at apex. They come out of the bud slightly involute, densely tomentose; when full grown are dark green above, covered with brown tomentum beneath. Stipules fugitive or wanting. Petioles short.

*Flowers.*—July, September. Rose or pale purple, perfect; borne in dense terminal panicles.

*Calyx.*—Tube bell-shaped, five-lobed.

*Corolla.*—Petals five, short-clawed, rose-tinted, obovate, inserted on the calyx, imbricate in bud.

*Stamens.*—Numerous, exserted, inserted on the calyx; filaments threadlike.

*Pistil.*—Ovaries five, superior, united at the base; style threadlike; stigma capitate.

*Fruit.*—Dry, consisting of five one-celled woolly carpels, united at base, encircled by the persistent calyx-cup. September.

The Steeple-bush is not badly named, for the flowering panicle is terminal, slender, and pointed. The pink spires bloom from the top downward; they have what is known as centrifugal inflorescence, the flowering impulse proceeds from the centre outward. As a consequence the flower cluster is never perfect; when the topmost flowers are open the lower ones are half-formed buds, and when the lower ones are in bloom the topmost are withered and brown.

The *Spiræa* flowers, as a rule, secrete little if any nectar, but they yield much pollen and are eagerly sought by the bees.

This Spiræa takes kindly to cultivation and will thrive in any ordinary position. It is especially valuable because of its late flowering.

Thunberg's Spiræa, *Spiræa thunbergii.*

Leaves 1′ to 2′ long.  Flowers ¼′ to ⅜′ across.

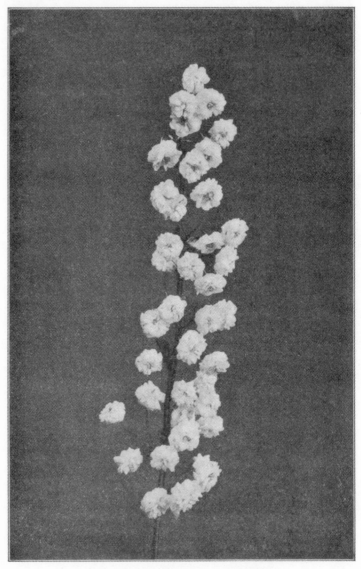

Plum-leaved Spiræa, *Spiræa prunifolia*.

## CULTIVATED SPIRÆAS

Apart from the native species which appear now and then in cultivation, there is a large number of distinctively garden Spiræas of great hardiness and of surpassing beauty. Time would fail to tell the tale of their loveliness; nor could space be allotted to make even a complete list of their numbers. There are, however, a few that stand out preëminent, and although their number may be enlarged by future hybrids and seedlings, it is scarcely conceivable that these should be supplanted. Grace, delicacy, personal charm and exquisite beauty may perhaps be permitted to hold their own against mere bigness—at least in the vegetable world.

We mention first, because it blossoms first, that species of rare and delicate beauty known as *Spiræa thunbergii.* The books report it as a dwarf, but when well placed and well fed it rises in compact and graceful form to the height of five feet. Of the entire group it is the first to bloom, coming out with *Forsythia* and *Magnolia stellata.* The leaves are one to two inches long, a quarter of an inch wide, and of a peculiar, pale, yellow green. It holds this airy foliage bright and clean throughout the summer; and when autumn comes, after many of its companions stand bare and leafless, it clothes itself first in purple bronze and then in orange and scarlet, and stands a figure of beauty until overwhelmed by the autumn storms. In its Japanese home it loves the rocky hillsides and high mountain valleys, and is widely distributed throughout the islands.

The well known double spiræa, *Spiræa prunifolia*, has long been a garden favorite in this country. This double variety was developed by the gardeners of Japan; the single form is probably not cultivated here. It, too, blooms early and the flowers are abundant upon the stem; so that the bush is extremely effective amid its companions. Its habit is rigid, the slender stems have not the grace so characteristic of many of the spiræas. The shining leaves are oblong, rounded at base, and pointed at apex, each one poised with a peculiar curve. In early autumn they turn a scarlet and orange, through which there appears a tone of brown in such a way as to give a wonderful depth and richness to the coloring.

However opinions may differ in regard to other species on the list, the horticultural world agrees that *Spiræa vanhouttei* is the finest of them all. It possesses a remarkable beauty of form; in bloom it stands like a great white fountain; in autumn its foliage runs through a bewildering maze of rich claret, deep red with purple tones, bright scarlet and orange fading to yellow. The origin of the plant is not clearly known; it is generally believed to have been derived from an Asiatic species, *Spiræa triloba*, which, however, is not its equal.

There are many dwarf varieties offered by the dealers, of which one of the best is that known as Anthony Waterer's Spiræa. This bears rose-colored flowers in flat corymbs, and blooms in midsummer. There are also magnificent spiræas on the Pacific slope, in Washington and in Oregon, which should appear among our ornamental plants either in their own persons or in hybrids.

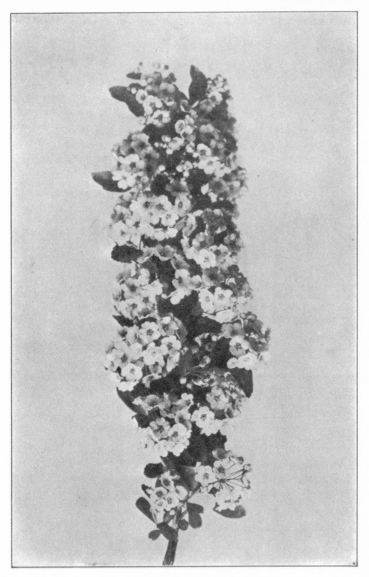

Van Hout's Spiræa, *Spiræa vanhouttei.*

Anthony Waterer's Spiræa.

## NINEBARK

*Opuláster opulifólius.   Physocárpus opulifólius.*

*Opulaster,* resembling a wild opulus, or cranberry-tree.
*Physocarpus,* bladder-fruit, in reference to the inflated
pods.

A shrub three to ten feet high, with recurved branches, smooth
twigs and foliage, the bark peeling off in thin strips ; found on
river banks and in rocky places.    Ranges from Quebec to Georgia, west to Manitoba and Kansas.    Often cultivated.

*Leaves.*—Alternate, simple, palmately veined, one to three
inches long, ovate-orbicular, obtusely or acutely three-lobed,
rounded, wedge-shaped or heart-shaped at base ; lobes irregularly crenate-dentate or crenate-serrate.    Stipules fugitive.   Petioles three-fourths to an inch long.

*Flowers.*—June.    White, rarely purplish, perfect, borne in
panicled, many-flowered hemispherical corymbs one or two inches
broad, which are terminal on short branches.    Pedicels slender,
glabrous or pubescent.

*Calyx.*—Bell-shaped, five-lobed, pubescent, persistent.

*Corolla.*—Petals white, five, rounded, inserted on the throat
of the calyx, imbricate in bud.

*Stamens.*—Thirty to forty, inserted with the petals ; filaments
white, anthers purplish.

*Pistil.*—Carpels five, on short stalks, alternate with the calyx-
lobes.

*Fruit.*—Follicles, glabrous, shining, three-eighths of an inch
long, inflated, acute, obliquely subulate-tipped, each containing
two to four seeds.    Borne in corymbs, each pedicel bearing five.
Seeds ovoid or globose, shining.

The Ninebark is now very generally planted in any
garden group of spiræas.    The flower cluster resembles
that of *Spiræa vanhouttei,* but not quite so many appear
on a flowering spray, and the blooming period comes a
little later.    The plant is a spiræa when it blossoms ;

Ninebark, *Opulaster opulifolius.*

Leaves 1′ to 3′ long.  Flower clusters 1′ to 2′ across.

Ninebark, *Opulaster opulifolius;* in fruit.

but after the petals drop its specific character shows itself and it is clear that its bladder-fruit name is deserved. For each small carpel begins to enlarge, in fact develops considerably beyond the needs of the seeds harbored within its protecting walls. Through changes of green and russet the inflated pods finally become purplish, and a second time the bush challenges attention because of the burden of fruit which weighs its slender branches almost to the ground. It is not altogether pleasant to see a plant so overpowered by its fruit. The Ninebark is sometimes used for hedges; it seems to bear the knife well and makes a leafy wall.

### PEARL BUSH. EXOCHORDA

*Exochórda grandiflòra.*

*Exochorda*, from *exo*, external, and *chorda*, a cord; suggested by the placental cords supposed to be external to carpels.

Exochorda, which appears in our gardens both as tree and shrub, undoubtedly ranks high among the ornamental plants that we have received from China. It inclines to long, slender spray, which very quickly grows out of bounds and becomes straggling, naked stems; but if properly pruned a compact and bushy form may easily be produced and just as easily retained.

The flowers somewhat resemble cherry blossoms, but where the cherry blossom shows a yellow centre, the Exochorda is curiously green, with a few white stamens set on the throat of the calyx. The plant is more

Exochorda, *Exochorda grandiflora*.
Flowers 1′ to 1¼′ across.

closely allied to the spiræas than to the cherries or the roses. The buds look like buttons; the flowers come out about the middle of May, and there is a charming contrast between the tender green of the young leaves and the snow white of the abundant bloom which

crowds upon the end of every twig. Mr. J. G. Jack, writing of Exochorda, says: "It is sometimes complained that the flowers lack individual interest, are cold and without anything to excite sentiment or admiration, except by the almost dazzling effect of the full bloom. But although the blossoms are formal and almost bold in effect and lack agreeable

Leaf of Exochorda, 2′ to 2½′ long.

fragrance, they appear after apple blossoms have faded and before Deutzia and Philadelphus flower, and certainly at this season we have nothing surpassing them in beauty. The flowers themselves are most interesting just as the buds are opening."

The fruit of Exochorda is composed of five small bony carpels adhering, in the form of a star, around the central axis. Young plants are often sterile, but as they get older they fruit abundantly; the seeds germinate quickly.

## KERRIA. CORCHORUS. GLOBE FLOWER

### *Kérria japónica.*

Named after Bellenden Ker, a British botanist.

This is the old-fashioned Corchorus of our gardens, a name originally applied through a misapprehension of the botanical affinities of the plant; a name that should be supplanted by Kerria, which sounds quite as well and is correct. Botanically the plant is allied to the spiræas.

The double-flowered form was the first introduced from Japan, and immediately became a great favorite. The blossoms are bright yellow and so very double that the name Globe Flower does not seem inappropriate.

Kerria. Double-flowered Form.

The single form from which the double was developed came later, and is the more beautiful of the two. It is an error to suppose that a double flower is always better than its type, for the multiplication of petals is frequently gained at the expense of grace and delicacy. In this single form the flowers, often an inch and a half across, are solitary, on slender stalks, and look not unlike great buttercups, only the petals are an orange yellow and not lustrous. The plant does best where it can have partial shade,

as the petals, curiously enough, bleach white in the sunlight, and in a sunny location it is rare to find a flower without one or more white petals.

The leaves are broad-lanceolate, long-pointed, deeply serrate-toothed, bright green above and paler beneath. There is a variety with single flowers and variegated leaves, but it is not the equal of either of the others. In winter the

Kerria. Single-flowered Form.

stems are such a brilliant green that they attract attention standing among the stems of other plants.

## BRAMBLE

*Rùbus.*

*Rubus,* the Roman name, kindred to *ruber,* red.

The Bramble is allied to the roses, and in many respects the likeness between them is marked; but the growth of the stem and the character of the fruit are personal and characteristic, and fully distinguish the genus from any other. In it are included the raspberries, black and red, also the blackberries.

The Bramble is a sort of compromise between a perennial herb and a shrub. The stems are indeed woody, but instead of living on from year to year and bearing an indefinite number of crops, as the currant or the gooseberry, they live but about a year and a half, and perish after maturing their fruit; while the roots live on indefinitely. The young stems make very rapid growth until they have attained their normal stature, then growth ceases. These stems are called canes, and are very noticeable in any vigorous black raspberry or blackberry bush, but not quite so marked in the red raspberry.

The fruit, likewise, will repay careful examination. In the centre of a *Rubus* blossom is a group of carpels set upon a slightly convex receptacle. After the petals fall and the seed vessels begin to enlarge, this convex receptacle enlarges too, and bears upon its sides and apex the numerous tiny drupes; one for each carpel of the blossom. They find themselves considerably crowded, and unite rather by pressure than by growth. In the case of the raspberries, the union of the receptacle with the calyx is stronger than its union with the drupes; so when the so-called berry is ripe the aggregation of little drupes slips off the receptacle and leaves it behind grown fast to the calyx. In the blackberry the conditions are reversed; the union of the receptacle with the drupes is stronger than with the calyx, so when the berry is ripe the drupes carry the receptacle with them. This is the explanation of the white core always found at the centre of a black-berry.

## PURPLE-FLOWERING RASPBERRY

*Rùbus odoràtus.*

Raspberry, from the Italian *raspo*, rough, on account of the roughness of the stem and leaves.

A straggling shrub with upright stems, three to five feet high, found by roadsides, in mountain paths and moist, shady places. Spreads rapidly by underground stems. Ranges from Nova Scotia to Ontario and Michigan, south to Georgia and Tennessee.

*Bark.*—On old stems pale, dull yellow, becoming loose and stringy. The recent shoots and flower branches are thickly covered with purplish glandular hairs, which continue up the petiole, along the midrib and primary veins on the under surface of the leaf, and thickly invest the flower-stalk and the calyx.

*Leaves.*—Alternate, simple, large, seven to nine, sometimes twelve inches broad, palmately three to five-lobed, cordate at base. Lobes serrate, acuminate; the middle one longer than the others. They come out of the bud plicate; shining, reddish, glandular-pubescent; when full grown are bright green, rough, hairy above and beneath. They remain unchanged until destroyed by the frost and storms. Petiole long, very pubescent, enlarged at base; stipules small, lanceolate, acuminate.

*Flowers.*—May to September. Perfect, borne in loose corymbs or panicles, rose purple, showy, one to two inches across; bracts membranous.

*Calyx.*—Deeply five-parted, densely covered with red glandular hairs; lobes tipped with a long slender appendage.

*Corolla.*—Petals five, rose purple, coming crumpled from the bud, inserted on the disk of the calyx.

*Stamens.*—Many, inserted on the calyx; filaments purple; anthers dull yellow, two-celled.

*Pistil.*—Many carpels inserted on a convex receptacle; style purplish; stigma white.

*Fruit.*—Each carpel ripens into a tiny red drupe, and together they form an aggregate fruit, depressed, hemispherical, acid. July, September.

The Purple-flowering Raspberry is very attractive as its pretty rose-like blossoms look out from a dense thicket by a mountain path; it is equally attractive when transferred from its wild-wood home to the garden. When permitted, a single bush will very quickly form a clump, for the underground stems send up abundant shoots. The young stems and shoots are clothed in velvet, so dense are the red hairs which beset them; but the bark of the oldest stems is a thing of shreds and patches. The blooming period extends from June to October, but there is never any great number of blossoms at one time. The spherical unopened buds are crowned with a flowing tassel made of the five long points of the calyx. The blossoms come out from the bud a soft rose purple, but quickly fade in the sunshine. In cultivation the plant should be given a shady place.

The fruit is a red raspberry that sits in a calyx-cup; about it is a fringe of dry stamens. Each little drupe

Purple-flowering Raspberry, *Rubus odoratus.*

Leaves 7′ to 9′ broad.   Flowers 1′ to 2½′ across.

is bright red, velvety with white hairs and crowned with a style. The drupes readily separate from one another and also from the receptacle; in flavor are a sharp acid.

The marked personal characteristic of *Rubus odoratus* is the astonishing abundance of glandular hairs upon the recent shoots, the leaves, the petioles, the flower-stalk and the calyx. Botanically, glands are cellular bodies containing some peculiar secretion, and situated on or below the cuticle, which covers the surface of a plant. Stalked glands are these little bodies elevated upon a stalk or stem.

## WILD RED RASPBERRY

*Rùbus strigòsus.*

Low, erect, three to six feet high, loving dry or rocky situations. Ranges from Newfoundland and Labrador to British Columbia, south in the Alleghanies to North Carolina and southwest to New Mexico. Suckers freely.

*Stems.*—Biennial, branched; new shoots densely clothed with weak glandular bristles and older stems with small hooked prickles. New shoots and branchlets red with a bloom; old stems pale, dull yellowish brown.

*Leaves.*—Alternate, pinnately compound; leaflets five in lower leaves, three in upper leaves, two and a half to three inches long; ovate or ovate-oblong, rounded at base, coarsely and irregularly serrate or slightly lobed, acute or acuminate at apex; lateral leaflets are sessile and bilateral; midvein, primary and secondary veins depressed above, prominent beneath; when full grown the leaves are a bright yellow green, smooth above, pale green or whitish, downy beneath. In autumn they become a rich vinous red, sometimes touched with yellow, or fall with little change of color. Petiole armed with tiny bristles and prickles. Stipules narrow and deciduous.

Red Raspberry, *Rubus strigosus.*

Leaflets 1′ to 3′ long.

*Flowers.*—May. Perfect, rose-like, about half an inch broad, borne in terminal or axillary, loose racemose or paniculate clusters, white; pedicels slender.

*Calyx.*—Persistent, tube short and broad; border deeply five-parted; segments acuminate.

*Corolla.*—Petals five, white, imbricate in bud, inserted on the disk that lines the calyx tube.

*Stamens.*—Numerous, inserted with the petals on the calyx.

*Pistil.*—Carpels numerous, crowded upon a convex receptacle, ripening into drupelets.

*Fruit.*—Consists of many drupelets that adhere and form an aggregate fruit, which falls away from the white spongy receptacle when ripe. Red, delicious. July.

The Red Raspberry of our hillsides and fence corners is the progenitor of all the cultivated varieties found in our gardens; and they really differ very little from it. At first the effort was made to acclimate varieties of *Rubus idæus*, the Red Raspberry of Europe, but this was not a success. Our climate seemed like the woodman's historic trap, especially adapted "to ketch 'em comin' and goin'." If the carefully imported plants survived our summers for a few years, they finally succumbed to our winters. Or, if sheltered from the severity of our winters, one hot dry summer finished them. They simply could not live here. Professor Card considers that over one hundred varieties have been planted, of which not more than eight or ten survive, and these in the gardens of amateurs. All the commercial varieties are either chance seedlings, careful hybridizations, or sports, of *Rubus strigosus*, and their name is legion. It is believed, however, that in several of the best there still lingers a strain of the European raspberry which never fails to improve the quality of the fruit at the same time that it affects the hardiness of the plant.

The root of all the raspberries belongs to that type which is called travelling ; that is, the suckers run out in every direction away from the central root, so that the new stems come up each year in fresh soil. This is nature's plan for providing "green woods and pastures new." It is evident that the raspberry in its wild state is continually changing its situation, and when domesticated it should be frequently taken up and replanted in fresh soil. The seeds are said to retain their vitality for a long time. The white raspberry of cultivation is probably a sport of the common red raspberry.

## BLACK RASPBERRY. THIMBLE-BERRY. BLACK-CAP

### *Rùbus occidentàlis.*

Straggling, prickly, with long arching stems ; growing by bowlders, in fence corners, by falling trees ; common throughout our range and widely cultivated.

*Stems.*—Biennial, slender, terete, recurved, ten to twelve feet long, purple, densely covered with whitish bloom ; often rooting at the tip ; sparingly armed with small hooked prickles. Old stems dull maroon.

*Leaves.*—Alternate, pinnately compound. Leaflets three, rarely five, two to five inches long ; terminal leaflet ovate ; lateral leaflets bilateral ; margins coarsely cut and irregularly serrate, apex acute or acuminate. They come out of the bud plicate, pale yellow green above, downy and glaucous beneath ; when full grown are bluish green above, whitish beneath. In autumn they remain unchanged until destroyed by the early winter storms. Petioles armed with small prickles. Stipules deciduous.

*Flowers.*—May, June. Perfect, white, borne in terminal corymbose clusters, on branchlets apparently borne on one side of the stem.

*Calyx.*—Five-parted, persistent ; tube short ; sepals acute, usually reflexed.

*Corolla.*—Petals five, white, small and fugitive, often emarginate.

*Stamens.*—Many, inserted on the calyx.

*Pistil.*—Carpels many, inserted on a convex receptacle ; style slender.

*Fruit.*—Each carpel ripens into a small drupe and together they form an aggregate fruit, which is black, shining, hemispherical, delicious ; when ripe this falls away from the receptacle, leaving that with the calyx. July, August.

In late summer the Black Raspberry bush shows clearly its bramble nature. The fruiting stems which in June were so vigorous, so crowded with clusters of ripening berries, are now faded, dishevelled, disheartened ; the corymbs of dried calyxes show where the berries were ; the life-impulse is departing from the stem, its vitality is exhausted, it is dying of old age.

Beside the dying stem stands youth and life and vigor in the person of the young cane springing from the centre of the bush and by a graceful arch meeting the ground two or three feet away. Its strong stem bears the bloom of youth ; its leaves fairly glow with life. Its poise is one of exquisite beauty ; but its nature is somewhat feline withal, for it resents disturbance and upon occasion will scratch. It has started on its full career ; this summer it will mature the buds which next year will produce the leaves and flowers and fruit of the plant, and then it, too, will go the way of its predecessors. The King is dead ! Long live the

Black Raspberry, *Rubus occidentalis.*
Leaflets 2′ to 5′ long.

King! The root of the bramble lives on indefinitely but its life functions in consecutive and ever renewed stems.

### HIGH-BUSH BLACKBERRY. COMMON BRIER

*Rùbus nigrobáccus. Rùbus villòsus.*

A straggling prickly bush with stems, both erect and recurved, three to eight feet high; found throughout the eastern portions of the United States and far northward in British America; known by its peculiar and pleasant fruit. Grows in thickets, along roadsides, in neglected fields. Multiplies abundantly by creeping roots.

*Stems.*—Biennial, shrubby, erect or recurved, angular, furrowed, three to eight feet high, armed with stout curved prickles, green or dark purple, with a bloom. Young branches, peduncles, stipules, petioles and veins beneath, pubescent and bearing numerous glandular-tipped hairs.

*Leaves.*—Alternate, compound, three to five-foliate. Leaflets ovate or lance-oblong, two to four inches long, rounded at base, unequally serrate, acute at apex; terminal leaflet somewhat heart-shaped and conspicuously stalked; the side leaflets also stalked; midrib and petiole armed with stout prickles. They come out of the bud plicate, dull reddish green, shining, hairy; when full grown are dark green above, paler, hairy and glandular beneath. In autumn they turn a rich vinous red, varying to bronze, purple or fading to orange. Stipules linear or lanceolate.

*Flowers.*—May, June. Of the rose type, white, showy, three-fourths to an inch and a quarter across, borne mainly in terminal, racemose, leafless panicles. Calyx persistent, deeply five-parted, its tube short and broad; petals white, obovate, much longer than the sepals; stamens inserted on the calyx. Pedicels glandular-hairy, an inch or two long, standing out at obtuse angles to the main axis.

*Fruit.*—An aggregate fruit consisting of many small, black, shining drupes borne on a long white axis which is the elongation of the receptacle. The drupes do not separate from the

High-bush Blackberry, *Rubus nigrobaccus.*
Flowers ¾′ to 1¼′ across.

receptacle, but both fall from the calyx together.   Sweet and aromatic.   August, September.

> The tangled blackberry, crossed and recrossed, weaves
> A prickly network of ensanguined leaves.
>
> —James Russell Lowell.

If you wish to enjoy the richness of the fruit you must not be hasty to pluck it.   When the children say with a shout, "The blackberries are ripe!" I know that I can wait.   When the children report, "The birds are eating the berries!" I know that I can wait.   But when they say, "The bees are on the berries!" I know they are at their ripest.   Then with baskets we sally forth.   *   *   *   Even now we gather those only which drop at the touch,—these in a brimming saucer, with golden cream and a soupçon of powdered sugar are Olympian nectar; they melt before the tongue can measure their full roundness; and seem to be mere bloated bubbles of forest honey.

—"My Farm at Edgewood."   Donald G. Mitchell.

Every one knows the Blackberry, the Common Brier, because of its marked tendency to inhabit and possess the earth. It springs up in any neglected place and, if undisturbed, takes possession and holds its own against all intruders. It loves the sea-shore, flourishes on the mountain side, is especially thrifty at the edge of woods, fairly riots in fields lately cleared or recently burned over, holds to the fencerows, and wanders along the roadside.

The species varies greatly in habit, but each and all forms possess a sturdy vitality which enables them to live in spite of discouragement. Sometimes, indeed, they discourage the farmer, for simply to cut them down is useless; they promptly scramble up again and can be eradicated only by uprooting. When the waste land is to be reclaimed, transformed into pasture, or meadow, or cultivated field, to uproot is praiseworthy; but to destroy this wild luxuriant growth, beautiful in leaf and in flower, grateful in fruit, glorious in its rich autumnal coloring,—simply to make a desolation, or to provide more space for ragweed and plantain and beggar-ticks,—is zeal without knowledge. Yet this is what happens nine cases out of ten when the rural street commissioner starts out upon his devastating career to improve the country roadside.

*Rubus nigrobaccus* is the prevailing form of the high-bush blackberries of the woods and fencerows of the north; from this wild, untamed, hardy stock has sprung the blackberry of cultivation. The well known Lawton, Kittatinny and Wilson varieties originated from wild seedlings found by the wayside and transferred to the garden.

The botanical history of this High-bush Blackberry is entangled and confused. The plant is really *Rubus villosus* of American botanists. It so appears in Gray's Manual, sixth edition. But in following out the rules of nomenclature adopted by the American Association for the Advancement of Science it was discovered that the name *Rubus villosus* belonged to another plant. Prof. L. H. Bailey was able to determine this by personally examining the herbaria of Linnæus and of Aiton. As a consequence our wild-wood brier became nameless, and finally received the Latin synonym of its common name—*nigrobaccus*,—blackberry. In studying the plant it is well to remember that the five-foliate leaves are found usually on young and sterile stems, the three-foliate upon the fertile ones.

Professor Bailey, in " The Evolution of our Native Fruits," published in 1898, writes as follows:

"Of the high-bush blackberry there are three general types or categories:

"(1) The common high-bush blackberry of the north, which has large, pointed, villous leaves and long, open, pubescent racemes. This is the plant which is ordinarily taken as the type of *Rubus villosus*, but strangely enough, although the common blackberry, it now has no scientific name. I, therefore, propose to call it *Rubus nigrobaccus*.

"(2) The leafy-cluster type of blackberry, which is characterized by a stiffer and mostly shorter growth, by smaller and usually narrower leaves, short and leafy flower clusters and the general, although not complete absence of villousness. This plant must now receive the name *Rubus argutus*, and its synonyms are *Rubus frondosus*, and *Rubus suberectus*.

"(3) The thornless blackberry type which must now be called *Rubus canadensis*, a synonym of which is *Rubus millspaughii.*"

Professor Bailey writes further as follows:

"Another form of the high-bush blackberry is a plant which Porter has named *Rubus allegheniensis* or the Mountain Blackberry. * * * Since Professor Porter has studied the plant in its native state for many years I shall accept the plant as a distinct species. I am the more inclined to this opinion since if the common high-bush blackberry were to be united to the Mountain Blackberry, *Rubus allegheniensis* would have to be taken as the type of the species; and I should consider it unfortunate to take a mountain form as the type of a common continental plant. This arrangement gives an analytical and perspicuous treatment to

Leafy-bracted Blackberry, *Rubus argutus*.

Flowers ¾′ to 1¼′ across.

the high-bush blackberries and should be the means of making the various forms better known. It goes without saying that in plants which are so confused as rubi, intermediate and perplexing forms will be found; but even these forms can be best understood when the plants are broken up into their reigning types."

In Britton's " Manual of the Flora of the United States and Canada " *Rubus argutus* and *Rubus frondosus* are considered as separate; *R. argutus* being the glabrate species, with the more southern habitat; and *R. frondosus* the Leafy-bracted Blackberry.

*Rubus nigrobaccus sativus*, the Short-cluster Blackberry, differs from the type in that it is lower, the leaflets broader, less distinctly long-pointed, fruits rounder and looser. It is the nondescript blackberry of open fields and is the parent of the larger part of the short-cluster or garden blackberries.

Although the Blackberry group is very confusing to an amateur, a few marked types can easily be determined; the High-bush, *R. nigrobaccus*, with its mountain form, *R. allegheniensis*, and its unkempt poor relation, *R. nigrobaccus sativa*, are not difficult to recognize. The corymbose *R. argutus*, synonym *R. frondosus*, can also be distinguished both in flower and fruit. The straggling Dewberry, *R. procumbens*, which once was one but now is many, can be readily recognized in its type.

But to distinguish among the varying and connecting forms which, grouped about these types, are now considered species, is the task of the expert. Moreover, the experts do not altogether agree among themselves. It is probable that the group will always be more or less of a problem to the classifying botanist. The fact that so many varieties have come into cultivation—that their seeds are scattered by the birds in out-of-the-way places; that the seedlings so produced will vary, returning to their type with modifications —obviously, will continue to confuse the situation.

In the meantime, the great types stand out clear enough for the amateur to enjoy; and if the variability of the family tends to drive the botanist to distraction, it also makes possible the production of a fruit unique in character and most delicious in flavor.

As a cultivated plant the blackberry is a purely American fruit; all the varieties have been developed from native wild plants; and we alone of all peoples prize " The blackberry that was the bramble born."

### RAND'S BLACKBERRY

*Rùbus rándii.*

This is a native of northern woods, ranging from New Brunswick to Maine and west to northern Michigan. Low and diffuse in habit; stems nearly glabrous and so soft and slender as to appear almost herbaceous; prickles few and weak, often wanting. Leaves are very thin, three or five-foliate. The flower cluster is long, many-flowered; the flowers about half the size of those of *Rubus nigrobaccus;* the fruit small, dry and seedy.

## LEAFY-BRACTED BLACKBERRY. LEAFY-CLUSTER BLACKBERRY

*Rùbus argùtus. Rùbus frondòsus.*

" A plant of comparatively stiff and straight growth, usually shorter than *R. nigrobaccus*, with narrower and more rigid leaflets. Stems stout, angled, with rather stout straight prickles, and the whole plant glabrous or only slightly villous, except in some of the very young parts. The flower clusters are short and leafy ; flowers about the size of those of *R. nigrobaccus*. Its range is wide, extending from New Brunswick and Lake Superior to Florida, Mississippi and Kansas. It is less common in the north than *R. nigrobaccus* but is more abundant in the south, and there is a southern variety."

—L. H. BAILEY.

## THORNLESS BLACKBERRY. MILLSPAUGH'S BLACKBERRY

*Rùbus canadénsis. Rùbus millspaùghii.*

" This plant has the general habit of *R. nigrobaccus*, but is distinguished by its long and slender petioles, mostly narrow and long acuminate leaves, long stipules, and especially by its lack of pubescence and general absence of thorns. It is apparently a well-marked species, growing throughout the country in the higher elevations from the Carolinas northward to Lake Superior."

—L. H. BAILEY.

The following account of this Blackberry is quoted by Professor Bailey in " The Evolution of our Native Fruits " from notes made by Mr. Kofoid, of North Carolina. " It seems to be very abundant where it occurs, forming dense thickets of upright stems five to eight

Leafy-bracted Blackberry, *Rubus argutus.*

feet in height. As late as the 29th of August we found
the fruit just turning a faint reddish tinge and quite palatable and sweet to a hungry man. Natives say that the
fruit becomes ripe and black in September. The berries
are large, long and slender and very sweet, lacking the
sharply acid or bitterish quality of the berries of the
lower mountains. There are no thorns or prickles.
One can go through the patches unscathed. * *
There are several botanical characters which distinguish this species from the common blackberry, aside
from the absence of thorns. It lacks almost entirely,
except on some of the young shoots, the conspicuously pubescent character of the common species. The
leaves are thin, and the leaflets sharply toothed and
prominently long-pointed. One of the most prominent
characters lies in the leaflet stalks. Upon vigorous
shoots the leaflets are five, and the three upper ones
have stalks from one to three inches long."

### MOUNTAIN BLACKBERRY

*Rùbus allegheniénsis. Rùbus villòsus*, var. *montanus.*

Similar to *Rubus nigrobaccus*, though smaller, stems
more slender, very prickly, branches commonly reddish, the younger parts glandular-pubescent. Fruit
dry with a somewhat spicy flavor, three-fourths to an
inch long, thimble-shaped, narrowing toward the tip;
drupelets small and numerous. Found on mountains
and high lands of the Atlantic states, throughout the
Alleghany region. In its typical forms this blackberry
is very well marked, but it frequently seems to grade
back to the type.

Dewberry, *Rubus procumbens.*

Flowers 1′ to 1¼′ across.

## LOW RUNNING BLACKBERRY. DEWBERRY

*Rùbus procùmbens. Rùbus canadénsis.*

" A strong-growing prickly plant, mostly with glabrous stems, which sometimes rise a foot or two above the earth and are then prostrate ; leaves medium to rather large, firm and thick, of three to seven oval or ovate, rather long-pointed and sharply doubly-toothed leaflets; racemes erect, with leaf-like bracts and from one to three-flowered, the central flowers opening first ; fruit variable, but usually globose or ovoid, with a few large and rather loose drupelets, shining black, sour, but becoming sweet at full maturity. This is the common dewberry of the northern states growing along the roadsides and on banks, the strong stems often reaching a length of five to eight feet. The species has a wide range, occurring as far south as Florida and west and southwest to Kansas, Oklahoma and Arizona. It is a very variable species, and it is probable that future observations may show that it should be broken up into two or three specific types.

—L. H. BAILEY.

This plant has had many names. It is the *Rubus villosus* of Aiton, the *Rubus canadensis* of authors, not Linnæus, and now it seems to have the name *Rubus procumbens.*

## RUNNING SWAMP BLACKBERRY

*Rùbus híspidus.*

" Stems scarcely woody but lasting over winter, perfectly prostrate and beset with small, reflexed, weak bristles, sending up many short and leafy flowering shoots; leaflets mostly three, obovate, blunt and shining, firm and thick in texture, and tending to be evergreen ; flowers small and few on leafless peduncles ; fruit of few grains, red or purple and sour."

—L. H. BAILEY.

Dewberry, *Rubus procumbens.*

Leaflets 2′ to 3′ long.

Running Swamp Blackberry, *Rubus hispidus*.

Leaflets ½′ to 1½′ long.

"Few trailing plants combine a better effect of flower and foliage than our Swamp Blackberry. Its common name suggests wet places as its chosen home, but it is also found in dry sandy soil. It blooms through the most of June. The foliage looks evergreen although it is not, and in the autumn it ranks with woodbine in the brilliancy of its changing tints."

—*Garden and Forest.*

## SHRUBBY CINQUEFOIL

*Potentilla fruticòsa.*

*Potentilla*, diminutive of *potens*, powerful, from the medicinal properties of some species. *Cinquefoil*, in reference to the five leaflets of some species.

Erect or ascending, much branched, very leafy, bark shreddy, six inches to four feet high; found in swamps, also in moist, rocky places. Ranges from Labrador and Greenland to Alaska, south to New Jersey, Illinois, Minnesota, in the Rocky Mountains to Arizona and in the Sierra Nevadas to California. Also in northern Europe and Asia.

*Leaves.*—Alternate, pinnately compound. Leaflets five to seven, oblong or somewhat oblanceolate, entire, acute or acutish at each end, one-half to three-fourths of an inch long, silky pubescent, margins revolute. Stipules ovate-lanceolate, acute, entire.

*Flowers.*—June to September. Cymose or solitary, bright yellow, about half an inch across. Calyx five-lobed, five-bracteolate; corolla of five nearly orbicular petals; stamens fifteen to twenty; style lateral, threadlike; achenes, disk and receptacle long-hairy.

The Shrubby Cinquefoil can very easily become a weed, for it has learned how to live under adverse conditions and its natural range is enormous. Controlled, however, it is an excellent plant to mass in

Shrubby Cinquefoil, *Potentilla fruticosa*.

Leaflets ½′ to ¾′ long.   Flowers ½′ to ¾′ across.

parks, as an undershrub, to brighten the dull places. Its midsummer bloom is also in its favor for garden planting.

## THE ROSE

*Ròsa.*

*Rosa* is the ancient Latin name of the flower.

Erect or climbing shrubs, generally with subterranean rootstocks, which send up suckers at some distance from the parent. Stems usually prickly; stalks and foliage often bearing aromatic glands; flowers usually fragrant.

*Leaves.*—Alternate, odd-pinnate, with stipules which grow fast to the petioles. Leaflets vary in number from three to eleven.

*Flowers.*—Solitary or in loose corymbs; pink, red, or white in our species.

*Calyx.*—Cup-shaped, or urn-shaped, constricted at the throat, becoming fleshy in fruit, five-lobed; lobes spreading, deciduous or persistent.

*Corolla.*—Petals five, obovate or obcordate, inserted upon the edge of the disk that lines the calyx-tube.

*Stamens.*—Many, inserted with the petals at the edge of the calyx-disk.

*Pistil.*—Made up of many separate carpels seated within the urn-shaped cup; ovaries hairy; styles distinct or united.

*Fruit.*—Achenes, numerous, enclosed in the berry-like fruiting calyx-cup, called a hip. This hip becomes pink or red or orange at maturity.

Six species of native wild roses are common within the range covered by this volume, besides two or three that "come out of the west" and frequently cross the border; there are in addition two acclimated species. The specific characters that differentiate them refer principally to the habit, the leaves, and the stem, rather than to the flower. All our native roses are single; all are pink. White flowers occasionally occur, but rather as an inconstant variation than as a specific character. The pink of the rose is unstable; it fades so quickly in the bright sunlight that in order to know the real color of the flower one must see it when opening. The blossom secretes no nectar; its fragrance-call to the bee is an invitation to gather pollen.

The fruit, which is peculiar and characteristic, consists of a hollow cup within which are closely packed many achenes, and protruding through a hole at the top are the remnants of the styles, one style for each achene. It is called a hip, and is the invariable fruit of the rose. Two views exist concerning it. Some consider it to be the calyx-tube which has become fleshy; others regard the fleshy part of the hip as the receptacle enlarged and hollowed so as to embrace and protect the achenes.

### MICHIGAN ROSE. CLIMBING ROSE. PRAIRIE ROSE

*Ròsa setígera.*

A climbing rose found in thickets and on prairies. Ranges from Ontario to Ohio, South Carolina and Florida, west to Wisconsin and Nebraska and southwest to Texas; has escaped from cultivation in New Jersey and Virginia. Grows rapidly; strong shoots reaching ten to twenty feet in a single season.

*Stems.*—Climbing or sprawling, several feet long, armed with scattered, straight or curved prickles, not bristly. Twigs, petioles, and peduncles often glandular-pubescent. Stems green or reddish, often dark purple with a bloom.

*Leaves.*—Leaflets three to five, one and a half to two and a half inches long, oval or ovate, acute or obtuse at apex, sharply

Michigan Rose, *Rosa setigera.*

Leaflets three to five.   Flowers 2½′ to 3′ across.

serrate, rounded at base; texture thick, veins and veinlets deeply depressed. Autumnal tints are a combination of bronze-purple, red, pink, orange and yellow. Stipules extremely narrow. Petiole prickly, glandular-pubescent.

*Flowers.*—June, July. Corymbose, varying from deep to pale pink, two and a half to three inches across, destitute of fragrance. Calyx-lobes ovate, acute, glandular, finally deciduous; petals obcordate; styles cohere in a protruding column, as long as the stamens.

*Fruit.*—Hip, red, globose, more or less glandular, three-eighths to half an inch in diameter.

*Rosa setigera* is our only native climbing rose and is the parent of the Baltimore Belle and other double climbing varieties. In its single state it is one of our most beautiful roses, with its clean handsome foliage and full clusters of flowers, deep rose pink as they first expand but very pale before they fall. Only one defect can be found, they are nearly scentless. The blooming season is late; when the flowers of nearly all other species have faded, these are in their prime.

Left to grow in a natural way, the stems will climb twelve or fifteen feet among the branches of other shrubs and small trees, and lift their flower clusters far above ordinary reach. If, however, the bush is planted alone and allowed to develop, the stems will rise three or four feet, then arch and bend over with tips trailing on the ground, presenting a unique and attractive appearance.

The colors that the leaves take on in autumn when the long arching stems turn purple and are coated with a glaucous bloom, present a bewildering confusion of green and purple bronzes, brightened with pink and rose and dull red, with yellow and orange.

The flowers are delightfully decorative. Cut the branches when the blossoms begin to appear, supply them abundantly with water and the buds will unfold day after day for a week, giving a most charming succession of opening roses; for the little branch seems scarcely conscious that it has severed connection with the root.

In cultivation, this child of the prairies requires a deep rich soil and generous treatment. Gardeners recommend that it be planted on the top of a bank that its long, vigorous and graceful shoots may grow in their own wild-wood fashion to cover it. So treated it is a thing of beauty throughout the summer.

*Rosa setigera* may be easily recognized among its companions at any season of the year by its long trailing stems; in summer by its three leaflets; in the blooming season by the rich flower clusters and also by the peculiar upright column which the styles make in the centre of the flower.

### MEADOW ROSE. EARLY WILD ROSE. SMOOTH ROSE

*Ròsa blánda.*

Low, erect, one to four feet high; found mostly in rocky places. Ranges from Newfoundland through New England to central New York, west to Illinois along the region of the Great Lakes. Stems a dark venous red; slender prickles sometimes present but not abundant; no spines.

*Leaves.*—Leaflets five to seven, an inch to an inch and a half long, oval or obovate, wedge-shaped or rounded at base, simply and somewhat irregularly serrate, obtuse or acute at apex, short-stalked; pale green above and slightly paler beneath. Stipules broad, dilated, entire or slightly glandular-toothed.

*Flowers.*—June, July. Stems one to three-flowered, rarely more, pink, two and a half to three inches across. Calyx-lobes acuminate, entire, hispid-pubescent, persistent and erect upon the fruit; petals obovate or obcordate, erose; styles distinct.

*Fruit.*—Hip, bright scarlet, globose or pyriform or obpyriform, glabrous, half to five-eighths of an inch long, crowned with the calyx-lobes.

The distinctive characters of *Rosa blanda* are its low habit, its unarmed stems, and its broad dilated stipules. The hip is globose or pyriform or obpyriform, wholly destitute of glandular hairs, and when mature still retains the calyx-lobes, which approach each other.

The Arkansas Rose, *Rosa arkansana*, was formerly considered a variety of *Rosa blanda* but is now regarded as a distinct species. Like the type it is low, and loves the meadows; but the stems, instead of being smooth, are densely prickly with very sharp and very slender bristles. The leaflets frequently number eleven. The stipules are narrow and the pink blossoms appear in corymbs, rarely if ever solitary. In habit and general appearance it is like the Meadow Rose, but it varies considerably in what are considered the specific characters. It is a rose of the prairies, ranging from Minnesota and Iowa to Nebraska, Colorado, Texas and New Mexico. The hips are little globes three-eighths to half an inch in diameter.

Early Wild Rose, *Rosa blanda.*

Leaflets five to seven. Flowers 2½′ to 3′ across.

## SWAMP ROSE.  CAROLINA ROSE

*Ròsa carolìna.*

Erect, stiff, five to seven feet high with rather distant, stout, commonly recurved spines, often with prickles scattered along the stem; old stems dull purple; common in low wet grounds and borders of streams and swamps.  Ranges from Nova Scotia to Florida and Mississippi, westward as far as Minnesota.  Suckers freely; makes clumps.

*Leaves.*—Leaflets five to nine, usually seven, varying considerably in outline, oval, ovate, ovate-lanceolate or obovate, one to two inches long, wedge-shaped or rounded at base, serrate, acute or obtuse at apex, often pubescent beneath.  In autumn they turn dull red of varying tints and shades; frequently darken in midsummer.  Stipules dilated.  Petioles often prickly.

*Flowers.*—June to August.  Bright pink, two to two and one-half inches across, borne in corymbose clusters.  Calyx-lobes lanceolate, acuminate, often dilated above, hispid-pubescent, spreading; after flowering deciduous; petals obcordate; styles distinct.

*Fruit.*—Hip, scarlet, globose or depressed-globose, three-eighths to one-half an inch long, glandular-hispid.  Clings all winter and remains in good color until March.

The Carolina Rose is one of the most abundant of our native roses.  At the blossoming time it seems to possess the swamps and waste lowlands.  It suckers freely; the underground stems travel fast and travel far, and no plant is companionless after the first year.

This is an excellent rose for park lanes and roadsides.  It is hardy, and will grow in good soil with only a moderate amount of water, and the flowering season is long.

Swamp Rose, *Rosa carolina*.

Leaflets five to nine. Flowers 2′ to 2½′ across.

Rose-hips. Upper, *Rosa blanda*; lower, *Rosa carolina*.

## LOW ROSE. PASTURE ROSE. DWARF WILD ROSE

*Ròsa hùmilis.*

Erect, bushy, six inches to three feet high; stems usually armed with sharp, slender, straight spines just below the stipules, and also more or less prickly. Found in dry or rocky soil from Maine and Ontario to Wisconsin, Georgia, Kansas, and Louisiana. Suckers freely.

*Leaves.*—Leaflets five, seven, one-half to one inch long, rather thin, ovate, oval or obovate, rounded or pointed at base, coarsely serrate, acute at apex, short-stalked or sessile, glabrous or pubescent beneath; not shining above. Autumnal tints red and orange, brilliant. Stipules narrow, entire. Petioles, pedicels and calyx usually glandular.

*Flowers.*—May to July. Solitary, or two to three together, fragrant, two to two and a half inches across, pink; pedicels and calyx usually glandular. Calyx-lobes lanceolate, acuminate or dilated at apex, usually lobed, spreading and deciduous; petals obovate or obcordate; styles distinct.

*Fruit.*—Hip, red, globose or depressed-globose, about one-third of an inch long, glandular-hispid, without the calyx-lobes. Clings to the branch throughout the winter.

In the middle west this little bush frequently becomes an undershrub and is often found almost entirely shaded. The flowering season is long; for it blooms very deliberately and has, moreover, the pleasant habit of putting forth a few stray blossoms in early autumn. The stem is not very strongly armed, the spines are few, but sharp as needles, and go straight to their aim. This rose is well adapted for coast planting; loves the cool moist air of the sea; is perfectly hardy and able to withstand the rigor of winter.

Pasture Rose, *Rosa humilis.*

Leaflets five to seven.  Flowers 2′ to 2½′ across.

Glossy Rose, *Rosa lucida.*

Leaflets seven to nine.   Flowers 2′ to 2¼′ across.

## GLOSSY ROSE. DWARF SWAMP ROSE

*Ròsa lùcida.*

Bushy, from three to six feet high ; found in wet places. Ranges from Newfoundland to New Jersey and westward. Suckers very little.

*Leaves.*—Leaflets seven to nine, one-half to one and one-half inches long, elliptic or obovate-elliptic, coarsely serrate, mostly acute at both ends, thick, shining above, slightly pubescent beneath. Stipules somewhat dilated, often glandular-toothed; prickles rather stout and flat, straight or slightly curved.

*Flowers.*—June, July. Few or solitary, about two inches across. Calyx-lobes usually entire.

*Fruit.*—Hip, scarlet, depressed globose, glandular-hispid, one-third of an inch long.

This rose and *Rosa humilis* so approach each other that much confusion exists with regard to them. In comparison with *Rosa nitida* the leaves are a lighter green ; in comparison with *Rosa humilis*, of thicker texture. The bush is adapted for borders of shrubberies ; the bright shining foliage and abundant bloom commend it in summer, and in winter a glow of color is diffused by its red fruits and its brownish red stems.

## NORTHEASTERN ROSE

*Ròsa nìtida.*

Bushy, one to two feet high ; stems and branches very densely covered with slender straight prickles nearly as long as the slender infrastipular spines ; found in low grounds and borders of swamps. Ranges from Newfoundland to Massachusetts ; often along the sea shore. Suckers freely.

*Leaves.*—Leaflets, seven to nine, short-stalked, one-half to an inch and a half long, oval or narrowly oblong, sharply serrate,

Northeastern Rose, *Rosa nitida*.

Leaflets seven to nine.  Flowers 1½′ to 2½′ across.

acute at both ends ; terminal leaflet sometimes slightly obovate and obtuse at the apex ; thick, bright green and shining. Autumnal tints orange and red, brilliant. Stipules usually broad, often glandular.

*Flowers.*—June, July. Spray one to three-flowered, roses deep pink, one and a half to two and a half inches across. Calyx and pedicels usually glandular. Calyx-lobes lanceolate, acuminate, entire, hispid or glandular, finally spreading, deciduous; petals often obcordate. Styles distinct. Fragrant.

*Fruit.*—Hip, scarlet, globose, about one-third of an inch high, glandular-hispid. Clings to the branches through the winter.

*Rosa nitida* is one of our most beautiful native roses. Its range is not very extensive and the plant seems not to be generally known. Although damp swamps and low moist grounds are its native home, transferred to the garden it grows freely, making a broad mass of bright foliage, and blooming with great profusion. One character which may aid to identify it are the red shoots thickly beset with slender red spines barely stouter than the red prickles. No other of our native roses has just this combination.

### SWEETBRIER EGLANTINE

*Ròsa rubiginòsa.*

Slender, four to six feet high, wands often longer, destitute of prickles but armed with stout, recurved spines. Naturalized from Europe ; found along roadsides from Nova Scotia to Virginia.

*Leaves.*—Leaflets five to seven, one to one and a half inches long, elliptical or oblong-ovate, rounded at base, doubly serrate, obtuse at apex ; smooth above, densely glandular-pubescent and resinous beneath ; very aromatic. Stipules one-half to five-eighths of an inch long, rather broad. Petioles prickly.

Sweetbrier, *Rosa rubiginosa.*

Leaflets five to seven.   Flowers 1¼' to 1½' across.

*Flowers.*—May, June. Solitary or in twos, an inch and a quarter to an inch and a half across, pink varying to white. Pedicels and calyx glandular-hispid. Calyx-lobes lanceolate, usually much-lobed, spreading, deciduous ; petals obcordate or obovate ; styles distinct.

*Fruit.*—Hip, scarlet, oval or pyriform, one-half to one inch long, glandular, without the calyx-lobes.

> I know a bank whereon the wild thyme blows,
> Where oxlips and the nodding violet grows;
> Quite over-canopied with lush woodbine,
> With sweet musk roses and with eglantine.
> —" Midsummer Night's Dream." SHAKESPEARE.

> With fairest flowers
> I'll sweeten thy sad grave ; thou shalt not lack
> The flower that's like thy face, pale primrose ; nor
> The azure harebell, like thy veins ; no, nor
> The leaf of eglantine, who not to slander
> Out-sweetened not thy breath.
> —"Cymbeline." SHAKESPEARE.

If the Sweetbrier did not come over in the May-flower it certainly followed hard upon; for we know that it bloomed in Pilgrim gardens long before the close of the seventeenth century. We can well understand that it was dear to the homesick wanderers, for this is the Eglantine of Chaucer, of Spenser, and of Shakespeare; the rose that is embedded in the very warp and woof of English life and so of English literature.

In spite of its fierce armament there is a certain delicacy about the Sweetbrier which gives it a charm peculiarly its own. The blossom is small and pale and in itself not fragrant; the delightful fragrance of the plant resides in the pale, amber, resinous glands which so thickly cover the under surface of the leaves as well as pedicel and calyx.

The long, thorny branches sprawl and scratch and seize and hold; and because of this the bush has very generally been banished from lawn and garden. It has fled to the roadside and there when June is young it unfolds its delicate blossoms and yields its delicious fragrance for the pleasure of any who pass by.

Of late years the gardeners have been at work upon the plant and they say they have hybrids much finer than the type. It may be so; but my allegiance holds fast to the wild creature of Chaucer and of Shakespeare, to "the jaws that bite" and "the claws that catch" of the old English gardens.

## DOG ROSE. CANKER ROSE. WILD BRIER

*Ròsa canìna.*

Erect or straggling, four to six feet high, wands sometimes ten feet long, usually armed with stout, short, hooked spines, not bristly but sometimes glandular. Native in northern Asia; naturalized from Europe. Escaped to roadsides and waste places from Nova Scotia to Virginia; abundant in the valley of the Delaware. Called Cat-whin and Canker-bloom.

*Leaves.*—Leaflets five to seven, an inch to an inch and a half long, oval or ovate, obtuse or rounded at base, serrate, obtuse at apex; smooth, rather thick, sometimes downy beneath. Stipules broad, glandular.

*Flowers.*—June, July. Solitary, or two to four in a cluster, pink, varying to white. Calyx-lobes lanceolate, much-cut, reflexed, deciduous; petals obovate or obcordate; styles distinct.

*Fruit.*—Hip, scarlet, long-ovoid, half to three-fourths of an inch long, usually glabrous, without the calyx-lobes.

The Dog Rose, naturalized from Europe, is common throughout New England and greatly resembles the Sweetbrier except that it lacks fragrance.

Dog Rose, *Rosa canina*.

Leaflets five to seven.  Flowers 1¼′ to 1½′ across.

Japanese Rose, *Rosa rugosa.*
Flowers 2½′ to 3½′ across.

## JAPANESE ROSE

*Ròsa rugòsa.*

The Japanese Rose is one of the best of our recent importations; its virtues are many, its defects few. It takes care of itself, requires very little attention, grows up strong and sturdy, makes a good hedge row. The large single flowers, both pink and white, bloom off and on from June to October; in fact they can be found in favored locations in early November. The great red hips are nearly as ornamental and effective as the roses themselves. The stout stems are thickly beset with prickles and bristles; the leaflets are five to seven, rough, dark green and shining above, whitish and pubescent beneath. The flowers are two and a half to three and a half inches across. Varieties with double flowers have been developed, and several good hybrids are offered by the dealers.

## JAPANESE TRAILING ROSE

*Ròsa wichuraiàna.*

This is distinctly a trailing plant, but may be so trained on a trellis as to figure as a climbing rose. It grows with astonishing rapidity, and will throw out wonderfully long shoots in one season. When the multitude of single white roses appear in June, against the background of shining, dark green foliage, the effect is exceedingly fine. The individual flower is exquisite; petals of the purest white surround a golden centre, and the whole gives forth a delicious fragrance. Mr.

Japanese Trailing Rose, *Rosa wichuraiana*.

Flowers 1½′ to 2½′ across.

J. G. Jack, writing shortly after the introduction of this rose, says of it: "As a rule, the stems trail closely along the ground, but the new stems of each succeeding year grow over the preceding ones, and where the tips get a chance to climb through the branches of some other shrub they take advantage of the support and become more or less raised. In fact, its habit is more like that of a trailing blackberry or dewberry than any other familiar object.

"Considering that its importation was undesigned or without a knowledge of its peculiar habit or value, the introduction of this rose has proved a very fortunate circumstance. Its dark, shining, evergreen-looking foliage will form a splendid covering for any rough piece of ground, and sandy or gravelly areas are likely to prove very congenial to the growth of the plant."

Many hybrids have been developed from the species; some double, some bearing larger clusters than the type, others really evergreen, and some admirable dwarf plants suitable for borders.

# POMÀCEÆ—APPLE FAMILY

## RED CHOKE-BERRY

*Arònia arbutifòlia.*

*Aronia,* modified from *Aria,* the Beam-tree of Europe.

An erect shrub, two to eight feet high, with slender branching stems and grayish brown bark; grows in swamps and wet woods, also in dry soil. Ranges from Nova Scotia to Minnesota, south to Florida and Louisiana.

*Leaves.*—Alternate, simple, one to three inches long, oval, oblong or obovate, rounded or wedge-shaped at base, serrulate-crenulate, obtuse or abruptly pointed at apex; when full grown are bright shining green above, pale, sometimes pubescent, often densely tomentose beneath. The midvein is glandular along the upper side. In autumn they turn a dark scarlet and orange or fall with little change of color. Petioles short; stipules deciduous.

*Flowers.*—May, June. Perfect, rose-shaped, white, or purple-tinged, one-half to five-eighths of an inch across; borne in terminal, compound, downy corymbs which are finally over-topped by the young shoots.

*Calyx.*—Urn-shaped, five-lobed, tomentose, adnate to the ovary.

*Corolla.*—Petals five, white, concave, spreading, imbricate in bud.

*Stamens.*—Numerous, inserted on the calyx-tube; filaments white, anthers pinkish purple.

*Pistil.*—Inferior, tomentose, five-celled; styles three to five, united at the base.

Red Choke-berry, *Aronia arbutifolia.*

Leaves 1′ to 3′ long.

Purple-fruited Choke-berry, *Aronia atropurpurea.*

Leaves 1′ to 3′ long.

*Fruit.*—Pome, sweetish, rather dry, one-quarter of an inch in diameter, globose, or somewhat depressed, red, not lustrous, bearing the remnants of the calyx-lobes and stamens. September, October; persistent until early winter.

The Choke-berries are distinctly ornamental plants. Their foliage color is good, being a rich shining green, so that the plant is attractive for its color alone. Three species are now recorded; and the specific differences lie in the fruit rather than in the leaves or flowers. The red-fruited species is the one most abundant in the south; the other two are northern. Why these berries are not attractive to birds is something of a puzzle: the flesh is somewhat dry, to be sure, but the flavor is agreeable; and yet the fact remains that birds pass them by, for others distinctly inferior and unpleasant. All the Choke-berries are excellent, country roadside shrubs.

Purple-fruited Choke-berry, *Aronia atropurpurea*, was long confused with *Aronia nigra*, from which it differs in habit, and in the color of its fruit. This is the tallest of the Choke-berries, sometimes reaching a height of twelve feet. In shape and size the leaves are not distinguishable from those of the other species of the genus; and the glandular midrib is a marked character common to them all. The flowers are white, about half an inch across, borne in terminal corymbs; calyx and pedicles tomentose. The fruit is not quite black, rather a deep purple; it remains on the bush until early winter.

The Black Choke-berry, *Aronia nigra*, is usually a lower bush than either of the others. It is found in swamps, or low woods, sometimes in dryer soil. The

Black Choke-berry, *Aronia nigra.*

Leaves 1′ to 3′ long.

leaves are obovate or oval, short-petioled, serrulate-crenulate, obtuse or abruptly pointed, shining green above, glabrous and yellow green beneath. They vary from two to two and one-half inches long, and the mid-rib is glandular along its upper surface. The flowers are white, about five-eighths of an inch across, bearing many stamens with pinkish purple anthers. The fruit is one-half to five-eighths of an inch in diameter, borne in clusters, of a shining black, and falls very soon after maturity. Ranges from Nova Scotia to Florida, and west to Ontario and Michigan.

### SHADBUSH. JUNE-BERRY

*Amelánchier botryápium.*

*Amelanchier*, the Savoy name of a different tree.

A shrub or small tree, the foliage and inflorescence densely white, woolly when young; found in swamps and on river banks. Ranges from New Brunswick to Florida and westward through the Mississippi valley.

*Leaves.*—Simple, alternate, pinnately veined, oblong, oval, ovate or ovate-lanceolate, rounded at base, acute at apex, finely and sharply serrate. They come out of the bud conduplicate, are densely white pubescent when young, nearly or quite glabrous when old. Autumnal tint yellow.

*Flowers.*—April, May. Perfect, white, borne in short rather dense racemes; pedicels and calyx covered with silky white hairs.

*Calyx.*—Calyx-tube campanulate, white, woolly, adnate to the ovary, five-lobed; lobes narrow, reflected, persistent.

*Corolla.*—Petals white, five, inserted on the calyx-tube, spatulate or linear, about half an inch long.

*Stamens.*—Many, inserted on the calyx-tube; filaments awl-like.

Shadbush, *Amelanchier botryapium.*

*Pistil.*—Ovary inferior, its cavities twice as many as the styles ; styles two to five, pubescent at base.

*Fruit.*—Pome, berry-like, one-fourth to three-eighths of an inch in diameter, sweet, delicious.   June, July.

In northern woods the Amelanchiers are conspicuous in early spring by the colors of their unfolding leaves; in one form these are red, in another silvery white, and their vernal beauty is increased by brilliant scarlet bud-scales and bracts, and by the silky white hairs which clothe the young growth.   Of the delicate beauty of the flowers of this tree it is not necessary to speak, for everyone who walks abroad in early spring knows the white flowers of the Shadbush which in April and May enliven the banks of swamps and upland woods all over eastern America.

*—Garden and Forest.*

The homely name of Shadbush was given to the *Amelanchier* group by the early inhabitants of our eastern states, because they flower at the time when the shad begin to ascend the tidal rivers.

The sixth edition of Gray's " Manual of Botany " considers most of the northeastern June-berries as varieties of *Amelanchier canadensis ;* but later botanists are inclined to regard these varieties as species.  However far the genus may be divided upon botanic differences, to the popular mind a Shadbush is a Shadbush, for its white bloom appears among the mist of opening buds and is unmistakable.   Its message is borne afar,—from rocky hillside over mountain valley, —that spring has come.   To the birds, likewise, a Shadbush is a Shadbush, for the family fruit has been preëmpted by the birds for ages and feeble human efforts to secure it have been outclassed from the first. It seems quite unnecessary to descant upon the delicacy of its flavor; it is so antecedently improbable that ordinary mortals should ever have an opportunity to enjoy it.

Low June-berry, *Amelanchier spicata.*

The Low June-berry, *Amelanchier spicata*, rises to the height of three feet from a long root creeping among rocks. The leaves are elliptic or oval, one to one and a half inches long, rounded at both ends, sometimes subacute at apex and sometimes subcordate at base, serrulate or dentate crenate, woolly when young. The flowers are borne in many four to ten-flowered racemes; the pomes are about a quarter of an inch in diameter.

The Round-leaved June-berry, *Amelanchier rotundifolia*, appears as both tree and shrub, and is distinguished by means of its leaves, which are broadly oval, ovate or nearly orbicular, serrate with large teeth, usually glabrous from the time of unfolding, though sometimes woolly. Its fruit is a little larger than that of *Amelanchier spicata*.

The Oblong-fruited June-berry, *Amelanchier oligocarpa*, is a low, glabrous shrub. The leaves are thin, narrowly oval or oblong, narrowed at each end, finely and sharply serrate. The flowers are borne in one to four-flowered racemes: the petals instead of being narrowly oblong are obovate or oblanceolate. The pomes are pear-shaped, dark blue purple with a heavy bloom, from one-fourth to three-eighths of an inch long. All of the species are early bloomers and all fruit sparingly.

Oblong-fruited June-berry, *Amelanchier oligocarpa*.

Leaves 1' to 3' long.   Flowers ¾' to ⅞' across.

## EVERGREEN THORN.   FIRE THORN

*Cotoneáster pyracántha.   Pyracántha coccínea.*

*Cotoneaster*, from *cotoneum*, quince, and *aster*, similar ;   like
a quince.   *Pyracantha*, from *pyr*, fire, and *acanthus*, thorn ;
alluding to the bright red fruit.

A thorny evergreen shrub, three to eight feet high, native to
southern Europe and western Asia, which about Philadelphia
and Washington has escaped from cultivation.   Young branchlets and petioles grayish pubescent.

*Leaves.*—Evergreen, one to two inches long, oval or oblanceolate, narrowed at base, crenulate, acute at apex ;  when full
grown are dark shining green, glabrous or slightly pubescent.
*Flowers.*—May.   Numerous, small, one-fourth of an inch
across, white, borne in terminal compound many - flowered
cymes, about an inch and a half across.
*Fruit.*—Haw, small, scarlet, depressed globose, bitter, ornamental.

A low evergreen shrub, especially handsome when
loaded with its bright red haws ; these remain on the
branches all winter if not eaten by the birds, who are
really fond of them.   It is also very pretty in spring
with its numerous corymbs of white flowers.   Its low
habit adapts it for planting on rocky slopes or in
sunny rockeries or for borders of shrubberies ; also
for low ornamental hedges or for wall-covering, as it
bears pruning well and is easily trained into any desired shape.   The plant thrives in almost any kind of
well drained soil, but prefers sunny positions.

Evergreen Thorn, *Cotoneaster pyracantha.*

Leaves 1′ to 2′ long.

## JAPAN QUINCE

*Pýrus japónica. Cydònia japónica.*

*Cydonia* from Cydon in Crete, where the quince was first brought into notice.

One of the most desirable of cultivated shrubs ; appearing in many varieties. The type has rigid thorny stems intricately branched, and bright scarlet flowers ; the variations occur more in size and color of flowers than in habit of shrub. Native of Japan.

*Leaves.*—Alternate, simple, pinnately veined, three to five inches long, ovate, ovate-lanceolate or oblong, wedge-shaped at base, crenately serrate, acute at apex. When full grown thick, smooth, leathery, dark shining bluish green above, pale yellow green beneath. Margin thickened and slightly turned inward. Petiole short, the leaf texture inclined to run down upon it. Autumnal tint deep bronze red. Stipules leaf-like, irregularly kidney-shaped, bilateral, crenately serrate ; found on growing shoots in September.

*Flowers.*—In shape and structure like apple blossoms. In color varying from deep reds to white.

*Fruit.*—Pome, full oval or globose, two to two and a half inches long ; stem deeply sunken in fruit. Olive green with reddish cheek, covered with white dots, hard, acid with typical quince flavor.

The brilliant bloom of the Japan Quince in the early spring always attracts attention ; the closely packed bright red blossoms set the bush aflame, and far away in the parks it fairly lights up the path. The plant has been known in this country for nearly a hundred years but has not yet received all the appreciation that it deserves.

To an unusual degree this shrub is clothed with its leaves. The branching habit is intricate ; the leaves

Japan Quince, *Pyrus japonica*.
Flowers 1½′ to 2′ across.

are always abundant. The leaf texture sometimes runs down the entire length of the short petiole; and upon the new shoots, which produce the strongest foliage, are crescent-shaped stipules, persistent and leaf-like. The bush would be desirable even if it never bore a flower. The leaves of new shoots take on a reddish tinge as they come out of the bud, and as these shoots are usually abundant, in midsummer there is often a fine display of color. As autumn comes on the bush again flames from afar; this time with the deep bronze red of its changing leaves.

The plant fruits considerably, one might almost say abundantly; but this is not very generally known because the fruit is so concealed by the leaves.

# CALYCANTHÀCEÆ—STRAWBERRY-SHRUB FAMILY

## CAROLINA ALLSPICE. STRAWBERRY-SHRUB. SWEET-SCENTED SHRUB

*Butnèria flórida. Calycánthus flóridus.*

*Butneria* in honor of Butner. *Calycanthus*, from *calyx*, cup, and *anthus*, flower, referring to the closed cup whici. contains the pistils.

A compact shrub, four to six feet high, native to the Alleghany mountains, and found along the shady banks of streams.

*Bark.*—Dull brown ; branchlets yellow brown at first ; swollen at the nodes.

*Leaves.*—Opposite, simple, three to five inches long, oblong, ovate or oval, entire or slightly ruffled, wedge-shaped or rounded at base, acute or acuminate ; midrib depressed above, all the veins prominent beneath. They come out of the bud face to face, bronze green, shining, slightly hairy above, with dense brown hairs beneath ; when full grown are bright green above, pale yellow green, slightly pubescent beneath. Their autumnal tint is a clear yellow. Petiole short, stout, grooved.

*Flowers.*—May to July. Perfect, reddish chocolate brown, solitary and terminal on very short, lateral, leafy branches.

*Calyx.*—Sepals many, narrow-oblong, united below into a fleshy inversely-conical cup, with some leaf-like bractlets growing from it, chocolate brown with a reddish tinge.

*Corolla.*—Petals many, reddish chocolate brown, thickish, narrow-oblong, in many rows, inserted on the top of the closed calyx-tube ; similar to the sepals.

*Stamens.*—Numerous, inserted just within the petals, short, in several rows, some of the inner ones sterile; anthers adnate, introrse.

*Pistil.*—Carpels several, enclosed in the calyx-tube, inserted on its base and inner face, resembling the rose-hip in structure.

*Fruit.*—A large, drooping, pear-shaped receptacle two inches long and one and one-fourth inches in diameter, to which the bases of petals, sepals and bracts are adnate, and which encloses few to many smooth, shining achenes.   September.

The Sweet-scented Shrub has been for years a garden favorite because of the strawberry fragrance of its flowers; even the stems and small branches emit a spicy perfume when bruised or broken.   The color of the flower is a reddish chocolate brown, but the tints are unstable and the flower fades as it gets older.   Also, as it ages the petals spread and flatten so as to make a loose rosette.   The behavior of the flower buds when the warm spring days come is most interesting. The scales quickly fall, leaving two tiny leaves that closely surround and thoroughly protect the little brown ball of the flower; and as it increases in size they enlarge, but they do not give up their protective attitude until both are well on toward maturity.

Many lovers of flowers have cultivated the Strawberry-shrub in their gardens; have delighted in the delicious fragrance of its blossoms; and have wondered that no fruit seemed ever to follow.   How the plant reproduced itself was a question; doubtless in some wonderful way which common people knew nothing about.   It is true that our common garden species rarely fruits in domestication; but there is another species native to the south which fruits abundantly; indeed, by so doing it has won its specific name *Butneria*

Strawberry-shrub, *Butneria florida*.

Leaves 3' to 5' long.

*fertilis.* The fruit is really very curious ; it hangs from the branch like a little closed bag and contains, packed within it, the smooth shining achenes.

*Butneria florida* was one of the earliest American shrubs taken to England and has long been a favorite there. It is easily grown ; the best location is one somewhat shaded ; and it prefers a rich sandy loam.

Smooth Strawberry-shrub, *Butneria fertilis.*

Fruit 3′ to 4′ long.

# HYDRANGEÁCEÆ—HYDRANGEA FAMILY

## WILD HYDRANGEA

*Hydrángea arboréscens.*

*Hydrangea*, of Greek derivation, meaning water vessel, so named from the shape of the small capsule.

Vigorous, four to ten feet high; found on rocky, river banks in southern New York and in New Jersey, very abundant in the valley of the Delaware, ranging south to Florida and west to Iowa and Missouri. Species variable. Ascends 4,200 feet in the mountains of North Carolina.

*Leaves.*—Opposite, simple, three to six inches long, ovate, rounded or cordate or broadly wedge-shaped at base, sharply dentate, acute or acuminate at apex; when full grown are bright green above, upper surface deeply corrugated, all the veins very prominent beneath, very reticulate, glabrous or pubescent.

*Flowers.*—June, July. Both fertile and sterile, borne together in terminal corymbose clusters. Exterior flowers of the clusters often without petals, stamens or pistils, but with enlarged and very conspicuous calyx-lobes; sometimes these sterile flowers are very abundant; sometimes there are none. Fertile flowers are small.

*Calyx.*—Tube obconic, adnate to the ovary, four to five-toothed, teeth minute, persistent.

*Corolla.*—Petals four or five, valvate in bud, pinkish cream.

*Stamens.*—Eight to ten, inserted on the disk; filaments threadlike, exserted; anthers pink; pollen abundant.

*Pistil.*—Ovary inferior, two to four-celled; styles two to four; ovules many.

*Fruit.*—Capsule small, two-celled, ribbed, many-seeded.

Wild Hydrangea, *Hydrangea arborescens.*

Leaves 3′ to 6′ long.   Flower clusters 3′ to 4′ across.

The general effect of our northern Hydrangea in bloom is a group of strong erect stems, each crowned by a pale, salmon pink cluster, made up of a multitude of tiny blossoms each about an eighth of an inch across. The stamens are exserted, and there are so many of them that in the flower cluster the stamens are much more prominent than the petals. The fragrance is pleasant, possibly a trifle heavy. The blossoms open irregularly, so that for some time any cluster will have a goodly number of buds mingled with the open flowers. While the flower cluster does not reach the regulation standard of an hydrangea, a standard based upon the abnormal development of sterile flowers in our cultivated species, nevertheless it does come up to no mean measure of beauty. Now and then a cluster shows a few marginal sterile flowers after the fashion of *Viburnum opulus*, but it rarely wastes its vitality in that way ; its fragrance and pollen are ample resources to attract its insect friends.

Our favorite, hardy, garden Hydrangea is *Hydrangea paniculata grandiflora*, a species developed by the Japanese from their wild form, *Hydrangea paniculata*. It is, indeed, a superb plant. The panicles are of enormous size and of great beauty ; in the best known form all the flowers are sterile. They run through a charming range of color: pale green, cream white, pale pink and lastly dull red. As this magnificent bloom appears in August and does not complete its color scheme until October, then remains upon the branches until beaten off by the storms of winter, there are definite and sufficient reasons for the popularity of the bush.

In southern Japan the shrub becomes a tree twenty-

Hardy Hydrangea, *Hydrangea paniculata grandiflora.*

five to thirty feet high, with stout stems and pendulous branches. The following notes from the Arnold Arboretum give a clear and detailed account of the plant as it now appears in its several forms:

" The first is the plant commonly known as *Hydrangea paniculata grandiflora*, with enormous panicles of sterile flowers. The bloom continues from late August until winter.

" The second appears to be the wild form of the first with much smaller panicles, appearing at the same time, only a few sterile flowers being scattered among the fertile flowers.

" The third is intermediate between these two and flowering at the same time, the panicle being nearly as large as that of the first and more showy than that of the second, by the presence of a larger number of large sterile flowers. This as a garden plant is, perhaps, the most desirable of the whole group.

" The fourth is similar to the second, from which it differs only in its time of flowering, which is during the first half of July or about six weeks earlier."

## GARDEN SYRINGA.   MOCK ORANGE

*Philadélphus coronàrius.*

*Philadelphus* is an ancient name applied to this genus by Linnæus for no obvious reason.

A beautiful shrub, native to central Europe, which is extensively cultivated and in some places has escaped from the gardens. Usually from six to twelve feet high.

*Stems.*—Young shoots pale golden brown, older twigs darker brown.

Flowering Branch of Syringa, *Philadelphus coronarius*.
Leaves 2′ to 4′ long.   Flowers 1⅛′ to 1½′ across.

*Leaves.*—Opposite, simple, two to four inches long, oval or elliptic, rounded or narrowed at base, sparingly denticulate, acute or acuminate at apex, three-nerved, veins depressed above, prominent below. They come out of the bud pale gray green, shining, densely covered with white hairs on the under surface; when full grown are deep dull green above, paler beneath. In autumn they darken purplish or fall with no change of color. Petiole short, grooved.

*Flowers.*—May, June. Perfect, cream-white, very fragrant, numerous, racemose at the end of the branches and twigs, one and one-eighth to one and one-half inches across.

*Calyx.*—Calyx-tube top-shaped, coherent with the ovary, four-lobed; lobes ovate, acute, longer than the tube, spreading, persistent, valvate in bud.

*Corolla.*—Petals four or five, rounded or obovate, white, convolute in bud.

*Stamens.*—Twenty to forty inserted on the disk; filaments white; anthers pale yellow.

*Pistil.*—Ovary inferior, four-celled; style four-cleft; stigmas oblong.

*Fruit.*—A four-valved capsule, many-seeded, surrounded by the persistent calyx and crowned by the persistent style. August, September.

The Syringa has merits. It withstands the hard conditions of city life; its blooming season is extended; the flowers are beautiful and deliciously fragrant; it holds its leaves late into the autumn. Each flower as it opens is a bell, maturing it becomes a star.

The blooming season is that of the roses,—together they are the last of the procession of spring flowers; when they have cast their petals to the wind, summer has come. Many shrubs fulfil their flowering duty and relapse into green insignificance to emerge again when autumn clothes them in gold and scarlet. But after June is past the Syringa charms no more; its fruit is

Large-flowered Syringa, *Philadelphus grandiflorus*.  Garden Form.

Flowers 2′ to 3′ across.

inconspicuous; its leaves cling late and fall with little change of color.

The books give southern Europe as the native land of the plant, but as a matter of fact it has been in cultivation so long that its origin is unknown. In northern Europe, it was first cultivated in Belgium, then introduced into England about the time of Gerard, 1597, who had plants of it growing in his garden, "in the suburb of Holborne in verie great plentie." It will grow in almost any location and is easily propagated by division of the root.

There is considerable confusion with regard to the two southern species, *Philadelphus inodorus* and *Philadelphus grandiflorus*. They seem to have changed names from time to time; and the individuals in our northern gardens appearing under these names are probably hybrids. In any case, there is now in cultivation a *Philadelphus* producing large scentless flowers —blooming a little after *Philadelphus coronarius*—which either is a native species or was derived from one.

# SAXIFRAGÀCEÆ—SAXIFRAGE FAMILY

## THE DEUTZIAS

No Deutzia is found native within the borders of the United States; the plants are principally Asiatic; of the sixteen species now known, one is found in Mexico, all the others in Asia. Their pretty name was given them by Thunberg in honor of his friend and patron Johann Van der Deutz. Nearly all are hardy shrubs, with rough bark, axillary flowers borne in racemes or corymbs, the leaves mostly ovate, acuminate, serrate, and more or less rough. Though hardy, some of them are easily forced under glass, by which means they are made to produce beautiful flowers at any time of the year, and in great abundance.

*Deutzia gracilis*, Bridal Wreath, is one of the smallest of the genus and possibly the best known. It is a low growing shrub, fairly burdened in May with masses of the most lovely, pure white flowers. One minor characteristic adds to their beauty, the yellow stamens are borne upon white filaments. Gardeners highly prize this species, as it can be easily forced, and this little white bush is always one of the attractive objects among Easter decorations.

*Deutzia scabra* has long been in cultivation and from it several favorite varieties have been produced. The

Deutzia, *Deutzia gracilis.*

Deutzia, *Deutzia scabra*.

leaves of the type are ovate to ovate-lanceolate, the panicles erect, two to four inches long, and the individual flowers white or tinged with pink.

This is cultivated in different forms; *Deutzia candidissima*, a variety of pure white flowers; the Pride of Rochester, which bears very large double white flowers; *Deutzia purpurea plena*, with double flowers, white within and purplish without. There are other species and many varieties; all are desirable, blooming, as so many of them do, in June and July. There are varieties with yellow and with variegated leaves.

# ITEÀCEÆ—VIRGINIA WILLOW FAMILY

## ITEA. VIRGINIA WILLOW

*Ìtea virgínica.*

*Itea*, the Greek name for willow ; because the leaves of this plant resemble those of the willow.

A stalwart shrub, four to ten feet high, growing in wet places ; twigs and inflorescence downy. Ranges from the pine-barrens of New Jersey to Florida, and west to Missouri and Louisiana.

*Leaves.*—Alternate, simple, one to three inches long, narrowly oval or oblanceolate, wedge-shaped at base, finely serrate, acute or acuminate at apex ; when full grown, bright green, smooth above, slightly hairy beneath ; midvein and primary veins depressed above, prominent beneath. Autumnal tints scarlet and crimson.

*Flowers.*—May, June. Perfect, white, borne in dense terminal racemes, two to six inches long. Pedicels short, downy.

*Calyx.*—Calyx-tube bell-shaped, five-lobed, base adherent to the ovary.

*Corolla.*—Petals five, white, linear, erect or slightly spreading, three-eighths of an inch long, the points inflexed, inserted on the disk that lines the calyx.

*Stamens.*—Five, inserted with the petals.

*Pistil.*—Ovary one, two-celled ; style slender ; stigma two-grooved ; ovules many.

*Fruit.*—Capsule two-grooved, oblong, slender, downy, many-seeded, tipped with the two-parted style.

*Itea Virginica* is coming into cultivation in parks and gardens. The flowers are white, borne in terminal

Itea, *Itea virginica.*

Leaves 1′ to 3′ long.   Racemes 2′ to 6′ long.

racemes ; they are small, but sufficiently abundant to make the bush very attractive during the flowering season.

The leaves color early ; they change from green to scarlet and crimson in midsummer and glow in this gorgeous panoply until late autumn. Even after the leaves of other shrubs have fallen they still cling to the stems, a body of solid crimson. Five species belong to the genus, but this is the only one native to North America.

# GROSSULARIÀCEÆ—GOOSEBERRY FAMILY

## PRICKLY WILD GOOSEBERRY. DOGBERRY

*Rìbes cynósbati.*

*Ribes*, of uncertain origin, the name of a plant supposed by the older botanists to be the Gooseberry; possibly from *riebs*, a German popular name for the currant.

A fine bush, three to four feet high, found in rocky woods from New Brunswick to North Carolina and west to Manitoba and Missouri. Thrives in all soils and exposures. Stems unarmed or prickly.

*Leaves.*—Alternate, often fascicled, three to five-lobed, nearly orbicular, one to two inches broad, heart-shaped at base, irregularly serrate or crenate; palmately veined, primary and secondary veins depressed above, very prominent beneath. They come out in clusters of three or four from a single bud; plicate, bright green, densely covered with white hairs; when full grown are bright green above, paler green beneath. In autumn they turn an orange, slightly touched with red, or drop with little change. Petioles slender, downy with glandular hairs. A sharp, slender, reddish brown spine is usually found just below the leaf cluster; sometimes two or three are together, sometimes none. Frequently spines are scattered along the stem; prickles are few or weak or none.

*Flowers.*—April to June. Perfect, produced from the same bud as the cluster of leaves, solitary, or two to three in a group, bell-shaped, green, small, rich in nectar; peduncles slender, pubescent.

Wild Gooseberry, *Ribes cynosbati.*

Leaves 1' to 2' broad.

*Calyx.*—Coherent with the ovary ; tube bell-shaped, slightly contracted at mouth, five-lobed ; lobes roundish, shorter than the tube, green sometimes touched with red ; when mature lobes recurve against the tube.

*Petals.*—Five, minute, green, obscurely three-lobed, obovate, borne on the calyx-tube, alternate with the calyx-lobes.

*Stamens.*—Five, inserted in the calyx-tube, slightly included, opposite the calyx-lobes ; filaments and anthers green, converging to the stigma.

*Pistil.*—Ovary one-celled, adnate to calyx ; style relatively large, undivided, hairy at base ; stigma capitate.

*Fruit.*—Berry, globose, several-seeded, brownish purple, prickly, rarely smooth, one-half an inch in diameter, crowned with the remains of the calyx ; of a pleasant flavor. August.

The Prickly Wild Gooseberry is a common undershrub in northern woods. It reaches the height of four feet and defends itself from man and beast by the many prickles on the lower part of the stems. Sometimes, however, the stem is entirely smooth save for the spines at the base of the leaves. The flowers are little green bells, rich in nectar, borne on slender one to three-flowered peduncles. The fruit is a brownish red berry, covered with prickles like a bur, though occasionally smooth. Reports from the Arnold Arboretum state that seedlings from the same plant may produce either smooth or prickly fruit. The berries when mature are sweet and pleasant, but the prickles are often very sharp. This is the commonest wild gooseberry east of the Mississippi River.

Eastern Wild Gooseberry, *Ribes rotundifolium.*
Fruit ¼′ to ⅓′ in diameter.

## GOOSEBERRY FAMILY

### GARDEN GOOSEBERRY. EUROPEAN GOOSEBERRY

*Rìbes ùva-críspa. Rìbes grossulària.*

Rigid, stocky, of thick branches, the fruiting ones without prickles; the spines are mostly triple, heavy and thick at the base, the central one three-eighths to one-half an inch long.

*Leaves.*—Orbicular, three to five-lobed, thick and very glossy, pubescent; petioles sometimes sparsely set with glandular-tipped hairs.

*Flowers.*—Peduncles short, one to two-flowered, pubescent or glandular. Calyx very pubescent, greenish; tube broad, bell-shaped; lobes broadly ovate, thickish, reflexed, petaloid. Petals inserted on the calyx-tube, obovate, reaching to the base of the anthers. Stamens shorter than the calyx-lobes. Ovary pubescent or glandular; style commonly two-cleft, hairy at base.

*Fruit.*—Berry, oval, large, yellowish green or red, minutely but roughly pubescent, often with scattered prickles or glandular tipped hairs.

This gooseberry is native to Europe, northern Africa and western Asia. It is the parent of the English gooseberries, and is widely cultivated throughout Europe; from it many varieties have been produced.

### ROUND-LEAVED GOOSEBERRY

*Rìbes rotundifòlium.*

Low shrub, branches commonly straight, with light colored bark; thorns mostly single, but very short, gray like the outer bark. Ranges from western Massachusetts and New York southward to North Carolina along the Alleghanies.

*Leaves.*—Orbicular, palmately veined, three to five-lobed, wedge-shaped at base, glabrous or slightly downy, ciliate on margin and veins; vernation plicate.

*Flowers.*—May, June. Perfect, greenish purple, borne on two to three-flowered short peduncles. Calyx-lobes narrow or oblong, spatulate, greenish or dull purplish, seldom reflexed ; petals obovate, small ; stamens longer than the calyx-lobes ; style two-cleft, downy.

*Fruit.*—Small, several-seeded, about one-fourth of an inch in diameter, smooth, purplish, of an agreeable flavor. July, August.

## NORTHERN GOOSEBERRY. HAWTHORN GOOSE-BERRY

### *Ribes oxyacanthoïdes.*

Low shrub, two to four feet high, branches slender, reclined, often crooked, reddish brown, commonly smooth, but sometimes with scattered prickles ; spines single or triple, rather slender and sharp, sometimes wanting ; found in wet woods and low grounds. Ranges from Labrador and Newfoundland to the North West Territory and south to New Jersey and Nebraska.

*Leaves.*—Solitary or in fascicles, alternate, simple, palmately veined, orbicular, wedge-shaped or heart-shaped at base, deeply three to five-lobed ; lobes incised and coarsely toothed, finely pubescent above and beneath, but commonly glossy when growing ; vernation plicate.

*Flowers.*—May to July. Small, perfect, greenish white or dull purplish, bell-like ; peduncles short, one to two-flowered.

*Calyx.*—Greenish white ; tube bell-like, coherent with the ovary, five-lobed ; lobes oblong or obovate, thin and petaloid, when mature recurved.

*Corolla.*—Petals five, dull purplish, broadly ovate or spatulate, inserted on the calyx-tube, alternate with the sepals, reaching half way to the anthers.

*Stamens.*—Five, inserted on the calyx-tube, slightly included.

*Pistil.*—Ovary coherent with calyx, one-celled, style single or slightly two-cleft, pubescent below, slightly longer than the stamens.

*Fruit.*—Round, several-seeded, perfectly smooth, with a delicate bloom, one-half inch in diameter, yellowish green or reddish when ripe, of an agreeable flavor. July, August.

Northern Gooseberry, *Ribes oxyacanthoides.*

## SWAMP GOOSEBERRY

*Ribes lacústre.*

Upright, the twigs and branches densely bristly, with straight slender prickles; spines weak, single, or several in a whorl, especially on young growth. In swamps and cold, wet woods. Ranges from Newfoundland to Pennsylvania, west across the continent.

*Leaves.*—Nearly orbicular, heart-shaped at base, thin, pubescent along the veins beneath, deeply five to seven-lobed, one to two inches wide; lobes incised-dentate, acutish; vernation plicate.

*Flowers.*—May, June. Small, perfect, greenish, borne in a nodding many-flowered raceme. Pedicels short, bracted at the base. Calyx greenish white, saucer-shaped, glandular-bristly; the lobes short, broad, and spreading. Petals fan-shaped, reddish, nearly as long as the calyx-lobes. Stamens short; anthers very short, each half-divided. Pistil cleft at summit; ovary glandular-hairy.

*Fruit.*—Berry, about one-sixth of an inch in diameter, reddish, covered with weak prickles, unpleasant. July, August.

## FETID CURRANT. PROSTRATE CURRANT

*Ribes prostrátum.*

A shrub with recumbent or prostrate stems, trailing and rooting; branches erect, thornless and without prickles; found in cold, damp woods. Ranges from Labrador, throughout New England and along the mountains to North Carolina, and westward to the Pacific Ocean; also in northeastern Asia and upon the islands of Japan.

*Leaves.*—Alternate, orbicular, two to three inches wide, cordate at base, palmately veined, five to seven-lobed; lobes ovate, acute, dentate-serrate; vernation plicate. Petioles slender, one to three inches long, base dilated.

*Flowers.*—May, June. Small, perfect, greenish, bell-shaped, borne in erect, slender racemes which appear from the same buds as the leaves. Pedicels short, glandular, bracted at base.

*Calyx.*—Coherent with the ovary, broad, bell-shaped, five-lobed ; lobes obovate or roundish, greenish white or purplish.

*Corolla.*—Petals five, small, spatulate or fan-shaped, greenish purple, inserted on the throat of the calyx.

*Stamens.*—Five, inserted on the throat of the calyx, alternate with the petals, short; anthers often purple.

*Pistil.*—Ovary coherent with the calyx, one-celled ; style two-cleft. Ovary, peduncle and pedicels covered with glandular-tipped hairs.

*Fruit.*—Small, pale red berry, glandular, bristly.

This is one of the intercontinental plants, found both in America and Asia. It may be recognized by its long, prostrate, trailing stems, its deeply heart-shaped leaves, its small greenish flowers borne in erect racemes, and its pale red currants, bristly glandular. Both plant and fruit emit a disagreeable odor when bruised. It does not take kindly to cultivation; it loves the cold, damp woods and languishes in warmth and sunshine.

### RED CURRANT

*Ribes rùbrum.*

Red Currant, *Ribes rubrum.*

The Red Currant of our gardens is undoubtedly of European origin and has been modified by cultivation ; nevertheless in essentials it differs very slightly from our own wild form. The parent bush was unquestionably an inhabitant of cool, moist, shady northern haunts, and to-day the self-same

bush is found in Europe, Asia and America. With us
*Ribes rubrum* inhabits a belt extending across the continent from Labrador to Alaska, and southward to
New Jersey, Indiana and Minnesota. In New England
and the Middle States, however, the wild currant bush
by the roadside is much more likely to be an escape
from the gardens than a direct member of the ancient
line.

## WILD BLACK CURRANT

*Rìbes flóridum. Rìbes americànum.*

Erect, three to five feet high. Ranges from Nova Scotia to
Manitoba, and southward to Kentucky, Iowa and Nebraska.

*Leaves.*—Alternate or clustered, three to five-lobed, nearly orbicular, two to three and one-half inches wide, palmately veined,
heart-shaped at base, glabrous above, downy and resinous-dotted
beneath ; lobes coarsely dentate-serrate, depressed above, ridged
below. They come out of the bud plicate, pale green and
downy ; when full grown are bright green above, paler beneath.
In autumn they take on a deep bronze, or fall with little change
of color.

*Flowers.*—April, May. Perfect, greenish white or yellow,
bell-shaped, three-eighths to one-fourth of an inch long, borne
in pendulous, loosely-flowered, downy racemes, which appear
from the same buds as the leaves.

*Calyx.*—Calyx-tube bell-shaped, coherent with the ovary,
border four to five-lobed ; lobes short, rounded, petaloid, greenish white.

*Corolla.*—Petals four to five, inserted on the throat of the
calyx, greenish white.

*Stamens.*—Four to five, inserted on the throat of the calyx,
alternate with the petals, included.

*Pistil.*—Ovary inferior, one-celled ; styles two.

*Fruit.*—Berry, globose-ovoid, black, smooth, one-fourth of an
inch in diameter ; crowned with the remnant of a calyx.

Wild Black Currant, *Ribes floridum.*

Leaves 2′ to 3½′ broad.

This species is rarely cultivated. In general appearance, and in flavor of fruit it resembles the Black Currant, *Ribes nigrum*, of the garden. It forms a graceful spreading bush, with luxuriant foliage and long, drooping racemes both of flowers and of fruit.

## GOLDEN CURRANT. BUFFALO OR MISSOURI CURRANT

*Rìbes aùreum.*

A bush of long, slender, upright or curving stems, growing along streams. Ranges from Minnesota to Missouri and Texas, westward to Oregon and California. Common in cultivation.

*Leaves.*—Alternate or tufted, one to one and a half inches long, simple, palmately veined, three to five-lobed, often broader than long, wedge-shaped or heart-shaped, or rounded at base; lobes rounded, toothed or entire; midvein and primary veins conspicuous. They come out of the bud convolute, pale green, downy and shining; when full grown are bright yellow green above, paler green beneath. Leaves of bearing shoots are commonly three lobed; lobes often short, broad, and entire. The autumnal tint is yellow dashed with red, and they change and drop comparatively early.

*Flowers.*—April, May. Perfect, yellow, cylindrical, borne in short, loose, leafy-bracted racemes. Fragrant, charged with nectar.

*Calyx.*—Coherent with the ovary; bright yellow, smooth; tube cylindric, one-half to an inch long, with five, spreading, recurved lobes.

*Corolla.*—Petals five, small, yellow with pink tips, inserted on the throat of the calyx.

*Stamens.*—Five, inserted on the calyx throat and alternate with the petals, slightly exserted.

*Pistil.*—Ovary inferior, one-celled; style long and slender, exserted; stigma capitate.

*Fruit.*—Globose berry, black, sometimes yellowish black, glabrous, shining, crowned with the remnant of the calyx, insipid. August.

## GOOSEBERRY FAMILY

This tall, vigorous, upright bush, found in unnumbered dooryards, is most attractive in early spring. The flowers and leaves start together, but the flowers get ahead, and the wand-like branches are thickly clothed with the flower clusters before the leaves make much headway. Its flame of yellow is due to the brilliant calyx; the tiny petals of the corolla are not very much in evidence.

The plant is graceful and hardy, sprouting freely from the roots. The leaves are inclined to drop early, which is its only defect as an ornamental plant.

Golden Currant, *Ribes aureum.*

Flowers ½′ to ⅝′ long.

# HAMAMELIDÂCEÆ—WITCH HAZEL FAMILY

*Hamamèlis virginiàna.*

*Hamamelis* is an ancient name with no obvious application to this plant. Witch is a modern spelling of the Saxon *wich* or *wych*. The meaning of the word in this connection is doubtful; it is good opinion, however, that it means pendulous, drooping; two trees are so named,—wych elm and wych hazel.

> Through the gray and sombre wood,
>     Against the dusk of fir and pine,
> Last of their floral sisterhood,
>     The hazel's yellow blossoms shine.
> —JOHN G. WHITTIER.

Amid the wild-wood pomp and circumstance of our northern autumn there is no more remarkable object than the Witch Hazel, which at the very moment of parting with its leaves breaks forth into an abundant bloom that clusters thickly about the stems and gives to November the aspect of April. The flower buds appear in August, they expand rarely in September, normally in October and November; and the flowers appear three or four together at the end of a short, brown, downy pedicel in the axil of a falling or fallen leaf. The flower is in fours; four lobes to the calyx; four long, crumpled, yellow petals; four fertile stamens

Witch Hazel, *Hamamelis virginiana.*

Leaves 4′ to 6′ long.

alternating with four scale-like, imperfect ones; only the pistil varies from the four-fold plan; the ovary is two-celled and two-styled. This late flowering of the plant seems an excess of zeal, for no growth takes place in the ovary until the following spring, and the ripening period is not forwarded thereby. The tiny last year's nuts slowly ripen as this year's flowers bloom, and are finally sent out from their woody pods with a projectile force which carries them several yards.

The Witch Hazel is to be looked for on the sides of deep ravines and at the edges of woodlands throughout our range.

# CORNÀCEÆ—DOGWOOD FAMILY

## DOGWOOD. CORNEL

### Córnus.

*Cornus*, horn, from *cornu*, referring to the toughness of the wood.

The Cornels with showy floral leaves are confined to the New World, the group being represented by the two flowering Dogwood trees, one in the east and the other in the west; also by the pretty little herbaceous Bunchberry, a familiar flower of our northern woods, and by another species resembling the last a Bunch-berry native to Alaska and the far northern parts of the continent. These are all that have come down to us from a very peculiar group of plants, which in earlier times were more widely scattered over the earth's surface than they are now. For the ancestors of our Flowering Dogwood occurred in Europe, where, however, their descendants have been unable to obtain a foothold.

*—Garden and Forest.*

The Dogwood makes a very attractive family group which consists of herbs, shrubs and trees. The trees are small and sometimes play at being shrubs; the shrubs now and then try to be trees; and the herbs are woody at base and apparently hope some day to be shrubs.

The highest and the lowest in the family produce flowers and fruit that are very similar. *Cornus florida*, the tree, and *Cornus canadensis*, the herb, wrap around their clusters of small flowers the superb white involu-

241

cre which makes the Dogwood tree the glory of the woods in spring-time, and the Bunch-berry the prize of the seeker. In the case of *Cornus florida* the flowers usually appear on the bare branches, but sometimes under favoring conditions the great white involucres linger until the leaves are nearly grown; but they never outstay their welcome, for few sights are prettier than a Dogwood tree bearing both leaves and flowers.

The other tree, *Cornus alternifolia*, and all the shrubs bear their flowers in flat cymose clusters, one to three inches across. The individual flower is a four-pointed

Single Flower of Dogwood, *Cornus baileyi*, enlarged.

star with four exserted stamens. The only flowering shrubs with which the dogwoods could be confused are the viburnums, but their flower is a star with five rounded divisions and five stamens. If it is remembered that the dogwoods are always in fours and the viburnums always in fives, the difficulty is removed.

The fruits of the family come in assorted colors; they range through bright scarlet, dark blue, pale steel blue, bluish white and pure white. In flavor they vary simply in degrees of unpleasantness, all being more or less acid, bitter and aromatic, and the bitter is of a particularly persistent and pervading kind.

Another family characteristic is the brilliant stems of many of the species. The most marked example is the White-fruited Dogwood, *Cornus alba* of Siberia, which is the species most generally cultivated in this country. The blood-red twigs and stems which glow throughout the winter, and deepen and flame as winter

Flowering Dogwood, *Cornus florida.*

Spread of the Flower-bracts 2′ to 5′.

merges into spring, are well known to even the most casual observer. This species is marked in many dealers' catalogues as *Cornus sanguinea*, but this is wrong. The real *Cornus sanguinea* is a European species having little of interest in the color of its bark, which becomes gray when old. The color of its fruit is black.

Our own *Cornus stolonifera* possesses the beautiful red twigs in so marked a degree as to give it the common name Red-osier Dogwood. *Cornus baileyi* and *Cornus asperifolia* have twigs of reddish brown; those of *Cornus alternifolia* and *Cornus circinata* are green; those of *Cornus amonum* dull purple. An extensive and pleasing range of winter coloring can be had by means of dogwoods alone.

## FLOWERING DOGWOOD

*Córnus flórida.*

The Flowering Dogwood is both tree and shrub, and its value as an ornamental plant is not exceeded by any other denizen of our gardens. Its flowers are *sui generis ;* the real flowers are the little green bunch in the centre of the four petaloid bracts which enwrap and protect them. The genesis of these great white bracts is interesting. They are simply four bud-scales and may be seen upon the flower buds which develop in late summer at the tips of the branches of any fruitful and flourishing individual. They endure the buffetings of storms; they brave the cold, the ice, the snow of winter; and when spring comes and other bud-scales, having completed their service, pass away unregarded, these simply take on a second growth,

Round-leaved Dogwood, *Cornus circinata.*

Leaves 2′ to 6′ long.   Cymes 1½′ to 3′ across.

carrying the weather-beaten winter portion of the old on the apex of the new. The notch on the end of the broad white bract is the bud-scale of the past winter. Search as you may, you can never find one without the dark scar. This is the insignia of service, the sign of work well done.

The original form of the Red-flowering Dogwood so frequently seen in parks and gardens came from Virginia; but the trees whose flower bracts vary from pure white are not rare. The bracts are not pretty or showy until fully developed, then they assume the pink of the wild rose.

## ROUND-LEAVED DOGWOOD

### *Córnus circinàta.*

A compact shrub six to ten feet high, in shady, often rocky, places, in rich or sandy soil. Ranges from Nova Scotia to Manitoba, south to Virginia, west to Iowa and Missouri.

*Stem.*—Twigs and branches green, warty-dotted.

*Leaves.*—Opposite, entire, two to six inches long, orbicular, or broadly ovate, sometimes broader than long, rounded or truncate at base, entire, acute or acuminate at apex. They come out of the bud slightly involute, pale green tipped with red, densely covered with white hairs; when full grown are bright pale green, slightly pubescent above, densely hairy beneath. In autumn they turn a dull yellow. Petioles one-half to three-fourths of an inch long.

*Flowers.*—May, June. Perfect, small, white, borne in rather dense flat cymes, one and a half to three inches across; pedicels downy.

*Calyx.*—Tube bell-like, four-toothed, coherent with the ovary.

*Corolla.*—Petals four, white, ovate, valvate in bud, inserted on a disk within the calyx.

Silky Dogwood, *Cornus amomum.*

Leaves 3' to 5' long.   Cymes 1½' to 2½' across.

*Stamens.*—Four, exserted, filaments threadlike; inserted with the petals.

*Pistil.*—Ovary inferior, two-celled; style slender; stigma capitate.

*Fruit.*—Drupe, globose, very pale blue or white with a bluish tinge, three-eighths of an inch in diameter; stone sub-globose, ridged. Bitter, aromatic. September.

This is one of the most attractive of the cornels. It reaches the height of six or ten feet; the branches are green and warty-dotted, the bright green leaves, large and roundish. It should be sought for in open rocky woods, and in cultivation will do best in a shady location. The flowers are rather large for a dogwood, and the fruit, light blue or bluish white, is too scanty to be effective, but the general effect of the plant is excellent.

## SWAMP DOGWOOD. SILKY DOGWOOD. KINNIKINNIK

*Córnus amòmum.   Córnus serícea.*

A shrub six to ten feet high, found in wet soil, low woods and along streams. Ranges from New Brunswick to Florida, west to Nebraska and Texas. Bark bitter and tonic.

*Stems.*—Shoots downy, green with reddish tinge. Winter twigs and branches purple; stems brown.

*Leaves.*—Opposite, simple, three to five inches long, oval, narrowly-ovate, or ovate-lanceolate, narrowed or rounded at base, entire, acuminate at apex; midvein and primary veins depressed above, ridged below. They come out of the bud slightly involute, pale green, with white woolly hairs; when full grown are bright shining green above, pale green, silky downy, often glaucous, beneath. Autumnal tints dull purple to deep red.

*Flowers.*—May, July. Perfect, cream-white, borne in flat cymes, one and a half to two and a half inches across.

*Calyx.*—Tube bell-like, four-toothed; coherent with the ovary.

Rough-leaved Dogwood, *Cornus asperifolia.*
Leaves 1½' to 5' long.  Cymes 2' to 3' across.

*Corolla.*—Petals four, white, narrowly oblong, acute, valvate in bud.

*Stamens.*—Four, exserted, filaments threadlike; inserted on disk, with the petals.

*Pistil.*—Ovary inferior, two-celled; style slender; stigma capitate.

*Fruit.*—Drupe, globose, pale blue, one-fourth to three-eighths of an inch in diameter; stone oblique, ridged. Bitter, aromatic. September.

The Silky Dogwood is the latest of the family to flower, usually coming into bloom about the twentieth of June. The leaves are slender, ovate, pointed, silky downy on the under side, especially when young. The flower cymes are rather smaller than those of the other dogwoods. The fruit is bright blue and usually abundant. The plant is very common at the north along the borders of swamps and in other low, wet places, where it forms a wide spreading bush eight to ten feet high. Its colored twigs and branchlets suffuse a purplish tint over the bush in winter, thus giving it a decided ornamental value.

## ROUGH-LEAVED DOGWOOD

### *Córnus asperifólia.*

Three to fifteen feet high, found in wet ground or near streams. Ranges from southern Ontario to Florida and west to Iowa, Kansas and Texas.

*Stems.*—Reddish brown; branchlets very rough, downy.

*Leaves.*—Opposite, simple, one and a half to five inches long, ovate-oval or elliptic, rounded at base, entire, acuminate at apex; when full grown densely rough-hairy above, pale and downy beneath. Petioles slender, rough-hairy.

*Flowers.*—May, June. Perfect, cream-white, borne in loose cymes; pedicels are rough-hairy.

Red-osier Dogwood, *Cornus stolonifera.*

Leaves 4′ to 6′ long.  Cymes 1′ to 2′ across.

*Calyx.*—Tube bell-shaped, four-toothed, coherent with the ovary.

*Corolla.*—Petals four, white, oblong-lanceolate, inserted on the disk.

*Stamens.*—Four, exserted ; filament threadlike, inserted with the petals.

*Pistil.*—Ovary inferior, two-celled ; style slender, stigma capitate.

*Fruit.*—Drupe, globose, white, about one-fourth of an inch in diameter; stone variable in shape. Bitter, aromatic. September.

*Cornus asperifolia* is a western and southern species, not occurring in New England or the Middle States. In habit and general appearance it resembles *Cornus stolonifera*, but the branches are brown instead of red, and the branchlets rough-hairy. It is a tall, hardy species.

## RED-OSIER DOGWOOD

### *Córnus stolonífera.*

Three to six feet high, found in wet places. Ranges from New Brunswick and Nova Scotia to British Columbia, south to Virginia, westward to Kentucky and Nebraska.

*Stems.*—Branchlets at first reddish, downy ; later dark red ; and in winter, stems, branches and twigs become a bright purplish red, smooth and shining. Stems lose much of their brilliant color when the leaves appear, to regain it again in autumn.

*Leaves.*—Opposite, simple, four to six inches long, ovate, ovate-lanceolate or oblong, rounded or wedge-shaped at base, entire, acute or acuminate at apex. They come out of the bud slightly involute, reddish, covered with white hairs above and below ; when full grown are bright green, somewhat downy above, paler green or white and somewhat downy below. In autumn they turn a bronze purple or dark red touched with orange, or yellow. Petiole dull red, slender, grooved, one-half to one inch long.

*Flowers.*—June, July. Perfect, cream-white, borne in flat cymes, one to two inches across ; pedicels downy.

Panicled Dogwood, *Cornus candidissima*.
Leaves 2½′ to 4′ long.  Cymes 1½′ to 2′ across.

*Calyx.*—Tube bell-like, four-toothed, coherent with the ovary.

*Corolla.*—Petals four, white, ovate-oblong, valvate in bud, inserted on disk.

*Stamens.*—Four, exserted; filaments threadlike; inserted with the petals.

*Pistil.*—Ovary inferior, two-celled; style slender; stigma capitate.

*Fruit.*—Drupe, globose, white or whitish, about one-fourth of an inch in diameter; stone variable in shape.

The Red-osier is a very common northern shrub found growing in company with *Alnus incana* along the watercourses. It spreads by means of underground shoots so that a single plant quickly makes of itself a thicket. In leaf, flower and fruit it resembles the Red-stemmed Dogwood of cultivation. Were it not surpassed by this Siberian species it would be cultivated for the beauty of its glowing red-purple stems and branches, which in winter look very warm, bright and cheerful against the snow. The fruit is white.

### PANICLED DOGWOOD

*Córnus candidíssima. Córnus paniculàta.*

Tall, spreading, often ten or twelve feet high, found along the borders of streams and on the margins of lowland woods and thickets. Ranges from Maine to North Carolina, west to Minnesota and Nebraska.

*Stems.*—Twigs, stems and branches smooth, gray.

*Leaves.*—Opposite, simple, two and a half to four inches long, ovate-lanceolate, wedge-shaped or obtuse at base, entire, acuminate at apex. They come out of the bud slightly involute, pale green tinged with red, slightly downy; when full grown are finely downy above and below; pale and sometimes glaucous below. Petioles slender.

Bailey's Dogwood, *Cornus baileyi.*

*Flowers.*—May, June. Perfect, cream-white, borne in loose-flowered somewhat paniculate cymes, one and a half to two inches across.

*Calyx.*—Tube bell-shaped, four-toothed, coherent with the ovary.

*Corolla.*—Petals four, white, lanceolate, inserted on the disk, valvate in bud.

*Stamens.*—Four, exserted; filaments threadlike, inserted with the petals.

*Pistil.*—Ovary inferior, two-celled.

*Fruit.*—Drupe, globose or slightly depressed, white, about one-fourth of an inch in diameter, stone sub-globose.

## BAILEY'S DOGWOOD

### *Córnus baileyi.*

This Dogwood is a native of the sand dunes of the Great Lakes, also found in moist ground from Pennsylvania to Minnesota and westward.

The species was long considered a form of *Cornus stolonifera* from which it can be distinguished " by the lack of stolons, by the much duller and brown bark, and the white fruit with a large flattened stone, and also by the white wooliness of the lower leaf surfaces. It appears on the sand dunes about the Great Lakes, often in the loosest, shifting, white sands." Flowers appear more or less abundantly all summer.

## ALTERNATE-LEAVED DOGWOOD

### *Córnus alternifðlia.*

The Alternate-leaved Dogwood is sometimes a tree and frequently a shrub. Unlike the other dogwoods its leaves are alternate and they often appear in a sort of tufted group. The stem and twigs are green and

Alternate-leaved Dogwood, *Cornus alternifolia.*

Leaves 2′ to 4′ long.  Cymes 1½′ to 2′ across.

in a group of dogwoods arranged for winter color give an excellent effect.

The leaves are slender-petioled, oval or ovate, acuminate or acute at apex, two to four inches long; dark green above, paler green and slightly pubescent beneath. The flower clusters are one and a half to two inches across, the petals lanceolate. The fruit is dark blue and a little less bitter than that of some of the other species, so that it is taken by the birds. The range extends from Nova Scotia to Georgia and west as far as Minnesota.

### RED-STEMMED DOGWOOD. WHITE-FRUITED DOG-WOOD

*Córnus álba.* (*Córnus sanguinea.*)

The Red-stemmed or Red-twigged Dogwood is one of the most satisfactory of cultivated shrubs. A native of northern Europe and northern Asia, it is perfectly hardy here, and the brilliant blood-red stems against a white background of snow, arrest the attention of the most unobservant. The flood tide of color is in February and March; as the leaves begin to appear the color fades and during the summer the stems are dull.

There is no objection to its common name; it is fitting and appropriate. Nor is there any objection to the botanical name, *Cornus sanguinea*, were that the name of the plant. But it is not, unfortunately; and furthermore, it never can be. That name has already been given to an entirely different species; it has been recorded in all the finding lists of Europe, and it will

Red-stemmed Dogwood, *Cornus alba.*

Leaves 3' to 5' long.   Cymes 2' to 3' across.

not, it cannot be changed. *Cornus alba* is the correct name; the bush having been named with reference to its fruit rather than its stems.

Dealers of acknowledged standing are extensively advertising the Red-stemmed Dogwood as *Cornus sanguinea* and the public is just as extensively buying it under the same name. " A name is a trifle and besides this one is fitting." No doubt " a rose by any other name would smell as sweet," but after all it is not quite pleasant that so gross an error should be so widespread; or that it should be so strongly entrenched among those who ought to know better.

Red-stemmed Dogwood, *Cornus alba*, in fruit.

# CAPRIFOLIÀCEÆ—HONEYSUCKLE FAMILY

## AMERICAN ELDER. SWEET ELDER

### *Sambùcus canadénsis.*

*Sambucus* is a word of doubtful origin and of no significance
as applied to this plant. An old explanation was that the
word is derived from *sambuke*, the Greek name of a musical
instrument supposed to have been made of the wood of this
plant. This explanation is now discredited.

A thrifty shrub, five to fifteen feet high, abundant on the
borders of streams, in moist places and along fences. Bark,
leaves and berries are reputed of medicinal value. Suckers
freely; the young shoot is a green withe. Common throughout
the northern states.

*Stems.*—Filled with white pith ; swollen at the joints. Branchlets green at first, then pale yellowish gray with more or less
bloom, later darker gray with yellow lines, finally dark or yellow
brown. Lenticels prominent.

*Leaves.*—Opposite, pinnately compound ; leaflets five to
eleven, almost sessile except the terminal which has a short peti-
olule, narrow-oblong or oblong-ovate, four to six inches long,
wedge-shaped or rounded at base, serrate, often entire toward
the base, acuminate or acute ; midrib and primary veins depressed above, prominent below ; lower leaflet sometimes lobed.
They come out of the bud pale green, shining, very downy ;
when full grown are dark green, glabrous above, pale green,
glabrous or somewhat downy beneath. In autumn they remain
unchanged until destroyed by heavy frosts. When crushed they
exhale a heavy odor. Petiole two to three inches long, grooved,

American Elder, *Sambucus canadensis.*
Leaflets 4′ to 6′ long.  Cymes 5′ to 8′ across.

swollen at base, the two coming together almost clasp the stem. Leaflets often have stipels.

*Flowers.*—June to August. Perfect, cream-white, star-like, three-eighths of an inch across, turning brown in drying, borne in flat, spreading, compound cymes five to eight inches across. Odor not unpleasant.

*Calyx.*—Adnate to the ovary; five-cleft; lobes minute, acute, white with reddish tips.

*Corolla.*—Cream-white, with small, short tube and flat border, five to seven-lobed; lobes rounded, greatly reflexed.

*Stamens.*—Five, inserted on the corolla and alternate with its lobes, exserted; filaments slender, white; anthers pale yellow, two-celled.

*Pistil.*—Ovary inferior, three to five-celled, one ovule in each cell; style three to five-lobed.

*Fruit.*—Berry-like juicy drupe, borne in broad flat cymes, dark purple, size of small pea, crowned with the remnant of the calyx, containing three to five nutlets. Flesh crimson with crimson juice; taste pleasant.

An elder or two
Foamed over with blossoms white as spray.
—JAMES RUSSELL LOWELL.

An infusion of the juice of the berry of the Common Elder is a delicate test for acids and alkalies. An infusion of the bruised leaves is used by gardeners to expel insects from vines. A wholesome sudorific tea is made of the flowers. The abundant pith is the best substance for the pith-balls used in electrical experiments; and the hollow shoots are in great use with boys for pop-guns and fifes.
—GEORGE B. EMERSON.

To one who in the ripening days of August fares through uncared for country roads, few bushes have more charm than the Elder. In every fence corner, bordering the tumbling stone walls, and in umbrageous clumps by the roadside, stand these spreading shrubs, with dull green foliage and heavy clusters of small purple black berries. Not seldom wild vines run riot through the gray clustered stems; and the clematis, the traveller's joy, tosses the white foam of its airy bloom over the full fruitage. The elderberry crop never fails; huckleberries and blackberries, other children of the wastes may have dried in the droughts of midsummer, but the little elderberries full of crimson juice crowd in close cymes upon every branch.
—MARTHA BOCKÉE FLINT.

The American Elder is one of the choicest of our native shrubs, and is such a familiar figure in northern fields and by northern roadsides that its beauty passes unnoticed, and the plant is foolishly and ruthlessly cut down even when no use is made of the land so despoiled. It marks a great advance in the intellectual cultivation of the individual when he is able to appreciate the beauty of familiar things, and does not wish to destroy an object simply because it is well known. There have been precepts carefully inculcated, that neat farming involved the destruction of every bush by the fence or wayside. Away with such unlovely wisdom! Why may not the fence line simulate the hedgerow and, with a little care, take virtually nothing from the cultivated field and add immeasurably to the beauty of the landscape? Why may not the roadside be an arboretum of its own locality?

In the flowering season the Elder equals if it does not surpass in beauty and effectiveness the finest of our garden favorites,—this bush "foamed over with blossoms white as spray." The high tide of bloom occurs in early July and marks the virtual closing of the great spring flowering period. The flowers cannot be used for indoor decoration,—they droop immediately upon being cut.

It is interesting to observe how the great flat cluster divides into fives. There are five large stems and four of these are of about equal size; the central one is not so long or so strong and it is this which gives the depressed look to the cluster. Each stem divides again into five, but one or two of the divisions usually outstrip the others.

Later, the bushes stand bowed with the burden of purple berries. People may be divided in opinion as to the merits of the fruit; the robins are not; with one accord they call them good and seek them tunefully and joyously. By way of domestic value, elderberries have been used in pies and puddings, but they are not sufficiently acid to be really palatable when used alone. The fruit is also responsible for the domestic elderberry wine, which certainly cheers and does not inebriate and is reputed to possess medicinal properties.

There is a golden-leaved variety which is very extensively planted; and which in midsummer lights up the fence corner or garden walk with a golden glow that is extremely effective amid the surrounding green.

## MOUNTAIN ELDER. RED-BERRIED ELDER

*Sambùcus pùbens. Sambùcus racemòsa.*

A shrub two to twelve feet high, twigs and leaves pubescent; the younger stems full of reddish brown pith; found in rocky places and in dry woods. Ranges from New Brunswick to British Columbia and Alaska, south to Georgia, southwest to Colorado and California.

*Stems.*—Young stems pale, dotted with many brownish lenticels; older stems brown, having a rough and warty appearance.

*Leaves.*—Opposite, pinnately compound; leaflets ten to fourteen, oblong-lanceolate or oval, three to five inches long, narrowed and often bilateral at base, sharply serrate, acuminate at apex; midvein and primary veins depressed above, prominent beneath; they come out of the bud pale green, shining and downy, when full grown are dark green, nearly smooth above, paler green and downy below. In autumn they remain late and fall with little change of color. Petioles reddish and grooved. Small red glands appear at the base of each petiole and at the base of some petiolules.

Red-berried Elder, *Sambucus pubens.*

Leaflets 3′ to 5′ long.

*Flowers.*—April, May.  Perfect, small, cream-white, turning brown in drying, borne in pyramidal compound cymes, odor heavy.

*Calyx.*—Tube adnate to the ovary ; border narrow, five-cleft ; lobes minute.

*Corolla.*—Cream-white, wheel-shaped, spreading five-cleft border, lobes rounded, greatly reflexed.

*Stamens.*—Five, inserted on the corolla and alternate with its lobes, exserted ; filaments slender, white ; anthers pale yellow, two-celled.

*Pistil.*—Ovary inferior, three to five-celled ; style short, three-lobed ; one ovule in each cell.

*Fruit.*—Berry-like juicy drupe, borne in pyramidal clusters, brilliant scarlet, size of a small pea, crowned with remnants of style and calyx, containing three to five nutlets.  Flesh yellow and unpleasant to the taste.  June, July.

The Red-berried Elder belongs to the group of early bloomers.  Its flower buds push out from their protecting bracts in company with those of the Shrub Yellow-root, the Forsythia and the *Magnolia stellata.* The flower cluster, instead of being broad and flat like that of the American Elder, is pyramidal.  The tiny flowers so dispose themselves that they seem like little balls with stamens protruding on every side.  The fruit is a brilliant scarlet, borne in great clusters, and frequently so abundant as to make the bush one mass of red; and as this magnificent display comes early— even before the American Elder comes into bloom—it has an increased value.  But under any circumstances, the fruiting bush is extremely ornamental with every branch tipped with a scarlet thyrsus.  A white-berried variety has been reported as occurring on the Catskill mountains.

The bush can be distinguished from *Sambucus cana-*

*densis*, if in bloom by the shape of the flower cluster; if in fruit by the brilliant scarlet of the berries; if without flowers or fruit, by the brownish pith of the small twigs which is a persistent character and will serve to determine the species.

## THE VIBURNUMS

Our northern Viburnums are a group of ornamental trees and shrubs which are rapidly winning their way into popular appreciation. Excellent in habit, foliage, flower and fruit, and perfectly hardy, they are valuable for lawn and park decoration, and also as roadside shrubs. The distinguishing characters are their flat clusters of small, white, rarely pink flowers and their showy panicles of fruit, which in ripening give most exquisite gradations of color. The individual flower is a five-pointed star, bearing five exserted stamens; the points of the star are considerably rounded. The only shrubs with which the Viburnums in bloom might be confounded are the dogwoods; but the individual flower of a dogwood is a four-pointed star, with the points intact. That slight distinction is a certain means of distinguishing the two.

Viburnum flower.

Two trees of the group, *Viburnum lentago* and *Viburnum prunifolium*, often appear as shrubs. They are attractive in foliage and in flower, and their fruit is sweet and edible.

One species of the genus has been developed into an extremely decorative plant and is the well known Snowball of our gardens.

The members of the family are conspicuous for their fine autumnal tints. These are bronze and purple, brightening into red or orange.

## HOBBLE-BUSH. AMERICAN WAYFARING-TREE

*Vibúrnum alnifòlium.   Vibúrnum lantanoìdes.*

*Viburnum* is an ancient name of unknown meaning.   Hobble-bush refers to the prostrate branches which often trip the unwary.

A low, irregular shrub with long, flexible, often procumbent, branches and large leaves; found in cold, moist woods.   Ranges from New Brunswick to North Carolina, west to Michigan.

*Stems.*—Bark purplish; branches often long and prostrate; branchlets densely covered with rusty, stellate pubescence. Branches often take root at the tips.

*Leaves.* — Opposite, simple, pinnately veined, orbicular or broadly ovate, three to eight inches across, heart-shaped at base, finely serrate, abruptly pointed at apex.   They come out of the bud involute, clothed with dense rusty down; when full grown are deeply corrugated above; midvein and primary veins scurfy with rusty stellate pubescence.   Autumnal tints are brilliant red and orange.   Petioles an inch to an inch and a half long, scurfy with rusty down, often showing small stipular appendages, but no real stipules.

*Flowers.*—May, June.   Of two kinds, perfect and neutral. White, borne in broad, compound, sessile, radiant cymes, three to five inches across; the outer and imperfect flowers more or less numerous, raised on longer pedicels and destitute of stamens and pistils.   They are circular disks, one-half to five-eighths of an inch across, having five, large, unequal, rounded lobes; the inner flowers are small and perfect.   Pedicels downy.

*Calyx.*—Tube adnate to the ovary; border five-toothed.

*Corolla.*—White; of the perfect flowers, rotate, five-lobed; lobes spreading; neutral rotate, lobes much enlarged.

*Stamens.*—Five, inserted on the corolla-tube; anthers exserted.

Hobble-bush, *Viburnum alnifolium.*
Leaves 3′ to 8′ across.   Cymes 3′ to 5′ across.

*Pistil.*—Ovary inferior, one-celled ; style short ; stigmas three-parted.

*Fruit.*—Drupe, ovoid-oblong, red darkening to purple ; one-seeded, half an inch long ; pulp soft. Stone three-grooved on one side and one-grooved on the other. September.

The flat hydrangea-like corollas of the neutral flowers on the margins of the flower clusters are an inch or more in diameter, and appearing above the half-grown leaves are extremely effective. The plant is good at all seasons, with its sturdy growth, its great leaves, its beautiful fruit changing through coral and crimson to purple.

The long branches often take root at the end and so form loops that, in the woods where it abounds, frequently catch the foot of the unwary, hence the name Hobble-bush. This unpleasant habit seems to be responsible for certain other not altogether complimentary names, as Witch-hobble and Trip-toe.

The rusty hairs which cover the growing shoots, the opening leaves, and the flower stems, are arranged in star-like clusters and are objects of great beauty under a magnifying glass. This peculiarity of stellate hairs is shared by the Clethra and also in a very marked degree by the Buffalo-berry.

The Hobble-bush is a better garden plant, or at least more manageable, when grafted upon *Viburnum dentatum* than upon its own roots.

## HIGH-BUSH CRANBERRY.   CRANBERRY-TREE.
## GUELDER ROSE

*Vibúrnum ópulus.*

An exceedingly handsome shrub with smooth branches, four to ten feet high, growing in low ground, along streams and on the borders of swamps.   Ranges from New Brunswick to Pennsylvania, and westward to Michigan, South Dakota and Oregon.

*Leaves.* — Opposite, simple, palmately veined, two to five inches long, one and a half to four inches wide, rounded or wedge-shaped at base, three-nerved, three-lobed; lobes divergent, sparingly toothed with unequal blunt teeth.   They come out of the bud involute, pale green tinged with red, shining and downy; when full grown are dark dull green, nearly glabrous above, paler green, somewhat pubescent, beneath, deeply corrugated above.   Petioles about an inch long, with one or two stipular appendages, which are more or less glandular.   Autumnal tints bronze purple and dull red.

*Flowers.*—May, June.   Of two kinds, perfect and neutral. White, borne in broad, compound, terminal pedunculate radiant cymes, three to four inches across, having five large, unequal rounded lobes.   The perfect flowers are small, about three-sixteenths across.   The neutral one-half to three-fourths of an inch across.

*Calyx.*—Tube adnate to the ovary ;  border five-toothed.

*Corolla.* — Cream-white, rotate, five-lobed ;  lobes rounded, spreading, imbricate in bud.   Perfect flowers a trifle more yellowish than the neutral.

*Stamens.*—Five, inserted on the corolla-tube, exserted.

*Pistil.*—Ovary inferior, one-celled ;  stigma three-parted.

*Fruit.* — Drupe, globose or oval, bright red, translucent, crowned by the limb of the calyx, three-eighths to half an inch long, intensely acid and slightly bitter ;  clings to the branch all winter.   Stone flat, orbicular, not grooved.   September.

The High-bush Cranberry loves the north, and along the sixtieth parallel encircles the globe with lit-

High-bush Cranberry, *Viburnum opulus.*

Leaves 2′ to 5′ long. Cymes 3′ to 4′ across.

Snowball, *Viburnum opulus sterilis.*

tle change of habit or character. It descends as far as the fortieth parallel and grows there fairly well.

In late May or early June a broad cluster of small white blossoms, which are the fruit-bearing flowers of the plant, appear at the apex of nearly every stem. At the margin of this cluster, arranged around these perfect blossoms in an irregular circle are numbers of cream-white disks variously rounded and lobed, destitute of stamens and pistils, apparently for show and not for use. These marginal flowers become conspicuously white a few days before the perfect flowers open. They are evidently a signal, a flag hung out to the insect world saying, "Come buy, come buy! without money and without price."

Its contribution to the beauty of the garden is greatest when in fruit. None of its neighbors can surpass it. Soon after the flowers have dropped, the berries are noticeable, and by the last of July they become a beautiful greenish yellow, touched with red. Later, the entire bush flames in scarlet, and so remains long into the autumn. The fruit is acid—so acid that the birds evidently do not care to set their bills on edge with it—containing also a marked trace of bitter; and has been used as a poor substitute for cranberries, whence its common name.

*Viburnum opulus* is the parent of the common Snowball, *Viburnum opulus sterilis*, of our gardens. Whenever any plant shows a few neutral flowers in its wild state, these can be increased indefinitely by cultivation and selection.

*Viburnum paucifolium*, the Few-flowered Cranberry-tree, differs from *Viburnum opulus* in its broader

Maple-leaved Viburnum, *Viburnum acerifolium.*

Leaves 3′ to 5′ long.   Cymes 2′ to 3′ across.

leaves and fewer flowers, all of which are perfect. The fruit is smaller and paler red. Its range is northern, reaching its southern limit in the mountains of Pennsylvania.

## MAPLE-LEAVED VIBURNUM. ARROW-WOOD

*Vibúrnum acerifòlium.*

A small bush, three to six feet high, found on sandy or rocky hillsides at the margin of woods; will grow in exposed positions. Ranges from New Brunswick to North Carolina and west to Michigan and Minnesota.

*Stems.*—Stems smooth, straight and slender; growing shoots and petioles somewhat pubescent.

*Leaves.*—Opposite, simple, palmately-veined, three-lobed, three to five inches long, orbicular or broad-oval, rounded or heart-shaped at base, coarsely and unequally toothed; lobes diverging, acuminate at apex. They come out of the bud involute, reddish, densely hairy; when full grown are dark green, downy above, paler and downy below. Autumnal tints are deep dull red varying to rose pink, sometimes fading to cream-white, very beautiful. Petioles an inch to an inch and a half long, downy, furnished near the base with two stipule-like appendages.

*Flowers.*—June. Perfect, cream-white, borne in loose terminal pedunculate cymes, two to three inches across.

*Calyx.*—Tube adnate to the ovary, five-toothed, teeth obtuse.

*Corolla.*—White, rotate, about three-sixteenths of an inch across.

*Stamens.*—Five, inserted on corolla-tube, filaments white, anthers yellow, oblong, exserted.

*Pistil.*—Ovary inferior, one to three-celled; style short, three-lobed.

*Fruit.*—Drupe, deep purple, about one-fourth of an inch long, clings to the branches throughout the winter; pulp thin. Stone lenticular, faintly two-ridged on one side and two-grooved on the other. September.

Downy Viburnum, *Viburnum pubescens.*

Leaves 2½′ to 4′ long.  Cymes 3′ to 3½′ across.

The Maple-leaved Viburnum so nearly resembles a group of young maples at the forest's edge as frequently to be mistaken for them. The bush at flowering time is exceedingly pretty; it grows in clumps and although the flower clusters are not large they are abundant and stand up well at the ends of the branches.

The autumnal coloring is fine, melting from dull red into rose pink, even upon occasion fading into cream-white. Rarely, an entire clump will be cream-white, or cream-white flushed with pale pink,—again a single bush will vary from old rose to cream-white. The effect is startling. Just what occasions this unusual white coloring is difficult to tell. The only other plant that I know, which sometimes does the same thing, is the Flowering Dogwood, whose normal autumnal tint is a brilliant scarlet; yet I have seen small trees in the depths of the woods clothed in white from crown to tip.

## DOWNY VIBURNUM

*Vibúrnum pubéscens.*

A compact shrub three to four feet high, with grayish slender branches and soft brown, downy twigs; found on dry rocky banks. Ranges from Quebec and Ontario to Georgia, west to Michigan and Iowa.

*Leaves.*—Opposite, simple, pinnately veined, two and a half to four inches long, ovate or oblong-ovate, rounded or heart-shaped at base, dentate-serrate or entire acute or acuminate at apex. They come out of the bud involute, pale green, shining and hairy; when full grown, thick, bright green above, paler green below; sometimes only downy on the veins beneath, often

Arrow-wood, *Viburnum dentatum.*

Leaves 1½′ to 3′ long.   Cymes 2′ to 3′ across.

clothed with a soft velvety pubescence. Autumnal tints deep purple brightening to red. Petioles short.

*Flowers.*—June. Perfect, white, borne in loose pedunculate cymes, one to three inches across, abundant.

Leaf of Downy Viburnum. Typical form.

*Calyx.*—Tube adnate to the ovary ; border five-toothed, acute.

*Corolla.*—White, rotate, five-lobed ; lobes spreading.

*Stamens.*—Five, inserted on corolla-tube, exserted.

*Pistil.*—Ovary inferior, style short, three-lobed.

*Fruit.*—Drupe, ovoid or oval, dark purple, one-fourth of an inch long ; pulp thin. Stone slightly two-grooved on both faces. August.

The Downy Viburnum is one of the smaller species of the genus, but it flowers superbly when grown in the open with abundance of light and air. The plant is also very fine in autumn, as the leaves turn a rich dark purple brightened with vinous red. The leaves vary greatly in shape, character of margin, and degree of pubescence.

### ARROW-WOOD

*Vibúrnum dentàtum.*

A compact shrub, six to ten feet high with ash-colored bark, smooth, obtusely angular branches ; the young shoots slender and very straight ; found in low moist grounds and on the border of rivers. Ranges from New Brunswick to Georgia and west to Michigan and Minnesota. Takes kindly to cultivation.

*Leaves.*—Opposite, simple, pinnately veined, one and a half to three inches long, broadly ovate, rounded or cordate at base, coarsely and sharply serrate, acute at apex ; strongly veined ; veins depressed above, prominent below. They come out of bud involute, green, slightly tinged with reddish brown, shining and

Withe-rod, *Viburnum cassinoides.*

Leaves 2′ to 4′ long.

downy ; when full grown are bright dark green above, paler beneath, with tufts of hair in the axils of the veins. The autumnal tint is dark bronze red. Petioles short.

*Flowers.*—June. White, perfect, borne in broad, flat pedunculate cymes, two to three inches across.

*Calyx.*—Tube adnate to the ovary ; limb five-toothed.

*Corolla.*—White, rotate, five-lobed ; lobes spreading.

*Stamens.*—Five, inserted on the corolla-tube, exserted.

*Pistil.*—Ovary inferior, style short, three-lobed.

*Fruit.*—Drupe, globose ovoid, dark blue, about one-fourth of an inch in diameter, flesh thin, dry, somewhat acid ; stone grooved on one side, rounded on the other. September.

*Viburnum dentatum* is now extensively planted in parks. In June when covered with great flat clusters  of snowy flowers, and later when these are succeeded by dark, shining, blue berries, the bush is most attractive and ornamental. These shining blue berries are eaten by birds, although it is hard to understand why ; they are dry, dull, tasteless, seedy things.

Leaf of *Viburnum molle.*

*Viburnum molle,* the Soft - leaved Arrow-wood, is a southern bush greatly resembling *Viburnum dentatum* and is sometimes found in Pennsylvania. It is perfectly hardy at the north and well worthy of cultivation.

### WITHE-ROD

*Vibúrnum cassinoides.*

A somewhat straggling bush, two to twelve feet high, with gray branches : twigs sometimes scurfy, sometimes glabrous ; found in swamps and wet soil. Ranges from Newfoundland to Manitoba, southward to Georgia and Alabama. Takes kindly to cultivation.

*Leaves.*—Opposite, simple, pinnately veined, ovate or oval, narrowed or rounded at base, crenulate, acute at apex, thick in texture, glabrous or nearly so. Autumnal tint first purple, then turns to a rich vinous red.

*Flowers.*—June, July. Perfect, white, borne in broad flat pedunculate cymes two to four inches across.

*Calyx.*—Tube adnate to the ovary ; border five-toothed.

*Corolla.*—White, rotate five-lobed ; lobes spreading.

*Stamens.*—Five, inserted on corolla-tube, exserted.

*Pistil.*—Ovary inferior, style short, three-lobed.

*Fruit.*—Drupe, globose to ovoid, dark blue, one-fourth of an inch in diameter, stone round or oval, flattened. September.

The best garden plant among our viburnums is *Viburnum cassinoides.* An inhabitant of northern swamps, it is distributed from Newfoundland to the Saskatchewan and southward to New Jersey. In its wild home it is a loose, straggling shrub, but in cultivation it takes on the graces of civilization and becomes compact, symmetrical, an ornament to the race and the flower of the family. The leaves are thick, leathery and rather dull green; the flowers, which are cream-white, are borne in broad five-rayed cymes four or five inches across. They are succeeded by abundant fruit which melts from pale green into bright rose, and then darkens into blue-black ; berries of the three colors often appearing at the same time.

Leaf of *Viburnum nudum.*

*Viburnum nudum,* the Large Withe-rod, is a bush of southern range which sometimes crosses our border. It resembles *Viburnum cassinoides,* but blooms a little later.

*Viburnum lantana,* the Wayfaring Tree of Europe, is

Wayfaring Tree, *Viburnum lantana.*

the first of the viburnums to bloom ; appearing early in May.

The inflorescence is a flat cyme two to three inches across; the individual flowers do not vary from the type, the leaves are thick dark green, and the fruit when ripening gives a succession of beautiful color through the range of pale green, glowing scarlet and dark blue-black. It has long been in cultivation, and is valuable because of its early bloom ; in other respects it does not excel our native species.

### SNOWBERRY

*Symphoricárpos racemósus.*

*Symphoricarpos,* fruit grown together; named from the clustered berries.

An erect shrub three to five feet high, with smooth, slender branches. Found in rocky places and on river banks from Nova Scotia to British Columbia, south to Pennsylvania and Kentucky. Widely planted as an ornamental shrub; suckers freely ; prefers limestone soils.

*Leaves.*—Opposite, simple, short-petioled, one to two and one-half inches long, oval or ovate, rounded at base and rounded or slightly acute at apex, entire or undulate; those of young shoots sometimes dentate. They come out of the bud involute, dull pale green, smooth, when full grown are dull dark green above, paler green below. In autumn they remain unchanged until caught by the heavy late frosts.

*Flowers.*—June to September. Perfect, small, white or pink bells, in axillary few-flowered clusters and in terminal clusters which are often leafy.

*Calyx.*—Tube nearly globular, adnate to the ovary, the border four to five-toothed.

*Corolla.*—Bell-shaped, one-fourth of an inch long, four to five-toothed, slightly gibbous at base, bearded at the throat, pinkish white.

*Stamens.*—Four to five, included, inserted on corolla, alternate with its lobes.

*Pistil.*—Ovary inferior, four-celled, two cavities contain aborted ovules, other two contain each a single ovule; style smooth, included.

*Fruit.*—Globose, pure white berry, loosely cellular, one-fourth to one-half an inch in diameter, four-celled, two-seeded, crowned with the remnant of the style which appears as a black spot, borne in clusters; berries of varying sizes. August to November.

The Snowberry is one of the favorites of old-time gardens, and is holding its own fairly well in the new. Throughout the spring-time it is simply a clean, bright little bush with a tendency to enlarge its circumference. Early in July it begins to put forth its clusters of tiny pink bells, which do not attract any particular attention; but which possess the power of transforming themselves as time goes on into clusters of snowy balls varying in size from small peas to small marbles; packed away among the leaves in charming confusion.

These white berries are the effective feature of the plant, and the bush is fairly well covered with them by the middle of August; although the blooming period continues for a month longer. At this time a border combination of Snowberry with *Rosa rugosa* is extremely good; the white berries of the one contrasting with the red hips of the other. The bush laden with its white burden is beautiful throughout the autumn, and holds its berries intact until they are destroyed by the frosts and storms of November.

The gardeners are in a way to develop the fruit at the expense of the beauty of the bush as a whole. The stems are extremely slender and delicate, and when

Snowberry, *Symphoricarpos racemosus.*
Leaves 1′ to 2½′ long.

the weight of the berries is too great for the stem to hold erect it is overburdened and its beauty is impaired.

### INDIAN CURRANT. CORAL-BERRY

*Symphoricárpos symphoricárpos. Symphoricárpos vulgàris.*

A shrub two to five feet high, branches erect or slightly curved, twigs purplish brown, usually pubescent. Found in rocky places and on river banks,—from the banks of the Delaware in New Jersey and Pennsylvania, south to Georgia and Texas, and west to Dakota. Cultivated.

*Leaves.*—Opposite, simple, short-petioled, one to one and one-half inches long, oval or ovate, rounded at base, rounded or acute at apex, margin entire or undulate, smooth above, softly downy beneath. They come out of the bud involute, dull pale green ; when full grown are dull dark green above, paler below. In autumn they remain unchanged until destroyed by the heavy frosts.

*Flowers.*—August. Perfect, small, greenish pink-tipped bells ; borne in dense clusters in the axils of the leaves ; filled with nectar.

*Calyx.*—Tube adnate to the ovary, five-toothed ; teeth short, persistent.

*Corolla.*—Bell-shaped, greenish pink, downy within, five-lobed.

*Stamens.*—Four or five, inserted on corolla-tube, and alternate with its lobes.

*Pistil.*—Ovary inferior, four-celled, only two of the cells with a fertile ovule, style bearded.

*Fruit.*—Berry, purplish red, ovoid-globose, three-sixteenths of an inch in diameter, four-celled, two-seeded, crowned by the remnants of the calyx, insipid, persistent after the leaves have fallen.

The abundance of fruit on the Indian Currant is little short of marvellous. The slender stems are fruit bearing for five or ten inches from the tip; the clusters

Indian Currant, *Symphoricarpos vulgaris.*
Leaves 1' to 1½' long.

of fruit appear in the axils of the opposite leaves and are so full and crowded that they surround the stem. As an example of this remarkable prolificness, a single fruiting stem seven inches long was found to bear fifteen double clusters, and each cluster had from seven to nine berries, making the total production about two hundred and fifty currants upon an average stem; many stems produced more.

In autumn these drooping wands of crimson berries adorned with leaves are most beautiful,—a bed of them enchanting. Moreover, these berries have great staying powers; the first heavy winter storms destroy the leaves which remain brown and curled until the winds carry them away,—but the clusters of berries are apparently undisturbed; they neither darken nor shrivel. Each tiny berry has a crimson skin, thin white mealy flesh, and two white bony seeds. The birds find nothing desirable about them and leave them entirely untouched.

### LONICERA. HONEYSUCKLE

*Lontcera.*

Named in honor of Adam Lonitzer, a German herbalist of the sixteenth century.

The *Lonicera* group commonly called honeysuckles are best known by the climbing vines which adorn our piazzas. Of erect shrubs *Lonicera tartarica*, the Tartarian Honeysuckle in its many varieties, is a favorite and deservedly so. It was brought to this country from Asia, as its name indicates; and has only here and there escaped from cultivation. *Lonicera xylosteum*, the Fly-honeysuckle of our gardens, is also an Asiatic spe-

Swamp Fly-honeysuckle, *Lonicera oblongifolia.*

Leaves ¾′ to 2′ long.

cies; and it, too, has sparingly escaped. It looks not unlike *Lonicera tartarica,* and bears its red berries well past midsummer. *Lonicera fragrantissima* is a species recently introduced whose value chiefly lies in its fragrant flowers which are produced in April. Midsummer finds it a leafy bush of rather pale green foliage.

Our northern *Lonicera* bushes are interesting but not so conspicuous in flower and fruit as to bring them very generally into cultivation. To be known they must be sought in their native wilds. There are four of them, *Lonicera cœrulea, Lonicera oblongifolia, Lonicera ciliata,* and *Lonicera involucrata.*

*Lonicera involucrata* is the largest of the four, and bears the largest leaves; its personal characteristic is the involucre which surrounds the fruit. It is really a Canadian plant and rarely crosses our northern boundary. *Lonicera cœrulea* is probably named for the curious, two-eyed, blue berry which it bears. *Lonicera ciliata* has a very downy leaf in early spring and a very glabrous one in midsummer. *Lonicera oblongifolia* has no marked distinguishing character, but is doing fairly well in cultivation, and gardeners are recommending it. The *Lonicera* fruit is a berry; it may be sweet or sour, but never fails to be bitter.

## SWAMP FLY-HONEYSUCKLE

*Lonicera oblongifòlia.*

An erect shrub, two to five feet high; found in bogs and swamps. Ranges from Quebec to Manitoba, south to Pennsylvania, and west to Michigan.

Blue Honeysuckle, *Lonicera cœrulea.*

Leaves 1½′ to 2′ long.

*Leaves.*—Opposite, simple, pinnately veined, three-fourths to two inches long, oval-oblong. Margin not ciliate, myrtle green above and gray green beneath, downy, pubescent when young, glabrous when mature.

*Flowers.*—May, June. Greenish yellow, perfect, half an inch long, slightly purple within, borne on a two-flowered peduncle in the axils of the leaves; peduncles long and slender; bracts minute or deciduous; fragrant, full of nectar.

*Calyx.*—Tube adnate to the ovary, ovoid; border slightly five-toothed.

*Corolla.*—Yellowish or purplish within, funnel-form, gibbous at base; border deeply two-lipped, lower lip linear, upper lip erect with four short lobes.

*Stamens.*—Five, inserted on the corolla.

*Pistil.*—Ovary two-celled, ovules many; style slender; stigma capitate.

*Fruit.*—Berry, crimson or purplish, one-fourth of an inch in diameter; two ovaries do not usually unite to form the fruit, although sometimes they do.

## BLUE FLY-HONEYSUCKLE. MOUNTAIN FLY-HONEY-SUCKLE

*Lonicera cærùlea.*

An erect dwarfish shrub one to three feet high; found in bogs and low lands. Shoots often bluish purple, pubescent with a bloom. Ranges from Newfoundland to Alaska, south to Rhode Island, and west to Wisconsin; also in Europe and Asia.

*Leaves.*—Opposite, simple, pinnately veined; one to one and one-half inches long, oval or obovate, rounded or narrowed at base, entire, obtuse at apex; when full grown sparingly hairy above, ciliate at margin, pubescent beneath. Petioles short.

*Flowers.*—June. Pale yellow, perfect, irregular, one-half to three-fourths of an inch long, borne on a two-flowered peduncle in the axils of the leaves; peduncles short; bracts awl-like.

*Calyx.*—Tube adnate to the ovary, ovoid; border slightly five-toothed.

Fly-honeysuckle, *Lonicera canadensis.*

Leaves 1′ to 2′ long.

*Corolla.*—Funnel-form, gibbous at base ; border five-lobed, nearly regular ; lobes longer than the tube.

*Stamens.*—Five, inserted on the corolla.

*Pistil.*—Ovary two-celled, ovules many ; style slender ; stigma capitate.

*Fruit.*—Ovaries of the two flowers unite and form an oblong or globose, bluish, two-eyed berry, half an inch long and about five-eighths of an inch across ; dark blue with a pale blue bloom ; bitter acid. July.

*Lonicera cœrulea* has this unusual characteristic ; it produces two perfect flowers in order to make one berry. The flowers are twins, but the pistils are separate, yet after the corollas have fallen the two ovaries enlarge and begin to grow toward each other and finally unite into a single berry, which shows its duplex origin by the two tiny so-called "eyes" at its apex, each of which is the remnant of a flower calyx. The double structure of the berry is clearly seen by a cross section, the line of cleavage between the two parts being very distinct. The fruit is drooping and usually hidden under the leaves. In taste a bitter acid, with the bitter much stronger than the acid.

In midsummer the new shoots have a bluish purple cast, which gives a certain bluish effect to the bush. It takes kindly to cultivation, and is recommended by gardeners.

### FLY-HONEYSUCKLE

*Lonícera canadénsis. Lonícera ciliàta.*

Three to five feet high, branchlets glabrous and marked with elevated lines which descend from the bases of the petioles ; found in moist woods. Ranges from New Brunswick to Manitoba, south to Connecticut and west to Pennsylvania and Michigan.

Tartarian Honeysuckle, *Lonicera tartarica.*

Leaves 1′ to 3′ long.

*Leaves.*—Opposite, simple, pinnately veined, ovate or oval, rounded or cordate at base, entire, acute or acutish at apex. Villous-pubescent when young, with margin strongly ciliate, glabrous when mature.

*Flowers.*—May. Greenish yellow, three-fourths of an inch long, perfect, borne on a two-flowered peduncle in the axil of the leaves ; peduncles slender; bracts minute.

*Calyx.*—Calyx-tube ovoid, united with the ovary ; border five-toothed.

*Corolla.*—Greenish yellow, funnel-form almost spurred at the base ; border five-lobed ; lobes nearly equal.

*Stamens.*—Five, inserted on tube of corolla.

*Pistil.*—Ovary two-celled, ovules many ; style slender ; stigma capitate.

*Fruit.*—Berries separate, red, one-fourth of an inch in diameter, borne in pairs ; the ovaries do not unite.

## TARTARIAN BUSH-HONEYSUCKLE

### *Lontcera tartárica.*

A glabrous erect shrub three to ten feet high. A native of Asia and common in cultivation ; has escaped quite extensively.

*Leaves.*—Opposite, simple, pinnately veined, one to three inches long, oval, oblong or ovate, rounded or heart-shaped at base, margin entire, not ciliate, apex acute or obtuse.

*Flowers.*—May. Pink to white, three-fourths of an inch long, perfect, solitary or in pairs, borne on a long, slender peduncle in the axils of the leaves ; bracts linear, often as long as the corolla tube.

*Calyx.*—Tubular, five-toothed.

*Corolla.*—Pink to white. Tube slender, with a peculiar enlargement at the base which is dark pink when the rest of the tube is pale pink ; border irregularly and deeply five-lobed and somewhat two-lipped ; upper lip three-lobed, lower lip two-lobed.

*Stamens.*—Five, inserted on the tube of the corolla.

*Pistil.*—Ovary two to three-celled ; style slender ; stigma capitate.

*Fruit.*—Berries separate, red or yellow. abundant, ornamental. July, August.

Tartarian Honeysuckle, *Lonicera tartarica*, in fruit.

The Tartarian Honeysuckles are most attractive bushes. One of their best features is the graceful outline of a finely-grown individual when the branches bend outward and downward almost to the grass. The flowers of the different varieties are white, pink, rose, or deep red, and possess a pleasant fragrance. They come into leaf early; the foliage is luxuriant and remains until late in the autumn; and the red or orange berries are very abundant and extremely ornamental. The berries have the translucent appearance of currants; in flavor they are a sweetish bitter, with the bitter inclined to remain somewhat unduly in the mouth. The birds seem to eat them very little, consequently they adorn the bushes for a considerable period.

### INVOLUCRED FLY-HONEYSUCKLE

*Lonícera involucràta.*

Northern shrub, three to five feet high; branches four-angular; found in deep woods. Ranges from Quebec to British Columbia and Alaska, rarely comes within the borders of the United States.

*Stems.*—Oldest stems are gray and ragged, the growing shoots yellow. Stems gray.

*Leaves.*—Opposite, simple, pinnately veined, two to six inches long, oblong, ovate, oval or obovate, rounded or wedge-shaped at base, entire, acute or acuminate at apex; pubescent when young. Petioles short, dark green above, paler beneath.

Leaf of Involucred
Fly-honeysuckle.

*Flowers.*—June, July. Yellowish, perfect, borne on a two to three-flowered peduncle in

Bush Honeysuckle, *Diervilla diervilla.*

Leaves 2′ to 5′ long.

the axils of the leaves. Involucre of four conspicuous and leafy bracts which at length surround the fruit.

*Calyx.*—Tube adherent to the ovary, slightly five-toothed.

*Corolla.*—Yellowish, funnel-form, one-half to three-fourths of an inch long, viscid-pubescent ; border five-lobed.

*Stamens.*—Five, inserted on tube of corolla.

*Pistils.*—Ovary two or three-celled, style slender ; stigma capitate.

*Fruit.*—Berries separate, globose or oval, nearly black, about one-third of an inch in diameter.

## DIERVILLA.  COMMON BUSH HONEYSUCKLE

*Diervílla trífida.  Diervílla diervílla.*

*Diervilla,* in honor of Dierville, a French surgeon who sent the plant to Tournefort.

A low shrub, two to four feet high.  Often forms dense, low masses of shrubbery on the borders of the forest.  Ranges from Newfoundland to the Saskatchewan, and through the northern states to North Carolina and Michigan.

*Leaves.*—Opposite, simple, pinnately veined, two to five inches long, ovate or oval, rounded at base, irregularly crenulate-serrate, slightly ciliate, acuminate at apex.  Dark green, glabrous above, paler green and glabrous beneath ; midvein and primary veins prominent.

*Flowers.*—May, June.  Perfect, small, yellowish, mostly in three-flowered clusters which are either terminal, or in the axils of the upper leaves.

*Calyx.*—Tube long, slender, adnate to ovary ; border with five linear, persistent lobes.

*Corolla.*—Narrowly funnel-form, tube slightly gibbous at the base ; border nearly regular, five-lobed, honey yellow or greenish yellow, downy externally, hairy within.

*Stamens.*—Five, exserted, inserted on the corolla ; anthers linear.

Weigela, *Diervilla rosea.*

*Pistil.*—Ovary inferior, two-celled ; ovules numerous ; style thread-like ; stigma capitate.

*Fruit.*—Capsule, glabrous, linear-oblong, three-fourths of an inch long, slender, beaked, crowned with the five calyx-lobes ; two-valved, many-seeded. September.

There are three species of Diervillas native to eastern United States, of which the Bush Honeysuckle is the northern species. It does not equal the cultivated forms in attractiveness and consequently is neglected.

## WEIGELA

*Diervílla rosea.*

*Weigela*, in honor of Weigel, a German botanist.

The Weigela of our gardens was discovered in China in 1844 by Robert Fortune. The first specimen which he saw is described as growing in a Mandarin's garden on the island of Chusan and characterized as a bush covered with rose-colored flowers which hung in clusters from the axils of the leaves and the ends of the branches. " I immediately marked it as one of the finest plants in northern China and determined to send plants of it home in every ship until I should hear of its safe arrival." From this beginning the Weigela has made its way until now it is one of the most prized of ornamental shrubs.

The bush has a tendency to straggling growth which may be wisely suppressed ; but to get the best results it should be allowed a fair degree of freedom, and then its graceful, curving branches laden with flowers almost if not quite reach the ground.

The dealers' catalogues now advertise varieties in great numbers, but *Diervilla rosea*, the plant of Mr. Fortune's devotion, is still the best known, and although the varieties differ from the type they have not yet surpassed it.

# RUBÌACEÆ—MADDER FAMILY

## BUTTON-BUSH. HONEY BALLS

*Cephalànthus occidentàlis.*

*Cephalanthus*, of Greek derivation, from *cephale*, head, and *anthos*, a flower ; the flowers growing in heads.

Strong, vigorous, erect shrub, varying from four to fifteen feet high ; stem often contorted ; found on the banks of slow-flowing streams and growing in swamps.   Ranges from New Brunswick to western Ontario and south to Florida, Texas and Arizona ; also on the Pacific coast.   Root large, stout, often contorted.

*Bark.*—Dark gray, cracked, flaky, surface plates thin and loose, even on small branches.   Branchlets at first brownish green or reddish brown, later pale dull brown, finally dark ashen gray.

*Leaves.*—Opposite or in threes, simple, three to six inches long, oblong-oval or ovate, rounded or wedge-shaped at base, entire, acute or acuminate at apex ; midvein, primary and secondary veins depressed above, very prominent beneath ; when full grown are thick, dark shining green above, paler, sometimes downy, beneath.   In autumn they turn a dull yellow or fall with little change of color.   Petioles one-half to one inch long, stout, grooved, sometimes twisted.   Stipules short, connecting the bases of opposite leaf stems.

*Flowers.*—July, August.   Perfect, white, fragrant, tubular, sessile, borne in dense spherical heads at the extremities of the branches ; often in groups of threes ; heads exclusive of styles about an inch in diameter ; filled with nectar.   Peduncles one to two inches long.   Remain in bloom a long time.

Button Bush, *Cephalanthus occidentalis.*

Leaves 3′ to 6′ long.   Flower balls 1′ to 1¼′ in diameter exclusive of styles.

*Calyx.*—Tubular, four-sided, four-toothed, hairy.

*Corolla.*—White, tubular, twice as long as the calyx, hairy within, four-toothed ; teeth imbricate in bud.

*Stamens.*—Four, borne on the tube of the corolla, alternate with the lobes, scarcely exserted ; anthers bicuspidate at base.

*Pistil.*—Ovary adnate to the calyx, two to four-celled ; style much exserted, long and thread-like ; stigma capitate.

*Fruit.*—A ball made up of many small capsules crowded together and each containing one or two seeds.

The Button-bush is a widely distributed plant, found growing by the side of standing water, often venturing in, and always loving the water about its roots. The leaves are large, rather coarse in texture, bright green and shining.

The flowers are the plant's distinctive attraction. It is apparent that the sphere is a common type of fruit-forms,—the apple, the cherry, the grape, the numberless capsules and seed-cases of spherical form attest the fact ; but it is not often that nature achieves a sphere in a flower or flower cluster. Yet the flower cluster of the Button-bush is a perfect globe, with thread-like styles protruding from every side. This little globe is made up of scores of tiny cream-white blossoms all crowded upon a central axis, and each one so full of nectar and so loved by the bees that one of the common country names of the bush is Honey Balls.

The plant is much used in European gardens, where the singularity of its flowering habit and its late season of bloom recommend it to planters. With us it is found by almost every roadside and should be protected and cherished.

# COMPÓSITÆ—COMPOSITE FAMILY

## GROUNDSEL-TREE

*Báccharis halimifòlia.*

*Baccharis*, the name of a shrub anciently dedicated to Bacchus ; without significance in its present use.

A branching glabrous shrub, three to nine feet high, the branchlets angled, sometimes minutely scurfy ; found on the sea-beaches, along salt marshes and tidal rivers, extending inland beyond saline influences. Ranges from Massachusetts to Florida and Texas.

*Leaves.*—Alternate, simple, three-nerved, midvein most prominent, one to three inches long, obovate or oblong, short-petioled or sessile, entire or few-toothed toward the apex. Leaves on the flowering spray smaller than the others ; when full grown are thick, bright green, glabrous. In autumn ney turn yellow or fall with little change of color ; persist until beaten off by first winter storms.

*Flowers.*—September, October. Diœcious. Calyx-tube adnate to ovary, the limb bristled; corolla tubular, five-lobed ray flowers absent; stamens five ; ovary one-celled ; style of fertile flowers two-cleft. In heads of terminal peduncled clusters of two to five ; those of the sterile plant nearly globose when young ; the bracts of the involucre oblong-ovate, obtuse, glutinous, appressed; the inner ones of the pistillate heads lanceolate, acute or acutish.

*Fruit.*—Achenes, with bright white pappus, one-fourth to one-half an inch long ; in two series of capillary bristles, much exceeding the involucre.

The Groundsel-tree, *Baccharis halimifolia*, is now conspicuous with its long, white, silky pappus. Although it belongs to the largest order of flowering plants, it is the only one in this vast order in our temperate climate that attains the dignity of treehood. In the Pines it grows from ten to fifteen feet in height, and in autumn is a very marked feature of the landscape. The abundant pure white pappus with which the plant is enshrouded at a little distance looks like a mass of white flowers strangely out of season in their rich setting of autumnal foliage.

—MARY TREAT, in *Garden and Forest.*
Vineland, N. J., November 17, 1888.

Shrubs which are in full bloom during the first weeks of October are not plentiful in our climate ; the muster roll includes the althæas, the hardy hydrangeas, the witch hazel and the groundsel-tree, together with sundry late blooming roses. The Groundsel-tree is valued for its fluffy fruit rather than for its inconspicuous flowers ; but any bloom at this period is welcome. It belongs to the *Compositæ*, the family of the asters, the daisies, the goldenrods and the sunflowers. The individual blossoms are minute and are gathered together in small heads without ray flowers, consequently are inconspicuous.

The plant is diœcious, that is, the pistillate and the staminate flowers are borne on different bushes. This is a kind of division of labor in the vegetable world ; many trees are of this nature, notably the willows. The particular and gratifying characteristic of the Groundsel-tree is that it is possible to plant two bushes side by side, watch them flourish throughout the summer and when blooming time comes in September, see one put forth its clusters of tiny pistillate flowers which look like little green buds with a pale top ; and the other put forth its staminate clusters which differ from the first only that the tops are a little more conspicuous. In the course of time, one green bush bears a

Groundsel-tree, *Baccharis halimifolia*.

Leaves 1′ to 3′ long.  Spray at the left, pistillate; at the right, staminate.

few dry remnants of flowers, the other bursts into a mass of fluffy white. All this can go on by the side of the garden walk and so clearly that he who runs to catch a suburban car may note and understand.

This fluffy appearance is due to the fact that each small seed after the fashion of so many of its family is a wind traveller; and is provided with means for its long journey in the shape of a feathery parachute made up of many white hairs, which makes a brave show upon the bush and finally takes the wings of the wind and sails away bearing the seed to "distant homes and unpeopled lands."

Fruit of Groundsel-tree.

The shrub is a native of sea-beaches and salt marshes, yet will grow almost anywhere; obviously, after a plant has acquired the ability to live on the seacoast, any other location must be an improvement. It bears close pruning and is a good ornamental shrub.

# VACCINIÀCEÆ — HUCKLEBERRY  FAMILY

## HUCKLEBERRY

" The huckleberries and cranberries take the place throughout the northern part of this continent of the heaths of the corresponding climates of Europe ; and fill it with not less of beauty, and incomparably more of use."
—GEORGE  B.  EMERSON.

" The huckleberry grows a second crop—a crop of color.    It is twice blessed—it blesses him that eats and him that sees."
—BRADFORD  TORREY.

" The name huckleberry is applied as a generic term to cover the fruit of all species of the two genera, *Gaylussacia* and *Vaccinium*.    In a restricted sense it is used locally to designate one or more species of the former genus, the name blueberry being then applied to fruit of *Vaccinium* species.    In other cases the term huckleberry is applied to black-fruited species of either genus.    The more general custom is to apply the name huckleberry to the fruit of all.

" The most important difference between these two genera is that in *Gaylussacia* the fruit is ten-celled, each cell containing a single seed, or properly a little stone, while in *Vaccinium* there are several seeds in each cell, these being small, and the fruit forming a pulpy berry.    The seeds of the former, while less numerous are far more troublesome than those of the latter.    The leaves and branchlets of *Gaylussacia* are clammy with resinous dots when young."
—FRED.  W.  CARD.

The Huckleberry family does not differ widely from the Heath family in respect to its leaves or its flowers; but in respect to its fruit,—bird and beast and man will assert in chorus that the difference is very great. For the huckleberry and the blueberry have ministered to the comfort of the birds and the refreshment of mankind for ages. The obvious difference between the two in popular estimation is that the huckleberry fruit is more "seedy" than that of the blueberry and consequently not so desirable for table use. As Professor Card so admirably explains, this popular opinion is based upon a structural difference in the fruit of the two genera.

The *Vacciniaceæ* seem, so far, to have successfully resisted all efforts at domestication. From time to time we read that some one has transferred a few bushes to his garden and that they have done well there; but oftener we hear and sometimes we see that transplanted bushes do not do well. It is probable that the untamed spirit of these wild creatures might be broken, were it worth while; but there is a more excellent way. The farmers have learned this in Michigan and in Maine and possibly elsewhere. The method is very simple—it consists in withdrawing grazing animals from fields where the *Vacciniaceæ* are native, permitting the bushes to take undisturbed possession; and then about once in five years burning the tract. Of course, the first year after the burning there is no crop, but in the second year the crop is enormous. As the demand for the fruit is steady, there seems no reason in the nature of things why careful and systematic treatment of natural blueberry lands should not be profitable.

Dangleberry, *Gaylussacia frondosa.*
Leaves 1½′ to 2¼′ long.  Fruit ⅓′ in diameter.

## DANGLEBERRY. TANGLEBERRY

*Gaylussácia frondòsa.*

*Gaylussacía*, named in honor of the chemist, Gay-Lussac.

A spreading bush, three to six feet high, found in moist situations by the side of lakes and at the edge of woods. Ranges from New Hampshire to Florida, westward to Ohio and southwest to Louisiana.

*Stems.*—Branches slender and divergent; recent shoots and fruit stalks pale green or pale reddish yellow; branches and stems are of a mahogany or bronze color, covered with a pearly epidermis.

*Leaves.*—Oblong, oval or obovate, one and one-half to two and one-half inches long, wedge-shaped at base, entire, slightly revolute, obtuse or acute, with a callous point at apex. When full grown are thin, pale green, glabrous above, glabrous or downy, pale or glaucous below, and sprinkled with minute resinous dots; midvein, primary and secondary veins prominent beneath. Autumnal tints are scarlet, crimson, and orange. Petioles short.

*Flowers.*—May, June. Perfect, few, greenish pink bells, borne on drooping pedicels one to three inches long which form a loose raceme. Each pedicel has a bract at base and two minute opposite bracts half way up.

*Calyx.*—Calyx-tube adnate to the ovary, five-toothed.

*Corolla.*—Broad, bell-shaped, one-eighth of an inch long, with five short angular teeth completely reflexed.

*Stamens.*—Ten, included; filaments smooth, shorter than the anthers; anthers awnless, tapering upward into tubes; cells opening by a terminal pore.

*Pistil.*—Ovary adnate to calyx, ten-celled, with one ovule in each cell; style as long as the corolla.

*Fruit.*—Berry-like drupe, globose, dark blue with a glaucous bloom, about one-third of an inch in diameter, sweet; nutlets ten. July, August.

The Dangleberry may be easily known by its large pale leaves which are glaucous beneath, and its loose

High-bush Huckleberry, *Gaylussacia resinosa*

Leaves 1′ to 2′ long.   Fruit ¼′ in diameter.

drooping racemes of flowers or of fruit. When neither in flower nor in leaf the reddish yellow wood of the new growth and the peeling, ashy gray bark serve as determining characters. The fruit has little value at the north, but in a milder climate is said to improve considerably in quality.

## BLACK OR HIGH-BUSH HUCKLEBERRY

*Gaylussácia resinósa.*

An erect shrub one to three feet high, branching freely with irregular straggling spray. Found on rocky hills and sandy ridges from Newfoundland to Georgia, westward to Wisconsin and Kentucky. Flowers and leaves densely covered with resinous dots. Species varies considerably.

*Stems.*—Young shoots downy, often deep red. Stems mahogany color beneath a pearly epidermis. Winter buds small, bright red.

*Leaves.*—Oval or oblong, rarely obovate, one to two inches long, wedge-shaped at base, entire, obtuse or acute at apex, mucronulate. They come out of the bud involute, shining, covered with minute resinous globules, pale green above and below; when full grown they are profusely covered with dots of yellow resin which give a yellowish flush to the under-surface. Autumnal tints are purplish, crimson and orange. Petiole short.

*Flowers.*—May, June. Reddish yellow bells, borne on short one-sided racemes, on terminal and axillary branches. Flower buds heavily covered with resinous dots.

*Calyx.*—Resinous; tube adnate to the ovary, five-toothed.

*Corolla.*—Ovoid conical or cylindric, five-angled, contracted at the mouth, dull red sometimes touched with yellow, five-toothed; teeth acute, slightly recurved.

*Stamens.*—Ten, included, filaments ciliate, anthers awnless, two-celled; cells prolonged into tubes opening by a pore at apex.

Dwarf Huckleberry, *Gaylussacia dumosa.*

Leaves 1′ to 1½′ long.   Fruit ¼′ to ⅓′ in diameter.

*Pistil.*—Ovary inferior, ten-celled, one ovule in each cell, many of which abort in fruit.

*Fruit.*—Berry-like drupe, black, shining, without bloom, sweet, one-fourth of an inch in diameter; nutlets ten.  July, August.

*Gaylussacia resinosa* produces the common huckleberry of the markets.  The fruit is sweet, firm, and

 shining black in color.  There are varieties which vary considerably from the type in respect to fruit; one has very sweet pear-shaped berries; another has glaucous leaves, and fruit covered with a glaucous bloom; a third has large bluish berries; and a fourth has white berries.

A species that so naturally divides into varieties would probably yield very readily to cultivation and produce a variety of superior fruit.  The

High-bush Huckleberry, in flower.

bush is now offered for sale as an ornamental shrub and gardeners report that it is growing in favor.

### DWARF HUCKLEBERRY

*Gaylussácia dumòsa.*

A shrub one to two feet high, from a creeping base, found in swamps.  Ranges from Newfoundland to Florida and Louisiana.

*Stems.*—Recent branches brownish downy, and somewhat viscid with a few glandular hairs.  Stems and older branches ashen gray.  Winter buds red.

*Leaves.*—Sessile, obovate-oblong, or oblanceolate, an inch to an inch and a half long, wedge-shaped at base, entire, ciliate with glandular hairs, obtuse or acute at apex, and ending in a small awl-like point; when full grown are bright green, thick and shining above, pale green, glabrous or downy beneath, and conspicuously sprinkled with resinous dots above and below; midvein and primary veins deeply depressed above. Autumnal tints purplish, scarlet, and orange.

*Flowers.*—May, June. Perfect, white, pink or red bells, borne in rather loose racemes. Bracts leaf-like, oval, persistent, as long as the pedicels.

*Calyx.*—Glandular, adnate to the ovary, five-toothed; teeth acute and fringed.

*Corolla.*—White, pink or red, bell-shaped, five-angled, five-toothed; teeth short and somewhat recurved.

*Stamens.*—Ten; filaments downy; anthers long, awnless, two-celled; cells prolonged into tubes opening at the apex.

*Pistil.*—Ovary inferior, ten-celled, each cell containing one ovule; style long and slender.

*Fruit.*—Berry-like drupe, depressed globose, black and shining, about one-fourth of an inch in diameter, rather insipid; nutlets ten. August.

The Dwarf Huckleberry, a small shrub from a creeping base, is not very abundant, nor is its fruit very good. Leaves, branchlets, flower stems and calyx are sprinkled with glandular and resinous dots.

## BOX HUCKLEBERRY

*Gaylussàcia brachýcera.*

A low shrub, six to fifteen inches high; branches erect; twigs smooth; leaves resembling those of the box. In dry woods, from Delaware and Pennsylvania to Virginia.

*Leaves.*—Evergreen, thick, leathery, smooth, not resinous, oval or oblong, one-half to one inch long, wedge-shaped at base, crenate-serrate, somewhat revolute, obtuse or acute at margin. Petioles short.

*Flowers.*—May. Small white or pink bells, in few-flowered racemes.

Box Huckleberry,
*Gaylussacia bra-
chycera.* After
Britton & Brown.

### DWARF BLUEBERRY. LOW-BUSH BLUEBERRY

*Vaccínium pennsylvànicum.*

A low bush, six inches to two feet high, found in dry, rocky, or sandy soil and often fringing wet lands. Ranges from Newfoundland to southern New Jersey and westward to Illinois and Michigan.

*Stems.*—Shoots green, branchlets a little angular, bark light green, warty with whitish dots ; stems reddish purple. Winter buds quite large, reddish purple.

*Leaves.*—Oblong or ovate-lanceolate, three-fourths to. an inch and a half long, acute at both ends, minutely serrate, rather thick texture, terminating in a callous tip. They come out of the bud revolute, deeply tinged with red, which color they retain for a considerable time ; when full grown are glabrous and shining above, smooth or slightly downy on the veins below ; finely and markedly reticulate. Autumnal tint scarlet and crimson ; fall early.

*Flowers.*—May, June. White bells, borne in few-flowered racemes. Bracts reddish.

*Calyx.*—Adnate to ovary, five-toothed.

*Corolla.*—Oblong, bell-shaped, slightly contracted at the throat, white or pinkish, five-toothed : teeth acute ; slightly reflexed.

*Stamens.*—Ten ; filaments short, hairy; upwardly prolonged into tubes ; cells opening by terminal pores.

*Pistil.*—Ovary inferior, ovules several ; style even with corolla.

*Fruit.*—Globular berry, one-fourth to three-eighths of an inch in diameter, blue with a bloom ; very sweet. The earliest of the blueberries.

This lowest and earliest of the blueberries delights in a thin, sandy soil, and carpets the ground in the openings in the pitch-pine woods with beds of rich soft green, which in May and June are decked with a profusion of beautiful flowers ; in July and August are loaded with delicious fruit, and in October turn to deep scarlet and crimson.

From its situation and exposure the berries ripen earlier than those of any other species. They are soft and easily injured in bringing to market, and liable when in mass to speedy decay.

—George B. Emerson.

Dwarf Blueberry, *Vaccinium pennsylvanicum.*

Leaves ¾' to 1½' long   Fruit ¼' to ⅜' in diameter.

*Vaccinium pennsylvanicum* is a dwarf, straggling bush, climbing to rocky heights or carpeting dry, sandy places. In winter its large, scaly, flower buds are easily distinguished from the leaf buds. The flowers appear a little before the leaves and are followed by large, pale blue, delicious berries, ripe by the last of June or in early July.

The immature clusters of fruit crowding at the very tips of the branches form a most enchanting combination of green, pink, purple, and blue.

Dwarf Blueberry, in flower.

The Canadian Blueberry, *Vaccinium canadense*, is a dwarf shrub resembling *Vaccinium pennsylvanicum*, but with broader and more downy leaves. The fruit is blue-black and ripens later than the common Blueberry. It is the last Blueberry to appear in the market and is most abundant in the British provinces.

*Vaccinium pennsylvanicum angustifolium* is a subarctic form with narrower leaves, found on the summits of the White Mountains, on the Adirondacks, at Quebec and northward.

*Vaccinium pennsylvanicum nigrum* is a variety with a rounder bell than that of the type; the berry black without bloom. It flowers a little earlier than the type.

Low Blueberry, *Vaccinium vacillans.*

Leaves 1′ to 2½′ long.   Fruit ₁₆³′ to ¼′ in diameter.

## LOW BLUEBERRY. BLUE HUCKLEBERRY

*Vaccinium vacillans.*

A stiff shrub, six inches to four feet high, found in dry, sandy soil. Ranges from New Hampshire to North Carolina and west to Michigan.

*Stems.*—Branchlets and smaller spray red or pink and contrasting in color with the yellowish green or pale gray of the twigs and branches. Winter buds red.

*Leaves.*—Obovate, oval or broadly oblong, one to two and one-half inches long, narrowed or rounded at base, entire or sparingly or minutely serrulate, acute or acuminate, with a small bristle at apex. They come out of the bud revolute, dull green tinged with red, which color they remain for some time; when full grown are dull light green, glabrous above, pale or glaucous beneath. Autumnal tint scarlet and crimson.

*Flowers.*—May, June. Pink or greenish white bells about one-fourth of an inch long, borne in racemose clusters; appear before the leaves are half-grown.

*Calyx.*—Tube adnate to the ovary, five-toothed.

*Corolla.*—Pink or white, oblong-cylindric, somewhat constricted at the throat.

*Stamens.*—Ten, filaments slightly hairy, anthers extending into long tubes; cells opening by terminal pores.

*Pistil.*—Ovary inferior; ovules several.

*Fruit.*—Globular berry, blue with a bloom, sweet, delicious flavor. Ripening somewhat later than *Vaccinium pennsylvanicum.* July to September. A variety with white fruit is known.

Mr. Jackson Dawson of the Arnold Arboretum describes this Blueberry as follows:

" The Low Blueberry, *Vaccinium vacillans,* is a shrub from one to three feet high, with a yellowish green stem and glaucous leaves, usually growing on high rocky ground and at the edge of woods. It bears an abundance of large sweet berries which are chiefly covered with a blue bloom, though I have found black varieties. The fruit and flowers are formed at the extremities of the last year's growth, which is from one to four inches long without leaves, so that a large part of the plant seems leafless. The ends of the branches are covered with fruit, however, which can be stripped off by the handful. As it is very prolific, the flowers of this species in May look much richer and more abundant than those of any of the others. The fruit is ripe from late July to September. The plant is well worth cultivation as an ornamental shrub, and for its valuable fruit."

*Vaccinium vacillans* may be distinguished from *Vaccinium pennsylvanicum* as a larger bush. The leaves are twice as large at least, dull green above, paler or distinctly glaucous beneath. The fruit begins to ripen when the best of *Vaccinium pennsylvanicum* is past. The berries are very similar; possibly those of *Vaccinium vacillans* are not quite so juicy or so sweet as the others.

## HIGH-BUSH BLUEBERRY. TALL BLUEBERRY. SWAMP BLUEBERRY

*Vaccinium corymbòsum.*

A shrub six to fifteen feet high, forming large, handsome clumps in swamps and moist woods. Ranges from Newfoundland to Virginia, west to Minnesota. Has many varying forms; produces the last market blueberry.

*Stems.*—Shoots and twigs yellowish green, somewhat angular when young. Stems and branches are bronze or copper color or tinged with purple or red or bleached to a gray; gradually the bark cleaves off, giving the stems a mottled look.

*Leaves.*—Alternate, simple, oblong or oval, one to three inches long, wedge-shaped at base, entire, acute at apex. They come out of the bud pale green or purplish, downy; when full grown are dark green, glabrous and shining above, paler and downy beneath. Autumnal tint brilliant scarlet and orange. Petiole short.

*Flowers.*—May, June. White or pale pink bells, borne in short pendent or nodding racemes, which appear on almost leafless branches of last year's wood. Bracts deciduous.

*Calyx.*—Adnate to the ovary; five-lobed.

*Corolla.*—White or pinkish, cylindric or slightly constricted at the throat, one-fourth to one-half an inch long, five-toothed.

*Stamens.*—Ten, anthers upwardly prolonged into tubes; cells opening by terminal pores.

*Pistil.*—Ovary inferior, ovules several, stigma small.

*Fruit.*—Berry one-fourth to one-third an inch in diameter, variable in color but typically blue with a bloom; pleasantly acid. July, August.

This Blueberry is described by Gray in three varieties, two of which Britton & Brown regard as sufficiently distinct to be considered species. These are *Vaccinium corymbosum atrococcum*, which differs from the type, principally, in more downy leaves, smaller and rounder flowers and berries black without bloom; and *Vaccinium corymbosum pallidum* which differs in having paler serrulate leaves, whitish or glaucous beneath. This form is common in the Alleghanies and has a southern habitat.

Mr. Jackson Dawson of the Arnold Arboretum writes of this Blueberry as follows:

"The High Bush Blueberry, *Vaccinium corymbosum*, forms handsome clumps of shrubbery from four to ten feet high in deep swamps and moist woods, but seldom reaches more than four feet in open pastures.

High-bush Blueberry, *Vaccinium corymbosum.*

Leaves 1′ to 3′ long.   Fruit ¼′ to ⅓′ in diameter.

The young branches are usually yellowish green, turning to a light gray when old or much exposed, while the bark on old stems becomes rough and peels off in shreds.

" The flowers are pretty, white bells, borne at the extremity of the branches of the previous year's growth. They appear in May and early June, and the fruit is ripe from August to late September. The latter is variable in shape, size, flavor, and color. Of many well marked varieties, one has large black fruit of a pleasant acid which seems exactly the flavor to add to a bowl of new milk. Another, a large one, has a delicate sugary flavor. I chanced upon a bush one day which was twelve feet high, loaded with berries of a beautiful blue, rich, juicy variety and half an inch in diameter, while some were even larger. In this swamp ten or twelve good forms of fruit might have been found and by careful selection and hybridization there is no reason why the High Bush Blueberry should not become an excellent and abundant fruit, as it is more easily cultivated than any of the others. A dwarf form of *Vaccinium corymbosum* which rarely grows more than eighteen inches high has large, fine, abundant fruit of a bluish black color."

The High-bush Blueberry has many virtues, and by no means the least is the gorgeous coloring that it assumes in late October. Then it becomes indeed a burning bush of the most brilliant scarlet and holds its leaves late into November. It should be more generally planted, for it is beautiful at all seasons, is not difficult to transplant, and will grow in any good garden soil.

Dwarf Bilberry, *Vaccinium cæspitosum*.
Leaves ½' to 1' long.

## DWARF BILBERRY

*Vaccínium cæspitòsum.*

A low much branched shrub, three to seven inches high; found on the summits of the White Mountains. Ranges from Labrador westward through subarctic America to Alaska, south in the Rocky Mountains to Colorado.

*Leaves.*—Obovate, one-half to one inch long, wedge-shaped at base, serrulate with small blunt teeth, obtuse or acute at apex, nearly sessile, shining green above and beneath. In autumn the leaves fall early.

*Flowers.*—June, July. White or pink bells; mostly solitary in the axils of the leaves; calyx five or four-toothed; corolla obovoid or oblong-obovoid, pink or white, five, rarely four-toothed; stamens ten, rarely eight.

*Fruit.*—Berry, globular, blue with a bloom, sweet, about one-fourth of an inch in diameter. August.

## BOG BILBERRY. BOG WHORTLEBERRY

*Vaccínium uliginòsum.*

Bog Bilberry, *Vaccinium uliginosum,*
in flower.

A low, stiff, much branched shrub, six to twenty-four inches high. Found on the summits of the high mountains of New England and New York mainly above the timber line, along the shore of Lake Superior and northward to Alaska. Also found in northern Europe and northern Asia.

*Leaves.*—Oval, obovate or oblong, one-half to one inch long, wedge-shaped at the base, entire, obtuse or retuse, nearly sessile; when full grown thick, bright green above, dull, pale, or glaucous beneath.

*Flowers.*—June, July. Pink bells, solitary or in clusters of two to four. Calyx four-lobed, rarely five-lobed; corolla pink, ovoid or urn-shaped, four-toothed; stamens eight, two-awned at the back, included.

*Fruit.*—Berry, globular, about one-fourth of an inch in diameter, blue with a bloom, sweet, not abundant. July, August.

## MOUNTAIN CRANBERRY. CROWBERRY

*Vìtis-Idæa vìtis-idæa. Vaccinium vìtis-idæa.*

A low evergreen shrub, three to eight inches high, with creeping stems and erect branches. Ranges from the higher mountains of New England and the coast of Maine to Labrador, westward to Lake Superior, British Columbia and Alaska; ascends 5,300 feet in the Adirondacks. Native in northern Europe and northern Asia; prefers peat soil; seeks the shelter of pine woods; makes beds and mats.

*Leaves.*—Crowded on the stem, one-fourth to two-thirds of an inch long, obovate or oval, obtuse at base, margin entire or sparingly serrate, slightly revolute, rounded or slightly retuse at apex; when full grown are thick, leathery, dark shining green above, paler, and dotted with blackish points underneath, glabrous or minutely ciliate toward the base. Petioles short.

*Flowers.*—June, July. White or pinkish bells, in short, terminal, secund racemes, nodding, longer than their pedicels. Bracts reddish.

*Calyx.*—Adnate to ovary, four-toothed.

*Corolla.*—White or pink, open bell-shaped, four-lobed.

*Stamens.*—Eight; anthers without awns, upwardly prolonged into tubes; cells opening by terminal pores.

*Fruit.*—Berry, globular, dark red, bitter-acid, about one-third of an inch in diameter; edible when cooked and used as a substitute for cranberries in the extreme north. August, September.

The Mountain Cranberry is one of those plants which since the glacial period has returned apparently unchanged to its northern home; and is found in

Europe, Asia, and America, well up toward the limit of the timber line. Like all the alpine and arctic plants it is dwarfed in stem and branch, although its flowers are lovely and fruit abundant.

This dwarfing of plants native to high mountains or northern latitudes is interesting from a physiological point of view. Professor Correvon, Director of the Alpine Garden of Geneva, Switzerland, writes concerning it as follows:

"In the first place physiological experiments have proved that it is during the night that the lengthening of tissues and the gradual expansion of the plant occurs. In the daytime the greater the insolation the less growth they accomplish, and, the Alpine night being so extremely cold, there can scarcely be any nocturnal development of mountain plants. It is under the influence of attenuated solar rays and during the warm dusks that the plants are able to increase. The hot and powerful sun of high latitudes causes the brilliancy and size of the corollas, but also prevents the equal expansion of stems and leaves. These latter have only the very short space of time between the setting of the sun and the beginning of the glacial night for their growth, and in addition they also profit by the short, cloudy, moist and tepid days that precede the setting in of winter to put forth new leaves and buds."

Mr. J. M. Macoun, of Ottawa, Canada, writing in *Garden and Forest* says:

"The fruit of the Mountain Cranberry is considered of no value in the warmer parts of Canada; but in the cold rocky woods of the north, along the

Mountain Cranberry, *Vaccinium vitis-idæa.*

Leaves ¼′ to ⅖′ long.  Fruit ⅓′ in diameter.

shores of Hudson Bay and the Arctic Ocean, it seems to gain size and flavor out of the very conditions that dwarf and destroy its less hardy competitors. For there it is acid, not acrid, and pronounced to be the equal, by those who have eaten it there, of the Cranberry. May not something be due to the appetite of the eater in that northern clime?

" It is true, however, that on the north shore of the Gulf of St. Lawrence the fisher folk gather it in large quantities for their own use, calling it the Low-bush Cranberry.

" In some places together with *Empetrum nigrum* it forms the sole food of the larger migratory birds as they return to the north in the spring. In the spring it is eagerly sought by the black bear, and on the islands in Hudson Bay and along the Arctic coasts the polar bear spends much of his time in tearing up the low evergreen plants in order to get at the fruit more easily; for it is on the under side and almost touching the earth that the berries are found in greatest numbers. Immense patches of ground covered with the dead plants may often be found, telling where bruin has been at work. All summer long the last season's fruit may be found mixed with the flowers or with the green berries, and is then eaten by many birds in preference to anything else."

Deerberry, *Polycodium stamineum.*

Leaves 1′ to 4′ long.  Fruit ⅜′ to ⅝′ in diameter.

## DEERBERRY. SQUAW HUCKLEBERRY

*Polycòdium stamíneum. Vaccínium stamíneum.*

*Polycodium*, many bells, referring to the abundant flowers.

A widely branching shrub two to five feet high, found in dry gravelly soil and under the shade of deciduous trees. Ranges from Massachusetts to Kentucky and Florida, west to Minnesota.

*Stems.*—Branches slender, green, downy at first, finally brown.

*Leaves.*—Oval, ovate, oblong or obovate, one to four inches long, rounded or heart-shaped at base, entire, slightly revolute at margin, acute or acuminate at apex; when full grown are light green above, pale or glaucous or slightly downy beneath ; midvein and primary veins very prominent beneath. Autumnal tints scarlet and crimson, or the leaves fall with little change of color. Petiole short, downy.

*Flowers.*—April, June. Very numerous, pure white bells, borne in graceful, leafy-bracted racemes.

*Calyx.*—Tube adnate to ovary, five-toothed.

*Corolla.*—Open bell-shaped, white, or white with a purplish tinge, or yellowish green, about one-quarter of an inch long, five-lobed.

*Stamens.*—Ten, exserted, anthers upwardly prolonged into tubes ; cells opening by a terminal pore.

*Pistil.*—Ovary inferior, five-celled ; style exserted.

*Fruit.*—Berry globose or pear-shaped, greenish white, yellowish or dull red, three to five-eighths of an inch in diameter, inedible. September.

The Deerberry is a plant of wide distribution, but is principally a bush of the Alleghanies. When removed from its wild-wood surroundings, given good soil and generous treatment, it develops into a charming garden plant. Its flowers may be distinguished by their very long, straight stamens, which project far beyond the short, spreading, corolla bells. The fruit is inedible.

### CREEPING SNOWBERRY

*Chiógenes serpyllifòlia. Chiógenes hispídula.*

*Chiogones*, snow born, in allusion to the white berries.

A trailing and creeping evergreen, with slender hairy branches and alternate two-ranked, oval or ovate, small leaves and solitary, axillary, small, greenish white flowers on short recurved peduncles. A native of cold, wet woods, it ranges across the continent from Newfoundland to British Columbia and southward to Michigan and North Carolina. The flowers appear in May and June, are bell-shaped; calyx four-cleft; corolla four-lobed; stamens eight; ovary four-celled. The berry is snow white, aromatic, many-seeded, rather mealy; usually minutely bristly.

Creeping Snowberry, *Chiogenes hispidula.* Leaves ¹⁄₁₂′ to ¼′ long.

### AMERICAN CRANBERRY

*Oxycóccus macrocárpus.*

*Oxycoccus*, sharp berry, of Greek derivation, referring to the sharp acid of the fruit. Cranberry is referred to a fancied resemblance between the stem, calyx, and petals, as the bud is about to unfold, and the neck, head, and bill of a crane; hence craneberry, soon corrupted into cranberry.

A trailing evergreen shrub with short, erect fruiting branches, alternate, nearly sessile leaves, and nodding slender peduncles, pale pink flowers. The leaves are dark green above, white or pale beneath, the margins revolute. Flowers appear in June in few-flowered clusters, slightly racemose. Calyx is four-parted; corolla four-parted, anthers exserted with very long terminal tubes; berry four-celled, red, acid. Found in bogs from Newfoundland to the Northwest Territory and southward to North Carolina, Michigan, and Minnesota. Extensively cultivated; produces the cranberry of the market. The Small or European Cranberry, *Oxycoccus oxycoccus*, also occurs in the extreme north, descending as far south as New Jersey and Michigan. A southern form appears in the mountains of Virginia and southward.

American Cranberry, *Oxycoccus macrocarpus*. Leaves ¼' to ½' long.

Professor Bailey, in " The Evolution of Our Native Fruits," writes of the cranberry as follows:

" The cranberry, the most unique of American horticultural products, was first cultivated, or rescued from mere wild bogs, about 1810. Its cultivation began to attract attention about 1840, although the difficulties connected with the growing of this new crop did not begin to clear away before 1850. Cape Cod was the first cranberry-growing region, which was soon followed by New Jersey, and later by Wisconsin and other regions. The varieties now known are over a hundred, all having been picked up in bogs, and the annual product from tame bogs in the United States is more than 800,000 bushels."

# ERICÀCEÆ—HEATH FAMILY

## LABRADOR TEA

*Lèdum groenlàndicum.   Lèdum latifòlium.*

*Ledum* is without significance as applied to this plant.

A low, evergreen, undershrub one to four feet high, growing in bogs and swamps and cold, damp, wooded glens.   Ranges from Greenland to British Columbia and southward to Massachusetts, New Jersey, Pennsylvania and Wisconsin.   Juices bitter, astringent and narcotic.   Root or subterranean stem very large.

*Stems.*—Recent shoots densely covered with rusty tomentum. Older branches reddish brown or copper-colored ; main stem very dark.

*Leaves.*—Alternate, simple, thick, one to two inches long, one-fourth to one-half an inch wide, oblong, pointed or rounded at base, obtuse at apex, margin entire, strongly revolute ; when full grown are pale green, slightly rugose, sparingly dotted with amber dots above, densely covered with soft brown wool beneath.   Those growing on branches near the ground are sometimes destitute of tomentum and are flat, short, elliptical and scattered, bearing resinous dots beneath.   Fragrant when crushed.   Petioles short.

*Flowers.*—May, June.   Perfect, white, three-eighths to one-half an inch broad ; borne in dense terminal umbels one to one and one-half inches across ; pedicels nearly an inch long, recurved in fruit, brown-hairy or tomentose, bracted at the base ; bracts deciduous.

*Calyx.*—Small, five-toothed, persistent.

*Corolla.*—Petals five, white, nearly or quite distinct, oval, obtuse, imbricate in bud.

*Stamens.*—Five to ten, hypogynous, exserted, filaments thread-like, white; anthers white, cells opening by terminal pores.

*Pistil.*—Ovary superior, ovoid, scaly, five - celled; ovules many; style threadlike, persistent; stigma five-lobed.

*Fruit.*—Capsule, a quarter of an inch long, oblong-oval, crowned with the style, downy, nodding, five-celled, five-valved, opening from the base. Seeds many.

Labrador Tea is an interesting example of a plant fitted to hold its own in a subarctic climate. In the first place, it is clothed in wool; it carries a thick woolly coat over its stems and on the under-surface of its leaves. This woolliness lessens the loss of water through the stomata. Then, too, the leaves are partly rolled up with the upper surface outward, so as to give the lower surface a deeply grooved form. This plant ranges far north into regions where the temperature even in summer often falls so low that the absorption of water by the roots ceases, since it has been shown that this stops a little above the freezing point of water. Exposed to cold dry winds the plant would then often be killed by complete drying up, if it were not for the protection afforded by the woolly, channelled, under-surfaces of the leaves.

—JOSEPH Y. BERGEN.

The name Labrador Tea is more than a botanist's fancy,—the resinous, astringent, and slightly bitter leaves really have been used at the north as a substitute for tea. There is no record that it is a good substitute; and in Russia where the leaves of an allied species are used instead of hops in the manufacture of beer, the beer so made causes headache and vertigo. Like all subarctic plants the roots are large in proportion to the spread of stem and foliage. The leaves are curiously recurved, a concession to the severity of the climate in its chosen home. The handsome clusters of white flowers are produced in May and June. It prefers a peat soil, and like most broad-leaved evergreens in our climate is the better for a slight winter covering, not as protection against winter cold, but against winter sunshine.

Labrador Tea, *Ledum grœnlandicum.*
Leaves 1′ to 2′ long.

## WILD HONEYSUCKLE. PINXTER FLOWER. PINK AZALEA

*Azàlea nudiflòra.*

*Azalea*, dry, arid, of Greek derivation, refers to the habitat of the plant. Pinxter is Dutch for Whitsunday and refers to the time of flowering.

A spreading shrub, two to six feet high, branched above, often simple below; grows in dry sandy or rocky woods, also loves the banks of sluggish streams and borders of swamps. Ranges from Maine to Florida, westward to Missouri and Texas. Variable in habit and in choice of location.

*Leaves.*—Alternate, crowded toward the end of the branches, simple, two to four inches long, oblong or obovate, acute at both ends, serrate, margin finely ciliate. They come out of the bud revolute, pale dull green, slightly hairy; when full grown are bright green, glabrous above, paler green and downy beneath. In autumn they turn dull yellow. Petioles short.

*Flowers.*—April, May, before or with the leaves. Perfect, showy pink or nearly white, faintly odorous, borne in terminal umbels developed from cone-like scaly buds which were formed the previous autumn. Pedicels hairy, erect, about three-fourths of an inch long.

*Calyx.*—Small, five-parted, persistent.

*Corolla.*—Varying from rose-color more or less intense to white, funnel-form, somewhat irregular; tube dark pink, scarcely longer than the lobes of the corolla, hairy, slightly glandular; border paler pink, five-lobed, somewhat two-lipped, one and a half to two inches broad.

*Stamens.*—Five, much exserted, declined; filaments slender, pink, often an inch and a half long; anthers awnless; cells opening by terminal pores.

*Pistil.*—Ovary superior, five-celled; style slender, pink; two to two and a half inches long, declined; ovules numerous.

*Fruit.*—Capsule, linear-oblong, erect, five-celled, opening down from the top, many-seeded.

Wild Honeysuckle, *Azalea nudiflora.*

Azaleas flush the island floors
And the tints of heaven reply.
—RALPH WALDO EMERSON.

Martha Bockeè Flint in " A Garden of Simples "
writes of *Azalea nudiflora* as follows :

" In secluded forest dells where the wood soil is
rich and damp, on the verge of black, peaty swamps,
and even on rocky hillsides, there blooms the most
beautiful of the Azaleas, the *Rhododendron nudiflora*.

No ' tree ' in its sub-arborescent
growth, it is truly a rose flower, for
the exquisite tints of the wild-rose
and the peach-blossom color its
clusters of airy bloom. . . . This
peerless azalea is familiarly known
in New England as the honeysuckle,
the swamp pink and the May apple.
The latter name comes from the irregular excrescence, pale green and
glaucous, growing on the leaves
when stung by an insect, which

Leaves of *Azalea nudiflora*.

there deposits its eggs. Cool, crisp,
and juicy, they are the delight of children, and put for
a day in spiced vinegar, make the first pickles of the
year.

" But the name by which this May Queen of our
northern flora is dearest to New Netherland families
is *Pingster-bloem*, the flower of Pingster or Whitsunday. In the seventeenth century, the rocky glens and
woodland glades of the island of Manhattan were all
aglow with this pink azalea, blooming over a period
long enough to connect it with that movable feast, by

Mountain Azalea, *Azalea canescens.*

Leaves 1½′ to 3′ long.

the Dutch revered only less than the festival of their own patron saint. With the prescribed religious observances the Pingster days had many features of the Saturnalia and were in that staid community a time of unwonted license. The slaves then had their holiday and held riot, awakening on the banks of the Hudson the wild echo of strains which had been chanted on the Congo and the Gambia. But the custom in Nieuw Amsterdam which is fairest in retrospect, and which lingered longest, was the gathering of the *Pingster-bloem*. . . . From the day's woodland revels, the youths and maidens returned laden with the branches of the *Pingster-bloem*, to adorn the houses. This yearly gathering of the Azalea is the nearest spontaneous approach to a May Day celebration which has ever thrived in our capricious climate. This may be explained not only by the matchless beauty of the sylvan spoil, but by the great reverence with which Whitsunday was regarded in every branch of the Christian church."

### MOUNTAIN AZALEA

*Azàlea canéscens.*

A mountain form, native to the Catskill and Shawangunk mountains and southward along the Alleghanies.

A branching shrub, four to fifteen feet high, the twigs glabrous or sparingly pubescent. Leaves oval, elliptic or sometimes obovate, wider and shorter than those of *Azalea nudiflora*, more or less soft canescent and pale beneath, and stiff hairy or pubescent on the veins, varying to nearly glabrous, the margins ciliolate-

Flaming Azalea, *Azalea lutea.*
Leaves 2′ to 3½′ long.

serrulate; pedicels glandular; flowers rose-color to white, very fragrant, expanding with or before the leaves; corolla border of two inches across; the tube rather stout, densely glandular but scarcely viscid; stamens exserted; capsule linear-oblong, narrowed above, glandular, one-quarter to one-third of an inch long.

## FLAMING AZALEA

*Azàlea lùtea. Azàlea calendulàcea.*

Four to fifteen feet high; erect, branches and twigs mostly smooth; in dry woods. Ranges from southern New York to Georgia on the slopes of the Appalachian mountains. Attractive in cultivation.

*Leaves.*—Alternate, simple, oblong, oval or obovate, wedge-shaped at base, margins serrulate and ciliolate-serrulate, somewhat revolute, acute at apex; when full grown bright green, glabrous or slightly hairy above; more or less downy or tomentose beneath. Petioles short.

*Flowers.*—May, June, with the leaves. Perfect, orange, yellow or red, very showy, slightly fragrant, borne in terminal umbels developed from cone-like scaly buds, which were formed the previous autumn.

*Calyx.*—Small, five-parted.

*Corolla.*—Varying from lemon to orange and red, funnel-form, somewhat irregular. Tube glandular-hairy, about the length of the corolla-lobes; border five-lobed, about two inches broad.

*Stamens.*— Five, long-exserted, declined, filaments slender, yellow; anthers awnless, cells opening by terminal pores.

*Pistil.*—Ovary superior, five-celled; style slender, three inches long, yellow.

*Fruit.*—Capsule, linear-oblong, erect, more or less downy.

Hardly inferior to any of the garden varieties is our native *Azalea calendulacea;* and one of the great sights of this continent for the lover of flowers is the slopes of the southern Alleghany mountains when they are blazing in June with the great flame-colored masses of this splendid plant.

*—Garden and Forest.*

Tree Azalea, *Azalea aborescens.*
Leaves 1′ to 2′ long.

## SMOOTH AZALEA. TREE AZALEA

*Azàlea arboréscens.*

The Tree Azalea under favorable conditions attains the height of six to ten feet. Although found in the mountains of Pennsylvania the plant is really southern and finds its most congenial home in the Carolinas and the Gulf states. The leaves are one to two inches long, obovate or oval, acute or acuminate at apex, margin entire and ciliate, bright green above, pale green beneath, fragrant in drying.

The flowers, which appear in June and July, are of the azalea type, white or tinged with pink, fragrant. The border is nearly regular, and the tube slender and glandular; stamens and style are red, long-exserted. The fruiting capsule is densely glandular, one-half to three-fourths of an inch long.

This is one of the most beautiful and most fragrant of the azaleas, and the length of its blooming period makes it desirable in cultivation.

## WHITE SWAMP HONEYSUCKLE. WHITE AZALEA. CLAMMY AZALEA

*Azàlea viscòsa.*

Four to six feet high, with numerous spreading branches, grayish bark and hairy twigs; the whole plant sticky and clammy; found in swamps, at the borders of ponds, on moist highlands. Ranges from Maine to Florida and from Ohio to Texas, not far from the coast. Variable.

*Leaves.*—Alternate, simple, obovate-oblong or oblanceolate, two to four inches long, short-petioled, wedge-shaped at base, entire, ciliolate at margin, obtuse or acute and bristle pointed at

Clammy Azalea, *Azalea viscosa.*
Leaves 2′ to 4′ long.

apex ; when full grown, light green above, often glaucous, more or less hairy, beneath.

*Flowers.*—June, July, after the leaves. Perfect, white, sometimes touched with pink, borne in terminal umbels developed from cone-like scaly buds which were formed the previous autumn ; all the parts viscid and glandular ; fragrant.

*Calyx.*—Minute, five-parted, glandular-bristly.

*Corolla.*—White, varying to pale pink, funnel-form, tube slender, very viscid, densely glandular ; border five-lobed, more or less two-lipped, one to two inches broad, shorter than the tube.

*Stamens.*—Five, exserted, declined ; filaments white, pubescent ; anthers orange, awnless, opening by terminal pores.

*Pistil.*—Ovary superior, glandular-bristly, five-celled ; style white, slender, pubescent, exserted.

*Fruit.*—Capsule, linear-oblong, about half an inch long, glandular-bristly.

The Clammy White Azalea is found abundantly on the borders of swamps, although it sometimes climbs the mountain side. The books report its color as white, but this is not always the case ; for some plants bear pure white flowers while others have pink or pale rose-colored blossoms ; sometimes the tube of a white one shows a flush of pink. The blossom is thickly covered with glandular hairs ; they are on pedicel, calyx, corolla, each one white crowned with a minute crimson ball.

It is late in August before the last blossom has faded on the White Honeysuckle that lives in a shaded nook by a northern swamp. Transferred to the garden the flowering period is shorter, but the bush belongs to the group of summer bloomers. The flowers are deliciously fragrant and this fragrance seems to reside in every part.

## CULTIVATED AZALEAS

It is well known that the charming Azaleas which glorify our lawns in the early spring are the product of the gardener's art. Their range of color is nothing less than marvellous. Through all the tints of buff and sulphur and primrose, through all the range of salmon and crimson and vermilion, fading from rose into white and deepening from lemon to orange, they make their bewildering way. Every morning is a fresh revelation of what subtle and varied color these gorgeous creatures can command ; and as the day ends the hawk moth, which looks like a humming-bird, poised upon wings whose motion is like the sleep of a top, hovers in the twilight above the blossoms seeking the nectar stored in the long tubes ; and so makes sure there shall be more Azaleas in days to come.

The story of their origin is most interesting, and in this life history our own plants bear a distinguished part. The entire American group possesses the characteristic known as variability. That means simply that a plant is in a state of " unstable equilibrium," and will respond to influences so subtle that our gross senses cannot divine what they are. The result is that in minor characters the plant is continually vibrating back and forth. It loves the swamp, but grows on the dry rocky hillside as if it desired no other home. Usually each flower has five stamens; some fine day a plant produces a cluster in which each flower has ten. Here the beautiful corolla-tube is smooth ; there it is covered with clammy hairs. These characters, moreover, do not persist with any degree of certainty.

357

Such a plant is the joy of the gardener, for its characters are not fixed and he can easily mould them to his purposes.

Our American Azaleas, notably *Azalea nudiflora*, *Azalea lutea* and *Azalea arborescens*, were sent to the Belgian horticulturists at Ghent early in the eighteenth century. They were first crossed with the *Azalea pontica* of southern Europe—strains from India, from China, from Japan, were introduced, and by a process of hybridization and selection a wonderful group known as the Ghent Azaleas was produced.

What the gardeners of Ghent began the horticultural world has continued; and now, in the selection of hardy Azaleas, one is embarrassed by the number of varieties from which to choose.

*Azalea mollis*, a rather recent introduction from Japan, is a form which is winning its way to favor because of its hardiness, its low spreading growth and its well-shaped, symmetrical head. The flowers of the type are flame-colored, but seedlings and hybrids furnish gorgeous blossoms of white, yellow, and orange. The plant is an early bloomer and is a very desirable species.

The Azaleas, like the rhododendrons, are intolerant of lime. It is futile to expect flourishing plants in a calcareous soil, for however well a bed may be prepared it is only a question of time when the surrounding lime leaches through. Nor is a stiff clay soil really suitable for the plant; although by digging wide and deep and filling in with sand and loam and leaf humus, suitable conditions can be created.

Rhodora, *Rhodora canadensis.*

Leaves 1′ to 3′ long.

## RHODORA

*Rhodòra canadénsis.*

Named from the Greek *rhodon*, a rose.

Early flowering, low, thin little shrub, one to three feet high, growing in cool bogs, by the side of sluggish streams, in damp woods and on wet hillsides. Ranges from Newfoundland to New Jersey, westward to central New York and Pennsylvania.

*Stems.*—Recent shoots straight, erect, pale yellowish brown, hairy. Older stems covered with an outer bark which peels off early and leaves a bright, copper-colored, smooth bark ; leaf-buds minute ; flower-buds terminal, scaly, yellowish brown.

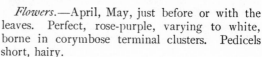

*Leaves.*—Alternate, simple, one to three inches long, oval or oblong, narrowed at base, entire, slightly revolute, obtuse or acute, often with a bristle at tip ; when full grown pale green above, paler and glaucous and downy beneath. In autumn they fall early with little change of color. Petioles short.

*Flowers.*—April, May, just before or with the leaves. Perfect, rose-purple, varying to white, borne in corymbose terminal clusters. Pedicels short, hairy.

Rhodora Leaf.

*Calyx.*—Minute, five-toothed.

*Corolla.*—Rose-purple, an inch to an inch and a half broad, two-lipped ; upper lip unequally two to three-lobed ; the lower divided to the base ; the segments recurved.

*Stamens.*—Ten, as long as the corolla ; filaments somewhat hairy ; anthers short, roundish, purple ; cells opening by terminal pores.

*Pistil.*—Ovary superior, five-celled, bristly ; style slender, purple, exserted ; stigma capitate.

*Fruit.*—Capsule, linear-oblong, five-celled, five-valved, many seeded.

Great Laurel, *Rhododendron maximum.*

Leaves 4′ to 7′ long.

Rhodora! if the sages ask you why
This charm is wasted on the marsh and sky,
Dear, tell them, that if eyes were made for seeing,
Then beauty is its own excuse for being.
Why thou wert there, O rival of the rose,
I never thought to ask; I never knew,
But in my simple ignorance suppose
The selfsame Power that brought me there brought you.
—RALPH WALDO EMERSON.

On the margin of some quiet swamp a myriad of bare twigs seem suddenly overspread with purple butterflies, and we know that the Rhodora is in bloom. Wordsworth never immortalized a flower more surely than Emerson this, and it needs no weaker words; there is nothing else in which the change from nakedness to beauty is so sudden, and when you bring home the great mass of blossoms they appear all ready to flutter away again from your hands and leave you disenchanted.
—THOMAS WENTWORTH HIGGINSON.

The Rhodora grows from one to three feet high, with each stem divided into four or five branchlets which are terminated by the encircling flower clusters. A native of swamps, it accepts the garden and will grow and spread if provided with a peaty soil and an open position. Like many others the flowers in order to be effective should be seen in masses. This is a genus of a single species; so far as known there is but one Rhodora.

### GREAT LAUREL. ROSE BAY

*Rhododéndron máximum.*

A tall shrub, sometimes a tree; found in low woods and along streams from Nova Scotia to Ontario and south to Georgia, chiefly along the mountains, often forming almost impenetrable thickets.

Leaves evergreen, alternate, four to seven inches

Hybrid Rhododendron.

long, oblong or lanceolate-oblong, dark green above, slightly paler beneath, acute or short-acuminate at apex, wedge-shaped at base. Flowers appear in June and July, pale rose varying to white, borne in corymbose clusters from scaly, cone-like buds formed the autumn before. Pedicels are glandular, viscid pubescent; corollas rather deeply five-cleft into oval obtuse lobes, rose-colored varying to white, sprinkled with yellowish or orange spots within; calyx-lobes oblong-obtuse; capsule oblong, puberulent.

Notwithstanding the many beautiful hybrids now in cultivation, our native Rhododendron is still a plant that charms by its most commended beauty. Its chosen home is a shaded nook by the side of a mountain stream ; its pale pink flowers ere they fall are overtopped by the shoot that started with the flower-bud, and the blooming period, beginning with us at the north in July, extends into late August.

Lapland Rose Bay, *Rhododendron lapponicum*—a dwarfed subarctic form, still lingers on the summits of the higher mountains of New England and New York.

### ALLEGHANY MENZIESIA

*Menzièsia pilòsa.*

Named in honor of Archibald Menzies, surgeon and naturalist, who in Vancouver's voyage brought the first known species from the northwest coast.

Erect shrub, two to five feet high ; found in mountain woods from Pennsylvania to Georgia. Twigs hairy and chaffy.

*Leaves.*—Alternate, simple, oval, oblong or obovate, one to two inches long, narrowed at base, margin entire, ciliate, obtuse

Sand Myrtle, *Dendrium buxifolium.*
Leaves ¼′ to ½′ long.

or acute with a glandular bristle at apex. When full grown rough-hairy above, slightly glaucous and often chaffy on veins below. Petioles short, downy.

*Flowers.*—May, June. Perfect, small, greenish purple bells, borne on slender pedicels, in few-flowered terminal umbels, developed from scaly buds. Pedicels threadlike, glandular. Calyx five-lobed, downy ; corolla urn-shaped ; stamens eight, included, filaments smooth, anthers awnless ; ovary four-celled. Capsules beset with short glandular bristles. Seeds many, pointed at each end.

### SAND MYRTLE

*Déndrium buxifòlium.   Leiophýllum buxifòlium.*

*Dendrium*, a tree, named according to the law of opposites.
*Leiophyllum*, smooth leaf.

A low, evergreen shrub with box-like foliage, widely branching, four to eighteen inches high. Native of the sandy pine-barrens of New Jersey and farther south.

*Leaves.*—Opposite, crowded, evergreen, simple, coriaceous, one-fourth to one-half an inch long, oval or oblong, acute at base, entire, somewhat revolute margin, obtuse at apex ; dark green and shining above, paler and black-dotted beneath ; mid-vein conspicuous ; other veins obscure.

*Flowers.*—April to June. Numerous, small, white or rose-colored, borne in small terminal umbel-like clusters. Bracts persistent.

*Calyx.*—Five-parted ; segments rigid, acute, persistent.

*Corolla.*—Petals five, ovate, spreading, white or pink.

*Stamens.*—Ten, exserted ; anthers reddish purple, two-celled.

*Pistil.*—Ovary superior, two to five-celled ; style slender, straight.

*Fruit.*—Capsule, ovoid, two to five-valved, splitting from the top.

This is an odd little evergreen bush which in blossoming time covers itself profusely with corymbs of tiny white flowers conspicuous for their purplish anthers. It fruits just as profusely as it blossoms.

## ALPINE OR TRAILING AZALEA

*Chamæcistus procúmbens.*

*Chamæcistus*, meaning ground-cistus.

A tufted, much-branched, trailing, dwarf, evergreen shrub with branches two to four inches long. Subarctic, found on the summits of the White Mountains, in Labrador, arctic America, Alaska.

*Leaves.*—Mostly opposite, crowded, evergreen, linear-oblong, one-sixth to one-fourth an inch long, margin entire, revolute, obtuse at apex ; dark green and shining above, paler beneath ; midrib prominent below. Petioles short.

*Flowers.*—July, August. Small, pink or white bells, solitary or clustered, from terminal buds.

*Calyx.*—Five-parted, segments purplish, ovate-lanceolate, persistent.

*Corolla.*—Broad bell-shaped, pink or white, with five obtuse lobes.

*Stamens.*—Five, included, inserted on corolla ; anthers didymous.

*Pistil.*—Ovary superior, two-celled, style short ; stigma capitate.

*Fruit.*—Capsule, subglobose, two to three-celled, many-seeded.

## MOUNTAIN LAUREL

*Kálmia latifôlia.*

*Kalmia* commemorates the labors of Peter Kalm, a pupil of Linnæus who was an enthusiastic admirer of the plant and who travelled in this country early in the eighteenth century.

A dense, broad shrub, five to ten feet high, with many stiff, crooked branches and a round, compact head ; tolerant of many locations and all soils except those containing lime. Ranges from Newfoundland to Hudson Bay, and along highlands and mountains southward to Georgia and Michigan. Root fibrous, matted; easily cultivated; foliage has the bad reputation of poisoning cattle.

*Leaves.*—Alternate or in pairs, or in threes, simple, evergreen, three to four inches long, oblong, wedge-shaped at base, entire, acute or rounded at apex and tipped with a callous point. They come out of the bud conduplicate; pale green slightly tinged with pink and covered with glandular white hairs; when full grown are thick and rigid, dark shining green above, pale yellow green beneath. They remain green and fall the second summer. Petioles stout, short, slightly flattened.

*Flowers.*—May, June, from buds which are found in autumn in the axils of the upper leaves in the form of slender cones of downy green scales. These buds develop a compound many-flowered corymb, four or five inches across, and overlapped at the flowering time by the leafy branches of the year. Buds and new flowers bright rose pink, afterward fading to pale pink or white and only lined with pink. Pedicels are red or green, hairy or scurfy and furnished with two bracts at base.

*Calyx.*—Five-parted; lobes imbricate in bud, narrow, acute, covered with glutinous hairs. Disk prominent, ten-lobed.

*Corolla.*—Saucer-shaped, rose-colored, white or pink, about one inch across. Tube short, with ten tiny sacs just below the five-parted border; lobes ovate, acute, imbricate in bud. The border is marked on the inner surface with a waving rosy line and is slightly purple above the sac. The buds are ten-ribbed from the sacs to the acute apex.

*Stamens.*—Ten, hypogynous, shorter than the corolla; at first held in the sacs of the corolla; filaments threadlike; anthers oblong, adnate, two-celled; cells opening longitudinally.

*Pistil.*—Ovary superior, five-celled; style threadlike, exserted; stigma capitate; ovules many in each cell.

*Fruit.*—Woody capsule, many-seeded, depressed, globular, slightly five-lobed, five-celled, five-valved; crowned with the persistent calyx, covered with viscid hairs. Seeds oblong.

The Laurels possess a remarkable adaptation for cross-fertilization. As each curious, angular, pocketed corolla-cup opens, the stigma appears erect in the very

Mountain Laurel, *Kalmia latifolia.*

Leaves 3' to 4' long.  Corymbs 4' to 5' across.

centre of the flower. The anthers are all hiding their youthful heads; in fact, every one of them is tucked into a pocket which fits it perfectly. The filaments are strained to a bow, and so delicately is the mechanism adjusted that a jar will release the anthers. Now comes the wandering bee, "voluble, velvety, vehement," and enters the flower. The soft body covers the stigma, the weight and the motion set the filaments free and the bee departs "a dusty fellow"—whose legs are "powdered with gold." In fact the bee carries off the greater part of the pollen of that flower and deposits some of it upon the stigma of the next flower visited; and so the process goes on through all the summer day.

The Laurel flourishes in gardens if only there be no lime there. The plant may be brought from the mountain side and if the roots are uninjured and the stems pruned back a little it will grow. It prefers leaf mould, but will grow in any good soil.

Laurel wood is very hard and solid, and in great demand for various purposes, one of which is indicated by the common name Spoon-wood.

*Kalmia angustifolia*, the Sheep Laurel or Lambkill, is found growing in company with *Kalmia latifolia*. It is a smaller bush, with narrower leaves and smaller blossoms. The blossom is of the kalmia type, with the saucer-shaped corolla, and the anthers caught in tiny pockets. Possibly it prefers moister soil than *Kalmia latifolia*, and is found in more open places. The flower clusters are lateral and a stem in full bloom looks like a flowery cylinder.

All the laurels are credited with poisoning young

Lambkill, *Kalmia angustifolia.*

Leaves 2′ to 5′ long.

animals.   Older cattle know enough to let them alone, but in early spring when the tender leaves are appearing, calves and young cattle, eager for green things, eat, and unless promptly treated, die.

The plants are a constant menace to the farmers on the mountains of Virginia, and the common names Lambkill, Calf Kill, Sheep Poison, clearly voice the "deep damnation" of rural opinion concerning them.

## SWAMP LAUREL.  PALE LAUREL

### *Kálmia glaùca.*

Low, slender-stemmed, evergreen, six to eighteen inches high; native of bogs and swamps.  Ranges from Newfoundland to Alaska, southward to New Jersey, Pennsylvania and Michigan.

*Stems.* — Smooth, yellow brown; branchlets two-ridged; ridges change position at each node.

*Leaves.* —Evergreen; opposite or sometimes in threes, an inch and a quarter to two inches long, a quarter of an inch wide, nearly sessile, oblong or linear-oblong, margin entire and revolute, apex acute, bright shining green above, glaucous or whitish beneath; midvein depressed, whitish above, prominent beneath.

*Flowers.* —April, May.  Of kalmia type, bluish pink, borne in simple terminal umbels of one to thirteen flowers.  Pedicel an inch long, slender, madder red; each subtended by a bract.

*Calyx.* — Five-parted; segments scarious margined, pink-tipped, imbricate in bud, persistent.

*Corolla.* —Saucer-shaped, about half an inch across, five-lobed, ten-keeled in bud, with ten tiny sacs in the saucer, into which the stamens are thrust.

*Stamens.* —Ten, shorter than corolla, filaments pink, stamens dark reddish brown, pocketed in the corolla sacs, springing forth by means of pressure and delivering pollen from terminal pores.

*Pistil.* —Ovary five-celled, ovules numerous; style slender, exserted; stigma depressed-capitate.

*Fruit.* —Depressed-globose capsule, glabrous about an eighth of an inch across.

Swamp Laurel, *Kalmia glauca.*

Leaves 1¼′ to 2′ long.

This exquisite little evergreen is found in company with *Andromeda polifolia*, and they bloom together. The flower is bright rose lilac, as it comes from the bud, fading later after the fashion of all the kalmias, but always beautiful. The blossoms are similar to those of the well known Mountain Laurel, but the flower cluster is much smaller, containing not more than a dozen flowers; each with a long slender pedicel. In northern Michigan this plant covers acres of swamp land and during the blooming period produces magnificent color effects.

Transferred to the garden the little Laurel improves in habit, is less straggling, but never becomes a compact shrub. It blooms much earlier than either *Kalmia latifolia* or *Kalmia angustifolia*, and is worthy of cultivation for that reason alone.

Mountain Heath, *Phyllodoce cærulea*. After Britton & Brown.

### MOUNTAIN HEATH. BRYANTHUS

*Phyllódoce cærùlea. Bryánthus taxifòlius.*

*Bryanthus*, from *bryon*, moss, and *anthos*, flower, because growing among mosses. *Phyllodoce*, a sea-nymph.

Low, evergreen, arctic-alpine undershrub, with yew-like leaves; found on the summits of the higher mountains of Maine and New Hampshire. Leaves alternate, linear, crowded, about a quarter of an inch long. Flowers pink or purplish bells, in nodding terminal umbels. Corolla oblong urn-shaped, five-toothed, contracted at the throat. Stamens ten, included ; ovary five-celled, style included ; capsule subglobose.

### CASSIOPE

*Cassìope hypnoìdes.*

*Cassiope* was the mother of Andromeda. The name has no obvious application to the plant.

An arctic-alpine, tufted, evergreen shrub with the aspect of a moss ; stems rising two to four inches high. Leaves loosely imbricate, linear, acute, flat above, convex beneath, one-twelfth to one-sixth of an inch long. The flowers are open bells, white or rose-color, one-fourth to one-third of an inch across, solitary, nodding on slender erect peduncles.

Cassiope, *Cassiope hypnoides.* After Britton & Brown.

Found on the summits of the higher mountains of New England and the Adirondacks of New York ; throughout arctic America, also in arctic Europe and Asia.

### SWAMP LEUCOTHOË

*Leucóthoë racemòsa.*

*Leucothoë,* a sea-nymph, one of the fifty daughters of Nereus : possibly referring to the plant as loving wet places.

Five to twelve feet high ; found in swamps and moist thickets. Ranges from Massachusetts to Florida and Louisiana, mostly near the coast. Suckers freely.

*Leaves.*—Alternate, simple, one to three and a half inches long, oblong to ovate, acute or rounded at base, serrulate, acute at apex, usually with a glandular point ; when full grown are glabrous, bright shining green above, paler, slightly pubescent on the veins beneath. In autumn they become a brilliant scarlet or vary through purple and scarlet and orange ; and remain until beaten off by storms. Petioles very short.

*Flowers.*—May, June, with or before the leaves. Perfect, white, bell-shaped, borne in one-sided racemes three to four inches long, which are mostly terminal, solitary or clustered ; pedicels short, bracted, jointed with the rachis. Fragrant.

*Calyx.*—Sepals five, distinct, acute, persistent, imbricate in bud, bracted.

*Corolla.*—White, oblong-cylindrical, contracted at the mouth, about three-eighths of an inch long, five-toothed.

*Stamens.*—Ten, included ; filaments white, awl-shaped ; anthers oblong, two-awned ; cells opening by terminal pores.

*Pistil.*—Ovary superior, five-celled, five-valved; style slender, exserted, stigma capitate.

*Fruit.*—Capsule, depressed-globose, surrounded by the persistent calyx and bracts. August, September.

*Garden and Forest* says: " The value of the northern native plant *Leucothoë racemosa* for the decoration of the parks and gardens of the northern states is very great. It is a hardy, fast-growing shrub which sometimes attains the height of ten feet; its slender branches are covered with dark green leaves which late in the autumn, long after those of every other tree and shrub cultivated in gardens have fallen, assume a brilliant and beautiful scarlet color. Its handsome, waxy, white, cup-shaped flowers are produced in long, erect, or slightly curved terminal racemes from buds formed the previous autumn, and covered during the winter with closely imbricated bracts. The splendid color of the leaves of this shrub in the late autumn

Swamp Leucothoë, *Leucothoë racemosa.*
Leaves 1′ to 3½′ long.   Racemes 3′ to 4′ long.

makes it one of the most desirable hardy plants for our northern gardens."

Although a swamp plant, *Leucothoë racemosa* can be readily cultivated; it needs peat soil or sandy loam, and a rather moist situation; given these it grows rapidly and becomes a broad bush. It is a tall, elegant, clean-limbed plant, attractive in winter because of the deep red of its twigs and branchlets. In springtime it bears racemes of small, fragrant, heath-like flowers, but its time of glory is late November, when it flames, a torch of scarlet, lighting up the swampy thickets, within sight of the sea, from Massachusetts to Florida.

### CATESBY'S LEUCOTHOË

*Leucôthoë catésbaei.*

An evergreen shrub, three to six feet high, found on the banks of streams. Ranges from Virginia to Georgia, westward to Tennessee. Is easily cultivated.

*Leaves.*—Alternate, simple, evergreen, leathery, lanceolate or ovate-lanceolate, three to six inches long, rounded at base, sharply serrulate, acuminate at apex; when full grown are dark shining green above, paler green below; midvein and primary veins conspicuous. Petioles greenish brown, about half an inch long.

*Flowers.*—April. Perfect, white, narrow bell-shaped, borne in axillary, densely-flowered racemes; central axis and pedicels white.

*Calyx.*—Sepals five, distinct, not imbricated in flower.

*Corolla.*—White, narrowly cylindric, constricted at throat, five-toothed.

*Stamens.*—Ten, included, filaments white, anthers yellow.

*Pistil.*—Ovary five-celled, style white, stigma green.

*Fruit.*—Capsule, depressed-globular, five-celled, five-lobed. Seeds many.

Catesby's Leucothoe, *Leucothoë catesbæi*.
Leaves 3′ to 6′ long.

Although Catesby's Leucothoë is a bush of southern range it is perfectly hardy at the north and is a valuable addition to our cultivated shrubs.

It blooms early ; the flower buds are developed in autumn in the axils of the persistent leaves of the year and look like cylindric cones about half an inch long, with close imbricate scales. As the weather grows cold these scales turn a deep red, the same color suffusing in a slighter degree the ends of the zigzag stems ; at the same time the upper leaves with their petioles often color as richly as the flower buds. The lower leaves for the most part retain their deep lustrous green color, and the contrast between the upper and the lower parts of the plant only adds to its beauty.

The recurved stems are three to six feet high, the evergreen leaves are thick and leathery ; and the white waxen bells are borne in crowded spike-like racemes. The plant prefers peat soil and damp situations, but will make the best of almost any location.

### WILD ROSEMARY. MARSH HOLY ROSE.

*Andrómeda polifòlia.*

*Andromeda*, a mythological name of fanciful application.

Slender, with stems but little branched, one to three feet high, foliage acid ; found in bogs. Ranges from Labrador and Newfoundland through arctic America to Alaska and British America, southward to New Jersey, Pennsylvania and Michigan.

*Leaves.*—Alternate, simple, linear-oblong or lanceolate, one and one-half to three inches long, narrowed at base, margins revolute, apex acute or obtuse, often with a small point ; when

Wild Rosemary, *Andromeda polifolia.*

Leaves 1½′ to 3′ long.

full grown are dull green, smooth above, white-glaucous beneath; midvein very strongly ridged beneath, petioles short.

*Flowers.*—May, June.   Perfect, tiny globes, white or tinged with pink, borne in few-flowered terminal umbels.   Bracts small, persistent.   Pedicels one-fourth to one-half an inch long.

*Calyx.*— Deeply five-pointed, persistent ;   lobes triangular-ovate, acute.   Disk ten-lobed.

*Corolla.*—White, globose, urn-shaped, about one-fourth of an inch in diameter, five-toothed ;   teeth recurved.

*Stamens.*—Ten, included ;   filaments bearded ;   anthers ovate, obtuse, awned, fixed near the middle ;   cells opening by a terminal pore.

*Fruit.*—Capsule, globose, five - celled, five - valved, many-seeded.

This plant is always fixed in some turfy hillock in the midst of swamps, as Andromeda herself was chained to a rock in the sea which bathed her feet as the fresh water does the roots of this plant.

—"Tour of Lapland."   LINNÆUS.

The lonely position of this little shrub in the midst of its native swamps seems to have impressed Linnæus to a wonderful degree ; and consequently he named it Andromeda—the rock-bound maiden.   It is a semi-aquatic, subarctic plant, and like so many of its kind knows no distinction between Europe, America or Asia, but is native to all.   Although it loves the cold deep swamps that border the limits of eternal snow, nevertheless when transferred to the garden border it will grow and flower as freely as in its native wilds.

The flowers are clusters of small globes usually white, but sometimes flesh-colored, and sometimes tipped with red ; they retain their beauty for nearly a month.

Mountain Fetter-bush, *Pieris floribunda.*

Leaves 1½′ to 3′ long.

## MOUNTAIN FETTER-BUSH

*Pieris floribúnda.*

*Pieris*, from Pieria, a town in Thessaly.

Evergreen, native to the Alleghanies, found in Virginia and southward; also hardy in northern gardens. From two to six feet high; with stems nearly erect and with very leafy branches.

*Leaves.*—Alternate, simple, evergreen, one and one-half to three inches long, leathery, oblong to ovate-lanceolate, rounded at base, serrulate and bristly-ciliate, acute or acuminate at apex; when full grown dark shining green above, paler and black-dotted below. Petioles short, bristly when young.

*Flowers.*—April, May. Perfect, white, five-angled bells, borne in terminal, slender, clustered, dense racemes about three inches long.

*Calyx.*—Five-lobed; lobes ovate-lanceolate, acute, valvate in the five-angled bud, persistent.

*Corolla.*—White, urn-shaped, slightly five-angled, five-saccate at base; five-toothed; teeth recurved.

*Stamens.*—Ten, included, filaments without appendages; anthers oblong, each with a slender awn on its back, two-celled; cells opening by terminal pores.

*Pistil.*—Ovary superior, five-celled; style slender, ovules many.

*Fruit.*—Capsule, ovoid-globose, sitting in the calyx and crowned with the slender style. Seeds many.

*Pieris floribunda* is one of the hardiest of the broad-leaved evergreens peculiar to the Alleghany mountains, and is a most charming ornamental shrub. The foliage is so dense that the stems and branches are concealed from sight. The flower buds practically mature the previous autumn, and stand all winter above the evergreen foliage, apparently without the slightest protection, ready to burst into bloom when the almanac says it is time. What is currently re-

Stagger-bush, *Pieris mariana.*
Leaves 2′ to 3′ long. Flowers $\frac{5}{12}′$ to $\frac{1}{2}′$ long.

garded as a late spring has little effect upon these flowers; the sun is up and so are they; sometimes they seem fairly to force the season. They are white, urn-shaped, five-angled cups, borne in long, branching racemes. The plant is worth cultivating, however, even if it should never bear a flower; the leaves are so green, clean, bright and glossy.

Gardeners recommend that the shrub be protected with evergreen boughs to prevent winter burning.

### STAGGER-BUSH

*Pieris mariàna.*

*Pieris*, from Pieria, the town in Thessaly where the Muses congregated; of no application to this plant. *Mariana*, because it was first described as a "Maryland shrub." Stagger-bush refers to its reputation for poisoning cattle.

A low shrub, one to four feet high; found in low, wet, sandy locations. Ranges from Rhode Island to Florida, mostly near the coast. Hardy throughout the north.

*Leaves.*—Simple, alternate, tardily deciduous, two to three inches long, oval or oblong, narrowed or rounded at base, margin entire, slightly revolute, acute or obtuse at apex; when full grown are shining dark green, coriaceous, smooth above, sparingly pubescent on the veins and black-dotted beneath. In autumn they turn an intense scarlet, and cling late.

*Flowers.*—April, May. Perfect, white, bell-shaped, borne in nodding lateral umbels on the many leafless branches of the preceding year, so forming a long compound inflorescence. Pedicels bearing one to three bracts.

*Calyx.*—Deeply five-parted; lobes lanceolate, acute, valvate in bud, persistent; disk ten-lobed.

*Corolla.*—White, or faintly pink, ovoid-cylindric, about half an inch long, five-toothed; teeth recurved.

*Stamens.*—Ten; filaments hairy on the outer side, two-toothed near the apex; anthers awnless, two-celled; cells opening by a terminal pore.

Privet Andromeda, *Xolisma ligustrina*, in fruit.

*Pistil.*—Ovary superior, five-celled ; style columnar ; stigma truncate.

*Fruit.*—Capsule, ovoid-pyramidal, small five-angled, five-celled. Seeds many.

The Stagger-bush is of somewhat straggling habit, yet very pretty and useful as a border shrub, blossoming profusely in early spring. The flowers are snow white waxen bells which appear in clusters from axillary buds crowded on the naked branches of last year's wood. The branches are wand-like ; and the leaves in autumn become intensely scarlet.

The plant was well known to our earlier botanists, and was first described as a Maryland shrub with the leaves of a euonymus and the flowers of an arbutus. It was sent over to England in 1736, and has been cultivated there for many years.

### PRIVET ANDROMEDA

*Xolísma ligústrina. Lyònia ligústrina. Andrómeda ligústrina.*

*Ligustrin*, the bitter principle of the Privet. Otherwise, these names seem to be without meaning.

Bushy, three to twelve feet high, growing in swamps and wet soil ; stem and branches light ash-colored with stringy bark. Ranges from New England to Florida and west to Arkansas.

*Leaves.*—Alternate, sometimes tufted, simple, oblong, obovate, oval or ovate, one to two and a half inches long, wedge-shaped at base, minutely serrulate or entire, acute or acuminate at apex ; when full grown glabrous or pubescent above, usually downy beneath. Petioles short, downy.

*Flowers.*—May, July. Perfect, small, white globes, borne in terminal or axillary, panicled leafless racemes. Pedicels thread-like, downy. Calyx-lobes triangular-ovate ; corolla an eighth of an inch in diameter ; stamens eight or ten, included ; ovary five-celled ; capsule depressed-globose, obtusely five-angled.

388

Cassandra, *Chamædaphne calyculata.*

Leaves ½′ to 1′ long.

Most plants furnish at least some provocation for the Latin names which they bear, but the Privet Andromeda seems most unfortunate of its class. The botanic name of this shrub appears in the books as "unexplained;" its English one is simply appropriated from those of two other plants.

Apart from its ill luck as to names it seems fortunate enough, for it is really a very pretty bush. In early spring it is conspicuous for its long panicles of tiny, white, globe-like flowers borne at the very end or upon the upper part of the branching stems. It is rare that a corolla so nearly attains a sphere. The flowers are borne upon leafless stems, and these continue leafless so that the fruit apparently is upon a dry branch.

### CASSANDRA. LEATHER-LEAF

*Chamædáphne calyculàta. Andrómeda calyculàta.*
*Cassándra calyculàta.*

*Chamædaphne*, ground or low Daphne. *Andromeda* and *Cassandra*, mythical terms without obvious application. *Calyculata* refers to the two bracts beneath the sepals as forming a secondary calyx.

Low, leafy, evergreen, from two to four feet high, forming large beds at the edge of swamps or in boggy meadows. Ranges from Newfoundland to Alaska, south to Georgia, west to Michigan and Illinois ; also occurs in northern Europe and Asia.

*Stems.*—Recent shoots covered with minute scurfy scales ; older stems dark copper color, smooth.

*Leaves.*—Alternate, evergreen, shining, leathery, one-half to an inch and a half long, oblong or oblanceolate, narrowed at base, obscurely denticulate and revolute at margin, acute or obtuse at apex, covered with scaly dots which are rust colored beneath ; upper leaves gradually smaller ; the uppermost reduced to mere bracts.    Petioles short.

*Flowers.*—April.    Perfect, solitary, white or tinged with rose purple, urn-shaped, borne on short pedicels in the axils of the small upper leaves, forming terminal one-sided, leafy racemes.

*Calyx.*—Sepals five, persistent, bracted at base.

*Corolla.*—White, oblong-cylindric, narrowed at the throat, five-toothed, one-fourth of an inch long ; teeth recurved.

*Stamens.*—Ten, included ; filaments flat, smooth ; anther-cells tapering upward into tubular beaks, awnless ; cells opening by terminal pores.

*Pistil.*—Ovary superior, five-celled, five-grooved ; style slender ; ovules many.

*Fruit.*—Capsule, depressed-globose, opening by five valves, two-coated ; outer coat splitting into five parts, inner into ten ; persistent throughout the winter, many seeded.    Seeds flattened, wingless.

The Cassandra often blooms before the snow is gone, but this is not difficult, because the flower buds were formed the summer before, and sometimes in late autumn they show the white tips of the corolla extending beyond the stiff sepals.   So well prepared are they that a few days of sunshine develop the flowers.   As the little bells become perfect in form and texture they droop upon their delicate slender stems and make a most charming wand-like spray.

The common name Leather-leaf is appropriate though not pretty ; Cassandra, the name of the daughter of Priam and Hecuba, is pretty but means nothing. The foliage effect of the plant is good, and this with its early flowers makes it worthy of cultivation.

## MAYFLOWER.  TRAILING ARBUTUS

*Epigæa rèpens.*

*Epigæa*, upon the earth, in reference to its trailing growth.

A prostrate or trailing shrub, with short branches and evergreen and reticulated leaves ; bristly with rusty hairs.  Found
in sandy or rocky woods and ranges from Newfoundland to the
Northwest Territories and southward to Michigan, Kentucky and
Florida.  Frequently forms patches.

Its local distribution is governed largely by the character of
the protecting vegetation, and also to a great extent by the soil ;
thriving best in light sandy or gravelly soil, but sometimes found
in clayey earth.  But one species beside *Epigæa repens* is known,
and that is a native of Japan.

*Leaves.*—Alternate, thick, evergreen, pinnately veined, one to
three inches long, ovate or nearly orbicular, cordate or rounded
at base, mostly glabrous above, hairy beneath, green both sides.
Petioles short, downy, slender.

*Flowers.*—April, May.  Perfect, or diœcious, pink or white,
in axillary clusters at the ends of the branches.  Sepals five,
oblong, persistent, dry, imbricated ; corolla salver-form ; limb
five-lobed ; stamens ten ; filaments slender ; anthers oblong,
awnless, opening lengthwise.  Style slender, its apex forming a
sort of ring and partly adnate to the five little lobes of the
stigma.  Capsule depressed-globular, five-lobed, five-celled, many
seeded.

The flowers appear in early spring, exhaling a rich spicy fragrance ; are dimorphous as to style and stamens, and sub-di-
œcious.

This is the famous Mayflower of Pilgrim devotion,
and although by many supposed to be distinctively a
New England plant, as a matter of fact ranges from
Newfoundland to the borders of Alaska, and from
Florida to Minnesota.  Probably no one would claim
that our Puritan ancestors were especially sensitive to

Trailing Arbutus, *Epigæa repens.*

Leaves 1′ to 3′ long.

the beauties of nature, but this clustered pink sweetness, smiling under the dry leaves of the forest and blooming ere the snow banks had disappeared in the hollows of the wood, touched even them. It must be placed to their credit that they named it well; however much they might have been assisted by the month of the calendar or the ship in the harbor; and it is not worth while to look too closely into the sources of their inspiration. So well have time and literature and imagination worked together that to most of us the Trailing Arbutus seems one of the historic assets of New England.

Sad Mayflower! watched by winter stars,
 And nursed by winter gales,
With petals of the sleeted spars,
 And leaves of frozen sails!

What had she in those dreary hours
 Within her ice-rimmed bay,
In common with the wild-wood flowers,
 The first sweet smiles of May!

Yet, "God be praised" the Pilgrim said,
 Who saw the blossoms peer
Above the brown leaves, dry and dead,
 "Behold our Mayflower here!"

"God wills it; here our rest shall be,
 Our years of wandering o'er,
For us the Mayflower of the sea
 Shall spread her sails no more."

O sacred flowers of faith and hope,
 As sweetly now as then
Ye bloom on many a birchen slope,
 In many a pine-dark glen.

—JOHN G. WHITTIER.

## WINTERGREEN

*Gaulthéria procúmbens.*

*Gaultheria,* named in honor of Gaulthier, a physician and botanist of Canada.

A small evergreen shrub, with stems creeping on or below the surface, and short, erect flowering branches three to five inches high bearing at their summits a crowded group of aromatic leaves. Found in cool, damp woods from Newfoundland to Manitoba and southward to Michigan and Georgia.

*Leaves.* — Alternate, evergreen, pinnately veined, two to two and a half inches long, oval, oblong or ovate, narrowed at the base, serrate with low bristle-tipped teeth, acute at apex ; shining ; when full grown dark shining green. The young leaves are a shining yellow green, often with a reddish tinge and deliciously aromatic.

*Flowers.*—Perfect, white or pinkish, small, bell-like flowers, axillary near the summit of the tiny erect branches. Pedicels with two bractlets. Calyx five-parted, persistent ; corolla urn-shaped,

Wintergreen, *Gaultheria procumbens.* After Britton & Brown.

five-toothed ; stamens ten, included, inserted at the base of the corolla ; filament dilated above the base ; anther-cells each two-awned at the summit, opening by a terminal pore. Ovary five-celled, five-lobed.

*Fruit.*—Capsule is enclosed by the calyx which thickens and turns fleshy so as to appear as a globular red berry ; many seeded.

The leaves of the Wintergreen as they put forth from the top of the upright stem are as near ambrosia as anything our northern climate can produce. The spicy aromatic flavor appears in leaf and stem and fruit, but is most delicate and delicious in the young leaves. One who has sought and eaten them in child-hood may wander far from his native home, may for-get much of his youth; but the picture of the leafy glade of the forest where he picked the Wintergreen, the carpet of shining leaves, the twin red berries hang-ing upon their stems, will never leave him.

The plant has several common names, Tea-berry, Checkerberry, Box-berry, Partridge-berry; the last is also given to *Mitchella repens*. The genus is mountain born and bred; its headquarters are the slopes of the Andes, where nearly one hundred species appear. In North America there is our own *Gaultheria procumbens* and two or three other species.

### RED BEARBERRY. KINNIKINIC

*Arctostáphylos úva-úrsi.*

*Arctostaphylos*, of two Greek words—a bear and a grape. *Uva-ursi* means the same; the fruit is a favorite food of bears.

Evergreen, with numerous trailing and spreading branches; the sterile ones two to three feet long, the fruiting branches shorter; twigs puberulent; mature stems red. Found on rocky hillsides and in dry sandy soils. Ranges from Labrador to Alaska, south to New Jersey, and westward across the continent through Pennsylvania, Illinois, Nebraska, Colorado and Califor-nia. Also found in Europe and Asia. Root large and creep-ing; juices astringent; leaves heavily charged with tannic acid.

*Leaves.*—Alternate, simple, thick, rigid, one-half to an inch long, spatulate, obtuse at apex, margin entire, base narrowed to a short downy petiole. They come out of the bud slightly revo-lute, pale, pubescent; when full grown are dark shining green, glabrous above and beneath. Midvein prominent, secondary veins finely reticulated.

Red Bearberry, *Arctostaphylus uva-ursi.*
Leaves ½′ to 1′ long.

*Flowers.*—May, June.   Perfect, small, nodding, white or pink bells, borne in few-flowered terminal racemes.

*Calyx.*—Reddish, persistent, five-parted ; lobes roundish.

*Corolla.*—Ovoid, constricted at the throat, hairy within, flesh colored or white, and pink tipped ; five-toothed ; teeth recurved, imbricate in bud ; about one-sixth of an inch long.

*Stamens.*—Ten, included ; filaments awl-shaped, hairy ; anthers large, purple, two-awned, opening by terminal pores.

*Pistil.*—Ovary free from calyx, surrounded with three fleshy scales.

*Fruit.*—Berry-like drupe seated in the persistent calyx, globose, red, glabrous, size of a large pea, with mealy insipid pulp and containing five bony nutlets.   They remain on the branches through the winter and serve as food for the wild birds.   July, August.

This low-growing evergreen that trails in thick mats over the inhospitable ground of barren uplands possesses a goodly number of wild-wood names. Very few plants of high degree can claim as many ; among them are Foxberry, Mealberry, Bear's Grape, Barren Myrtle and Bilberry. This too is the Kinnikinic of the western Indians who smoke the leaves and believe the practice secures them from malarial fevers. A curious corruption or an echo of *uva-ursi* exists in a rural name for the plant " universe."

The flowers appear in May, and the urn-shaped, flesh-colored, rosy-mouthed bells are succeeded by astringent red berries, mealy and flavorless ; but which have the virtue of staying on the bushes all winter and no doubt comfort and sustain many a hungry bird and possibly an errant bear. In winter the shining leaves darken to chocolate above, and become reddish beneath. The plant is said to be easily cultivated and will thrive in almost pure sand.

Heather, *Calluna vulgaris.*

*Mairània alpìna*, Alpine or Black Bearberry, is an Alpine species closely allied to *Arctostaphylos uva-ursi*. Its leaves are deciduous, its flowers white, and its drupes black. It seeks the summits of the higher mountains of New England and crosses the continent from Labrador to British Columbia.

## LING. HEATHER

*Callùna vulgàris.*

*Calluna*, Greek, from *kalluno*, to brush or sweep ; brooms being made of it.

Low straggling evergreen forming tufts and mats ; the branches ascending three to fifteen inches. Found along the coast, in sandy and rocky soil, from Newfoundland to New Jersey ; naturalized or adventive from Europe.

*Leaves.*—Opposite, minute, linear, sessile, about one-sixteenth of an inch long, imbricated in four rows, usually two-auricled at the base, three-angled, grooved on the back.

*Flowers.*—July, September. Perfect, bell-like, lilac-pink or white, small, borne in terminal one-sided, dense, spike-like racemes.

*Calyx.*—Sepals four, colored like the petals, oblong, about an eighth of an inch in length, concealing the corolla. Four bracts at the base.

*Corolla.*—Bell-shaped, pink or white, four-parted, slightly twisted, persistent, shorter than the sepals.

*Stamens.*—Eight, filaments short, anthers brown, oblong, attached to the filaments by their backs, opening by a longitudinal slit, each sac with a dorsal reflexed appendage.

*Pistil.*—Ovary depressed-globose, eight-angled ; style slender, exserted.

*Fruit.*—Capsule, four-sided, four-celled, four-valved, few seeded ; seeds ovoid.

*Calluna vulgaris* is believed to be identical with the Scotch Heather, and although thoroughly established through the British maritime provinces and the coast regions of Maine and Massachusetts, is probably of remote European introduction.

# CLETHRÀCEÆ.—WHITE-ALDER FAMILY

## WHITE-ALDER. CLETHRA. SWEET PEPPERBUSH

*Cléthra alnifòlia.*

*Clethra*, of Greek derivation, meaning alder, in reference to the resemblance between its foliage and that of the alder.

Late flowering, three to ten feet high, frequently cultivated. Found in masses, growing in low or wet places, along the banks of streams, sometimes in swamps where the roots are submerged in early spring or after heavy rains. Ranges from Maine to Florida, mostly near the coast.

*Stems.*—Slender, straight, not much branched, at first pale green and stellate-downy, then dull, pale, brownish yellow ; finally dark, yellowish brown.

*Leaves.*—Alternate, simple, pinnately veined, three and a half to four inches long, obovate, narrowed or wedge-shaped at base, sharply serrate at least beyond the middle, acute or obtuse at apex. Midvein and primary veins depressed above, prominent below. They come out of the bud slightly involute, pale green tipped with reddish brown, glabrous and shining above, densely hairy beneath ; when full grown are deep dark green above, dull yellow green beneath. In autumn they turn a bright clear yellow. Petioles half an inch long.

*Flowers.*—August, September. Perfect, white, fragrant, borne in solitary or clustered slender racemes four to six inches long, which are either terminal or appear in the axils of the upper leaves. Central axis and pedicels pubescent, hairs in starry-like groups.

Clethra, *Clethra alnifolia*.
Leaves 3½′ to 4′ long. Racemes 4′ to 6′ long.

*Calyx.*—Five-lobed ; lobes oblong, obtuse, nerved, downy, imbricate in bud, persistent.

*Corolla.*—Petals five, slightly united at the base, white, obovate or oblong, imbricate in bud.

*Stamens.*—Ten ; filaments white, smooth, slender ; anthers sagittate, extrorse in bud but inverted in the flower, two-celled ; cells opening by pores at the base.

*Pistil.*—Ovary superior, three-angled, three-celled, downy ; style slender, exserted, three-cleft at apex ; ovules numerous.

*Fruit.*—Capsules, crowded in stiff, erect racemes, subglobose, three-lobed, three-celled, one-eighth of an inch in diameter ; each sits in persistent calyx, crowned with persistent style.

*Clethra alnifolia,* naturally a swamp plant, takes very kindly to cultivation and possesses a peculiar value in that it shows its long spikes of fragrant white flowers late in summer when other shrubs are largely out of bloom. The buds are arranged upon a long axis, and they begin to open at the base, consequently the flowering period is extended. The blossoms have a delightful spicy fragrance, are full of nectar and are eagerly sought by the bees.

Two peculiarities of the Clethra are of interest to a botanist. One is the character of the hairs found upon the stems and flowers ; under a common magnifying glass these can be seen to be arranged in very perfect stars. The other is the way that the arrow-headed anthers reverse their position ; in the bud they look out from the centre of the flower ; in the blossom they look in.

The bush is a favorite of gardeners because it will grow in poor soil and in shade ; thus possessing a general utility value, at the same time that it has a high personal value.

Lilac, *Syringa vulgaris.*

# OLEÀCEÆ—OLIVE FAMILY

## THE COMMON LILAC

*Syrínga vulgàris.*

*Syringa* from *sirinx*, the native name in Barbary.  Lilac
is from *lilag*, the Persian word for a flower.  The plant was
cultivated in England in 1597.

The year that the Lilac was brought to America is
in doubt, but we know that as early as 1652 it, together
with the Snowball, was the modest ornament of many
a cottage yard.   When the tide of emigration set westward the Lilac was the first flowering plant that
bloomed by the side of the log house in the frontier
settlement.  Brought from New England along with
the household goods, it made one of the Penates of
the new home.  At the time of fullest bloom and
greatest fragrance, women and children came to the
country church with lilac-spray in hand, and the fragrance of the flower mingled with the sound of prayer
and of sacred song.   After a little the White Lilac
made its way into the new settlement, a welcome addition to be sure, but never for one moment a rival in
the hearts of the people of the flower they so deeply
loved.   As the frontier line moved on toward the
setting sun, the Lilac went with it until there came a
day when it reached the region of long, hot, dry

Persian Lilac, *Syringa persica.*

summers, and at this point the Lilac faltered in its march. For this is a native of the highlands; it loves cool, moist summers, and although centuries of cultivation have inured it to many changes, it has not yet learned to flourish in heat and drought. Its native land is somewhat in doubt, but it is accredited in the books to the mountainous region of central Europe from Piedmont to Hungary. It was made known to European botanists by a plant brought from Constantinople to Vienna toward the end of the sixteenth century. Extremely showy, of easy culture and perfectly hardy, the shrub spread rapidly throughout the gardens of Europe. In the survey of the royal gardens of Nonsuch, planted in the time of Henry VIII., there is mentioned a fountain "set round with six lilac trees, which bear no fruit, but only a very pleasant smell."

The well known White Lilac is but a variety of the Common Lilac. The Persian Lilac, *Syringa persica*, is native to the region extending from Caucasus to Afghanistan, and was brought into Europe in 1640. Its flowers are rose-lilac, deliciously fragrant and borne in open thyrses. This appears in a white variety; also in one with cut leaves, *Syringa laciniata*.

A third species, long known, is Josika's Lilac, *Syringa Josikæa*, so named in honor of the Baroness Von Josika, who discovered the plant in Transylvania. It is an upright shrub with spreading branches and purple twigs; the leaves are elliptic-lanceolate, about three inches long, bright shining green above and whitish beneath. The flowers are bluish purple.

Privet, *Ligustrum vulgare.*

Since the discovery of the affinity that exists between the plants of northeastern Asia and northeastern America a number of north China, Japanese and Manchurian lilacs have been brought into this country. From these has been evolved an astonishing number of varieties, double-flowered and single-flowered, in color melting from deep rose to blush and white, or running through all the changes of a lilac which, losing its pink by successive stages, attains at last a cool pure blue. But after all is told, notwithstanding the doubles and the singles, "my heart is in the highlands," and there is no Lilac like the old Lilac—which gave its name to the color.

The French gardeners took up the Lilac upon its first appearance in Europe, and in Paris it has been for a hundred years a favorite forcing plant.

## PRIVET. PRIM

*Ligústrum vulgàre.*

The Privet of old English gardens, a native of both Europe and Asia, has been very generally introduced into this country as a hedge plant. The plant, however, is so well adapted for city life that gardeners are beginning to use it not for a hedge merely, but as an ornamental shrub. Its virtues are many,—it bears a smoky atmosphere with composure and increases in stature ; is remarkably free from insect pests and from disease ; the foliage, a dark handsome green, remains until destroyed by the storms of winter. On the southern shore of Lake Erie it is fresh and bright and

*Forsythia suspensa.*

beautiful well into December ; indeed, it is the last plant to succumb to winter storms ; it just misses being an evergreen. When permitted, it will develop into a shapely bush six to ten feet high.

The flower cluster is a thyrsus, in general effect a diminutive copy of a lilac cluster ; fragrant, with a rather heavy odor. The individual blossom is in shape very like a small, white, lilac blossom ; in fact, the family characters are apparent and the relationship somewhat emphasized. The fruit is a small black berry. Flowers are rarely seen in hedge rows as they appear on new wood and that is usually cut away when the hedges are trimmed. Several species are in cultivation.

### FORSYTHIA

*Forsythia.*

Since the Forsythia was introduced into this country it has ever been counted a permanent and valuable addition to our ornamental shrubs. Its golden bells gleam in the April sunlight and transform the brown bush into a glowing mass of color. The bloom precedes the leaves, but before its splendor has passed the leaves are half grown.

Three forms of the plant appear in our gardens. One, *Forsythia viridissima*, a stiff, upright little bush well covered with yellow bells in the spring but not noticeable at any other time. This is the form first introduced into Europe, and first brought here. The second is distinguished by the long, slender, graceful branches which rise and curve and droop and sometimes trail upon the ground. This appears in the dealers' catalogues under whatsoever name their fancy prompts,— *Forsythia suspensa, Forsythia seiboldi, Forsythia fortunei.* It is good opinion that *Forsythia suspensa* should be regarded as the specific form and *Forsythia seiboldi* and *Forsythia fortunei* varieties. As the three stand side by side in the Arnold Arboretum the difference seems to be mainly a matter of foliage ; in habit they are very much alike. The leaves of the *F. suspensa* group are both simple and trifoliate ; those of *F. viridissima* are always simple. There is an intermediate form,— probably a hybrid, which carries the

Leaf of *Forsythia viridissima.*

leaf of *F. viridissima* slightly modified and whose branches have somewhat the grace of *F. suspensa ;* this is known as *Forsythia intermedia.* A third form is of recent introduction ; it comes from Albania, is named *Forsythia europæa* and is distinguished by small, ovate-lanceolate, quite entire leaves.

Simple Leaf of *Forsythia suspensa.*

As the flower buds are formed the summer before, in order to get the best results the bushes should be pruned some little time after the flowering period. Then every new shoot will be laden with flower buds which will give an excellent account of themselves the following April. If the plants are pruned in winter the flowering spray is very largely removed.

## OLIVE FAMILY

Forsythia was introduced from China about the end of the eighteenth century and first bloomed in England in the gardens of the king at Kensington; it was named in honor of William Forsyth, director of the royal gardens.

# LAURÀCEÆ—LAUREL FAMILY

## SPICE-BUSH. CAROLINA ALLSPICE. BENJAMIN-BUSH

*Bénzoin bénzoin.   Líndera bénzoin.*

Named for John Linder, a Swedish botanist of the eighteenth century.   *Benzoin* refers to its aromatic odor, somewhat resembling that of gum-benzoin.

Tall, well-shaped, four to twelve feet high.   Found in damp woods throughout New England, westward as far as Michigan and Kansas and southward.   Leaves, fruit and bark are aromatic. Easily cultivated.

*Bark.*—Branchlets at first bright green, smooth, later olive green, sometimes pearly gray, finally grayish brown.   Branches are long, tapering and brittle.

*Winter buds.*—Flower and leaf buds distinct.   Leaf buds small, one-eighth of an inch long, acute, solitary.   Flower buds globose, in groups of two to five.

*Leaves.*—Alternate, simple, pinnately veined, three to six inches long, one and one-half to three wide, oval, oblong-oval, or obovate, wedge-shaped at base, entire, abruptly acute, sometimes rounded at apex ; midvein, primary and secondary veins depressed above, prominent beneath.   They come out of the bud revolute, ciliate at margin, pale green ; when full grown are dull dark green above, pale or glaucous green below.   In autumn they turn a clear bright yellow.   Petiole about half an inch long, terete.

*Flowers.* — March, April ; before the leaves.   Polygamo-diœcious, greenish yellow, small, borne in almost sessile umbel-like clusters in the axils of last year's leaves.   Each cluster is made up of secondary clusters of four to six flowers, surrounded by an involucre of four deciduous scales.

Spice-bush, *Benzoin benzoin*, in flower.

Spice-bush, *Benzoin benzoin*, in fruit.
Leaves 3′ to 6′ long.  Fruit ½′ long.

*Calyx.*—Six-parted, yellow ; segments oblong, obtuse, spreading, imbricate in bud.

*Corolla.*—Wanting.

*Stamens.*—Staminate flowers with nine stamens in three rows, the inner filaments one to two-lobed and gland-bearing at base ; anthers two-celled, opening by two uplifted valves. The pistillate flowers with fifteen to eighteen rudiments of stamens in two forms, and a globular ovary, with short thick style.

*Fruit.*—Drupe, oblong, or obovoid, scarlet, shining, half an inch long, borne singly or in clusters of two to five. Flesh thin, yellow, aromatic ; seed large, oblong.

The Spice-bush begins and ends its sylvan year in yellow. The pale blossoms fairly cover the branches in April, coming forth in company with the first maples and early elms. The late October finds it a glow of sunshine from the yellow of its changing leaves.

The shrub is erect and trim and so easily cultivated that it is worthy of a place in yard or lawn ; it is also excellent for roadside planting. The leaves are large and beautiful and the plant is thickly clothed with them when it grows in a damp, shaded location. But where it produces most foliage it bears the least fruit ; like many other plants it develops the one at the expense of the other. The bush is aromatic in bark, fruit, and leaf, and possessed some reputation in times past for medicinal qualities.

There is a notable difference in the yellow color of the flowers on different bushes. Ordinarily, stamens and pistils are produced in separate flowers and these flowers are usually found on different plants. The staminate flowers have not only the yellow calyx but the yellow anthers as well—this brightens them to a marked degree ; the pistillate flowers are duller.

# THYMELEÀCEÆ—MEZEREUM FAMILY

## LEATHERWOOD. MOOSEWOOD

*Dírca palústris.*

*Dirca* is the name of a fountain of ancient Thebes. Leatherwood refers to the tough, fibrous bark.

Much branched, two to six feet high, found mostly in wet, shady places. Ranges from New Brunswick to Virginia and westward to Minnesota and Missouri. Juices acrid, producing nausea.

*Stem.*—Twigs yellowish green, smooth ; bark of mature stems golden brown ; inner bark tough, fibrous, and of great strength.

*Leaves.*—Alternate, simple, two to three inches long, one and one-half wide, oval or obovate, wedge-shaped at base, entire, obtuse at apex ; midvein and primary veins depressed above, prominent beneath. They come out of the bud involute, pale yellow green, downy, when full grown are pale yellow and smooth. In autumn they turn a clear yellow. Petioles short ; the bases conceal the buds of the next season.

*Flowers.*—April, before the leaves. Perfect, light yellow, borne three or four in a cluster, from a bud of three or four dark hairy scales, which form an involucre, from which soon after proceeds a leafy branch.

*Calyx.*—Corolla-like, tubular, funnel-shaped, truncate, the border wavy or obscurely four-toothed.

*Corolla.*—Wanting.

*Stamens.*—Eight, in two rows, inserted on the calyx-tube, above the middle, exserted, the alternate ones longer ; filaments very slender ; anthers large, ovoid.

*Pistil.*—Ovary superior, one-celled, one-ovuled ; style thread-like, exserted ; stigma capitate.

*Fruit.*—Drupe, reddish, oblong-oval, pointed at both ends, containing one large, shining, brown seed.

A marked peculiarity of *Dirca palustris* is the character of its thick porous bark. This is soft and pliant and to outward appearance innocent enough, yet its tenacity and toughness are astonishing. If one wishes to know exactly how this bark behaves he has only to break a stem from the bush and attempt to go away with it. The wood is easily broken, it offers no great resistance ; it is in managing the bark that madness lies. For that bark will neither yield nor give ; it is soft, you can indent it ; it is pliant, will move as you wish ; but it simply will not part. Its fibres are a wonderful example of a natural string, and the Indians who used it for bow strings and fish lines and in the manufacture of baskets well understood its properties.

*Dirca* blooms early and the fruit matures quickly, but is so hidden among the leaves and falls so soon that it easily escapes notice. The books call it a drupe, but that seems a courtesy title only, for the flesh is exceedingly thin and very leathery.

The petioles are swollen at the base sufficiently to conceal and protect the brown velvety buds of next year's leaves. There is no terminal bud, the stem ends in a point ; the bud which will continue next year's growth is axillary. What decorative value the plant has lies chiefly in the yellow green of its foliage, which might be used advantageously to brighten a dark place.

Leatherwood, *Dirca palustris.*

Leaves 2′ to 3′ long.

## DAPHNE. SPURGE LAUREL. MEZERON

*Dáphne mezèreum.*

*Daphne,* the name of the nymph transformed by Apollo into a laurel.

Low, hardy, one to four feet high ; a native of Europe and Asia which has escaped from cultivation and is now found sparingly in Massachusetts and New York, also in Canada.

*Leaves.*—Alternate, simple, thin, three to five inches long, oblong-lanceolate or oblanceolate, narrowed at base, entire, acute at apex, smooth, bright green.    Petioles very short.

*Flowers.*—April, before the leaves.    Perfect, rose-purple, rarely white, very fragrant, borne in sessile clusters of two to five, on the shoots of the preceding year.

*Calyx.*—Salver-shaped ; tube about half an inch long, downy ; lobes four, spreading, about as long as the tube.

*Stamens.*—Eight, in two rows, included, inserted on the calyx-tube ; filaments very short.

*Pistil.*—Ovary superior, one-celled ; style short ; stigma large, capitate.

*Fruit.*—An oblong-oval red drupe, a quarter of an inch long.

*Daphne  mezereum* is widely  distributed,  common over  nearly  the  whole  of  Europe  and  northern  Asia

*Daphne mezere-um*, in flower.

and found in the Arctic regions.   For centuries it has been a favorite garden plant in Europe, but in this country is too rarely seen.   It is of erect habit, one to three feet high, with rigid branches ; in summer each is crowned with a tuft of narrow deciduous leaves.

The flowers appear before the leaves, in numerous clusters of two or three, along the wood of the preceding year, and are

422

Mezeron, *Daphne mezereum.*

Leaves 3′ to 5′ long.

succeeded by large, red, handsome berries. This is a very attractive little shrub, which thrives in any good garden soil. A variety with white flowers is known and there is another which blooms in the autumn.

The bark has medicinal properties, and is now used as one of the ingredients in the compound of Sarsaparilla.

### DAPHNE

*Dáphne cneòrum.*

*Daphne cneorum* is one of the sweetest plants that grows. Its native home is the calcareous soil of the southern Alps; it is also found in Hungary and Transylvania. In those rocky highlands it seems to have touched the feelings and stirred the fancy of the people, and is there known as the Pearl of the Mountains.

The sweet-scented pink blossoms are borne in close terminal clusters on each of the many branches. In outward appearance an individual flower looks not unlike an individual lilac blossom. The apparent corolla is a long tube with a spreading four-lobed border, and is about the size of a lilac corolla. As there is but one of the floral envelopes, the perianth must be called a calyx. Under favorable conditions these blossoms are produced from early spring until late autumn.

The leaves are olive green, persistent, alternate, somewhat crowded on the stem, about three-fourths of an inch long. The roots are fine and threadlike and spread vigorously in a rich sandy soil.

Daphne, *Daphne cneorum.*

Leaves ¾′ to 1′ long.

Like so many evergreens removed from their protecting forests it sunburns in our winters; yet will not endure thick covering. Gardeners recommend a slight sprinkling of straw over it which will give protection from the sun, and yet allow the air to circulate freely.

# ELÆAGNÁCEÆ—OLEASTER FAMILY

## SILVER BERRY. ELÆAGNUS

*Elæágnus argéntea.*

*Elæagnus*, sacred olive ; the Greek name of an entirely different plant.  *Oleaster* is a Latin word, which is interpreted wild olive tree ;  derivation doubtful.

Silvery-scaly, much-branched, six to twelve feet high.  Ranges from Minnesota to South Dakota, Utah, and Montana.  Stoloniferous.

*Stems.*—Young twigs covered with brown scurf, which finally becomes silvery.

*Leaves.*—Alternate, simple, one to four inches long, elliptic to lanceolate, wedge-shaped at base, undulate or entire, acute or obtuse at apex, densely silvery on both sides.  Petioles short.

*Flowers.*—May, July.  Perfect, numerous, borne solitary, or in clusters of two or three, in the axils of the leaves; silvery without, pale yellow within, fragrant.

*Calyx.*—Tube bell-shaped ;  border four-lobed, silvery without, pale yellow within ;  lobes ovate, valvate.

*Corolla.*—Wanting.

*Stamens.*—Four, borne at the throat of the calyx-tube; filaments short.

*Pistil.*—Ovary one-celled ;  style linear, long.

*Fruit.*—Drupe-like, ovoid, silvery, dry and mealy, edible.

The Silver Berry is one of the best of the woody plants with light colored foliage.  Its range is northern, consequently it is rather difficult to cultivate, since subarctic plants seem less tolerant of heat, than plants of more temperate range are of cold. The flowers are whitish without and yellow within, not very beautiful but delightfully fragrant. The chief attraction of the bush is its silvery foliage, whose metallic lustre is due to an immense number of tiny white hairs arranged in starry groups, and so compactly placed that they look like a covering of silver.

Of cultivated species the Garden Elæagnus or Wild Olive Tree, *Elæagnus angustifolia*, a native of southeastern Europe and western Asia, is one of the best. This is believed to be the veritable wild olive of the classic authors. It is often called the Jerusalem Willow; not without reason, for it certainly looks very like a willow. The Portuguese call it the Tree of Paradise, basing their admiration largely upon the rare fragrance of the flowers. These are silvery without and yellow within, borne in the axils of the leaves, two or three together. The silvery whiteness of the foliage renders the plant conspicuous wherever it may be. The reddish oblong fruit, which somewhat resembles a date, is said to be common in the markets of the Levant. In its native land the plant is a tree; here it is both tree and shrub.

The Long-stemmed Elæagnus, *Elæagnus longipes*, has recently been introduced into this country from Japan, and is highly recommended by gardeners. Another excellent species for cultivation is *Elæagnus umbellata*, which in foliage closely resembles *Elæagnus longipes*. The specific difference is found in the fruit. The leaves of both species are a beautiful dark green above and silvery white beneath. There are many other in-

Silver Berry, *Elæagnus argentea.*
Leaves ¾′ to 2′ long.

troduced species under observation in nur eries and experiment stations which will no doubt in time give an excellent account of themselves.

## BUFFALO-BERRY. RABBIT-BERRY

*Lepargyrǽa argéntea. Shephérdia argéntea.*

*Lepargyrǽa,* of Greek derivation, silvery-scaly. *Shepherdia* in honor of John Shepherd, once curator of the Liverpool Botanic Garden.

Slender, growing from six to fifteen feet high, peculiar for the silvery pubescence which covers stem and leaves. Branches are covered with gray bark, twigs silvery white, often terminating in thorns. Ranges from Minnesota to Kansas and Nevada, northward to Manitoba.

*Leaves.*—Opposite, oblong or oblong-lanceolate, one to two and a half inches long, about half an inch wide, somewhat pointed at base, margin entire, obtuse at apex, silvery-stellate-pubescent above and below. Petioles about five-eighths of an inch long.

*Flowers.*—April, May. Small, yellow, diœcious, fascicled at the axils of the leaves of the preceding season. Staminate flowers with a four-parted perianth and eight stamens; filaments short. Pistillate flowers with a four-lobed perianth, bearing an eight-lobed disk at its mouth which nearly closes it; style somewhat exserted.

*Fruit.*—Drupe-like, oval or ovoid, scarlet, sour, about onefourth of an inch long, edible.

The Buffalo-berry is an interesting plant, whose native home is the far west, but which takes very kindly to eastern cultivation. A marked characteristic is the peculiar metallic lustre of its leaves, which is produced by a starry white pubescence that so covers their surfaces as to make them look as if sheathed with silver. This pubescence is sometimes brown, but usually white, and is not confined to the leaves alone, but

Garden Elæagnus, *Elæagnus angustifolia.*

covers pedicels, petioles and twigs as well. This gives the bush a very decorative effect, clothed as it is in grayish white, among the surrounding green.

The flowers appear during April and May in small, compact clusters at the axils of last year's leaves. They are not especially beautiful, but by their numbers they make the plant attractive at the flowering season. The fruit is scarlet or crimson, the size of currants, and often so abundant as to redden the entire bush; in flavor an agreeable acid, just a trifle astringent.

The difficulty in cultivating the plant for its fruit lies in the fact that it is diœcious; both pistillate and staminate bushes are essential to success.

### CANADIAN BUFFALO-BERRY

*Lepargyrǽa canadénsis. Shephérdia canadénsis.*

A thornless shrub, three to eight feet high ; the young shoots brown scurfy, later becoming white ; found on gravelly banks and sterile soils where little else will thrive. Ranges from Newfoundland to Alaska, southward to Maine, New York, Michigan and Utah. Hardy in its native wilds under very adverse conditions ; but difficult to transplant.

*Leaves.*—Opposite, ovate or oval, one to two inches long, pointed at base, margin entire, obtuse at apex. Somewhat silvery-stellate-pubescent above, densely so beneath ; often much of this pubescence is brown. Petioles short, also stellate-pubescent.

*Flowers.*—April, June. Small, diœcious, yellowish, borne in clusters at the axils of last year's leaves. Staminate flowers with a four-parted perianth and eight stamens. Pistillate flowers with a four-lobed perianth, bearing an eight-lobed disk at its mouth which nearly closes it ; style somewhat exserted.

*Fruit.*—Drupe-like, oval, red or yellowish, about a quarter of an inch long, the flesh insipid. July, August.

Buffalo-berry, *Lepargyræa argentea*
Leaves 1′ to 2½′ long.

# LORANTHÀCEÆ—MISTLETOE FAMILY

## AMERICAN MISTLETOE

*Phoradéndron flavéscens.*

*Phoradendron*, tree-thief, because of its parasitic habit.

A many-jointed, much branching, yellowish green shrub, six to twelve inches high, parasitic on the branches of deciduous leaved trees; notably the tupelo and the maples. Of southern range, yet appears in the southern counties of New Jersey, Pennsylvania, Ohio, Indiana and Illinois, as well as throughout the south.

*Leaves.*—Opposite, obscurely three-nerved, three-fourths to one and a half inches long, oval, oblong or obovate, wedge-shaped at base, obtuse at apex, thick, yellow green above and beneath. Petioles short.

*Flowers.*—May, July. Diœcious, in short catkin-like jointed spikes, usually several to each short fleshy bract or scale, and sunk in the joint. Calyx globular, three-lobed; in the staminate flowers a sessile anther is borne on the base of each lobe, transversely two-celled; each cell opening by a pore or slit; in the pistillate flowers the calyx-tube adheres to the ovary; stigma sessile. Berry globose, white, fleshy.

Our American Mistletoe is not the same species as the European Mistletoe, though greatly resembling it. Its range is southern, yet it appears sparingly within our northern lines.

The name Tree-thief is well deserved, for the plant

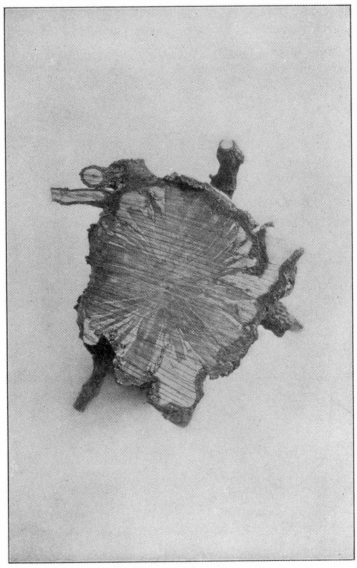

Cross-section of a Branch of a Maple Tree upon which a Mistletoe was established; life size.

At this point the diameter of the branch is doubled. The lighter parts of the wood are Mistletoe, and the branchlets are all Mistletoe.

lives upon juices that it has not elaborated and is supported by root and trunk that are not its own. When a Mistletoe is fairly established upon a branch it eats into the very structure of the wood; the branch is

Fruiting Spray of American Mistletoe.

enlarged at the point of contact—often its diameter is doubled. Our plant has fallen heir to the sentiment and the folk-lore of Europe, and figures to a greater or less extent in our Christmas decorations.

# MYRICÀCEÆ—BAYBERRY FAMILY

## SWEET GALE. DUTCH MYRTLE

*Myrica gàle.*

*Myrica*, of Greek derivation, but of obscure application to this plant.

Erect, three to five feet high, and forming tangled patches; growing in places which are inundated through a part of the year. Ranges from Labrador and Newfoundland through New England and the Middle States as far south as Virginia and along the Great Lakes to Minnesota. Roots long, matted.

*Stems.*—Branches and upper part a rich dark purple, polished and shining. On old and lower stems the outer bark cracks and rolls horizontally, becoming rough, and in color pale.

*Winter buds.*—Leaf buds minute. Staminate aments in the axils of the upper leaves in short, ovoid, pointed buds.

*Leaves.*—Alternate, simple, one and one-half to two and one-half inches long, oblanceolate, wedge-shaped at base, partly entire but serrate toward the apex, which is a little pointed. They come out of the bud revolute, pale green, slightly hairy, dotted with pale amber resinous dots above and below; when full grown are a dull dark green, glabrous above, downy on the veins below and sprinkled with minute, yellow, resinous dots above and below. Fragrant.

*Flowers.*—April. Mostly diœcious, individual flowers solitary under a scale-like bract. Staminate flowers borne in catkins an inch or more long, terminal; scales on short stalks, covered with resinous dots. Stamens three or four; anthers large, opening with four valves. Pistillate catkins are ovoid; scales triangular; stigmas two-lobed, purple, threadlike.

437

Sweet Gale, *Myrica gale*, in fruit.

Sweet Gale, *Myrica gale*, in flower.

*Fruit.*—Nuts in imbricated heads; each nut two-winged by means of two fleshy ovate scales which are attached at the base.

Although a denizen of cold northern swamps, the Sweet Gale is wonderfully tolerant of changed conditions, and will grow on a dry, gravelly, exposed ridge. Like the Bayberry, the leaves are densely covered with small resinous dots which are the source of their fragrance.

## BAYBERRY. WAXBERRY

*Myrica carolinénsis. Mérica cerifera.*

*Myrica*, the ancient name of an unknown shrub.

Stiff, crooked, growing in miniature thickets; found in every variety of situation and soil; from dry, rocky hills to sandy plains, from the border of marshes to the edge of the sea-shore; varies from three to eight feet in height. Ranges near the coast from Nova Scótia to Florida and Alabama; sparingly found on the borders of the Great Lakes.

*Bark.*—Brownish gray, dark and pale irregularly mixed; young stems golden brown, somewhat hairy and covered with resinous dots. Leaf buds minute, globular, reddish brown.

*Leaves.*—Alternate, or irregularly scattered or tufted, simple, two to three and one-half inches long, obovate or oblong, narrowed at the base, entire, or with three or four serrate teeth near the apex which bears a tiny point at the end. They come out of the bud revolute, pale green tinged with red, shining, covered with white woolly hairs, thickly covered with pale amber resinous dots; appear rather late; when full grown are leathery, shining, bright green, resinous, dotted on both sides, fragrant. In autumn they darken to a bronze purple or fall with little change of color.

*Flowers.*—May. Diœcious, individual flowers without calyx or corolla, solitary on a scale-like bract. Staminate flowers expand with the leaves, borne in stiff, erect catkins less than an inch long, on last year's wood; scales roundish, loose; stamens

Bayberry, *Myrica carolinensis.*

Leaves 2′ to 3½′ long.

three to four ; anthers divided.  Pistillate catkins small, erect ; scales oval, pointed ; ovary bearing two awl-shaped stigmas.

*Fruit.*—Dry, waxy berries or drupes, one-eighth of an inch in diameter, borne in clusters of four to nine, on short stalks.   At first green, then blackish, finally pale gray, almost white, consisting of a stone coated with dry wax which has a slightly aromatic taste.   They persist for two or three years.

At the mouths of their rivers, and all along upon the sea, and near many of their creeks and swamps, the myrtle grows, bearing a berry of which they make a hard, brittle wax of a curious green color, which by refining becomes almost transparent.   Of this they make candles, which are never greasy to the touch and do not melt with lying in the hottest weather ; neither does the snuff of these ever offend the sense like that of a tallow candle, but instead of being disagreeable if an accident puts the candle out, it yields a pleasant fragrance to all who are in the room, insomuch that nice people often put them out on purpose to have the incense of the expiring snuff.

—ROBERT BEVERLY in " History of Virginia."

This little shrub when planted along the shore withstands the ocean winds and storms perhaps better than any other plant known in cultivation, and can be made to do good service in establishing plantations by the sea side.   It is now coming largely into use for that purpose, as it affords protection to more attractive specimens which may be planted to leeward. Beginning with a hedge of these Myricas, plantations may often be established where without something of this nature the task would be hopeless. Almost any bleak and barren exposure can be covered in this way and become comparatively beautiful.

—LUCIUS D. DAVIS in " Ornamental Shrubs."

The fruit, leaves, and recent shoots of the Bayberry are fragrant with a balsamic odor which comes from the minute, transparent, resinous dots with which the recent shoots and under surface of the leaves are profusely covered.

Bayberry wax is obtained by boiling the berries in water.   The wax dissolves, rises to the surface and hardens on cooling; it is estimated that about one-third of the weight of the berries consists of wax.   In the early days of the settlement of this country this wax had a commercial value.

In the renaming of plants according to the rules of the American Association of Science, the Bayberry has lost its specific name of *cerifera* and gained that of *carolinensis; cerifera* is now given to a southern tree, the Wax Myrtle.

## SWEET FERN

*Comptònia peregrìna. Mýrica asplenifòlia.*

*Comptonia*, in honor of Rev. Henry Compton, bishop of Oxford.

Fragrant, round-headed, about two feet high, growing on hillsides and in the openings of woods. Ranges from New Brunswick to the Saskatchewan, occurs abundantly throughout New England and the Middle States and on the Appalachian range. Roots long, creeping ; suckers freely.

*Bark.*—Young stems green or yellowish or reddish brown and sprinkled with tiny resinous dots ; the older stems yellowish brown with shining surface, somewhat hairy ; oldest are reddish purple or coppery brown.

*Winter buds.*—Leaf buds minute, globular, hairy. Pistillate aments crowded at the summit of the stems, stiff, erect, one-fourth of an inch long, cylindrical, pale brown, hairy.

*Leaves.*—Alternate, simple, fragrant, three to six inches long, less than an inch wide, pointed, cut into obtuse or pointed lobes by sinuses reaching to the midrib, margin of these lobes entire, somewhat reflexed. They come out of the bud conduplicate, pale green ; when full grown they are dark lustrous green ; midrib depressed above, prominently ridged and pubescent beneath, secondary veins small but also ridged. Petioles short ; stipules half an inch long, auriculate or half heart-shaped, often with a pair of smaller stipules below. Leaves, petioles and stipules densely sprinkled with minute, yellow shining resinous dots.

*Flowers.*—April, May.   Diœcious, often monœcious ; the individual flower without calyx or corolla, solitary under a scale-like bract.   Staminate catkins one-half an inch long, borne at the end of the branch.   Scales kidney or heart-shaped with long point.   Pistillate catkins globular, and bur-like.   Ovary one-celled, surrounded by eight long awl-shaped persistent scales. Stamens two to eight ; filaments somewhat united below ; anthers two-celled.

*Fruit.*—Nut, ovoid-oblong, smooth, shining, surrounded by bristly scales.   September.

This is a plant that looks like a fern and grows like a bush ; fragrant even when flowerless.   An inhabitant of the north, it goes south by way of the mountain tops.   The pleasant spicy fragrance which it diffuses is due to the vast number of minute grains of resin which are profusely sprinkled over leaf and stem.

The long slender pinnatifid leaf certainly suggests a fern ; so that the common name seems significant and appropriate.   The foliage is very attractive ; the plant thrives in sterile soils, flourishes at the seaside, and is certainly worthy of cultivation.

Sweet Fern, *Comptonia peregrina*
Leaves 3′ to 6′ long.

# FAGACEÆ—BEECH FAMILY

## CHINQUAPIN

*Castànea pùmila.*

From Castanea, a town in Thessaly, or from another town of that name in Pontus ; the ancient name of the genus.

A shrub, rarely a tree, growing in dry soil.   Ranges from New Jersey to Florida, from Pennsylvania to Texas.

*Leaves.*—Alternate, simple, pinnately veined, veins very prominent beneath, three to six inches long, wedge-shaped at base, sharply serrate, acute at apex.   They come out of the bud pale green, shining and woolly; when full grown are dark green and smooth above, densely white tomentose beneath.   In autumn they turn a bright, clear yellow.   Petioles short, stout, slightly angled.   Stipules fugitive.

*Flowers.*—June, July : monœcious, fragrant.   Staminate catkins erect or somewhat spreading, three to five inches long, about a quarter of an inch in diameter.   Pistillate flowers are borne in prickly involucres at the base of the staminate catkins.

*Fruit.*—Nut small, ovoid, brown, enclosed in a prickly pointed bur.   Kernel sweet.

The Chinquapin is a bush that in its best estate is twelve feet high, although it fruits at three. The leaves are of the chestnut type, sometimes six inches long, and underneath are densely covered with cream-white woolly hairs.

The burs are small, about an inch in diameter, some-

Chinquapin, *Castanea pumila*.

Leaves 3′ to 6′ long.

times less ; the size varying with the number of enclosed nuts, which frequently are two, though normally
one.   In fruiting this chestnut apparently makes up in
number what it lacks in size ; it is more prolific branch
for branch than our common chestnut *Castanea den-
tata*.   The plant is southern ; it crosses the border
in New Jersey and Pennsylvania, but its chosen home
is upon the slopes of the southern Alleghanies.

# BETULÀCEÆ—BIRCH FAMILY

## HAZEL-NUT. AMERICAN HAZEL

*Córylus americàna.*

The husk of the hazel resembles a cap ; whence its English name from the Saxon *haesle*, a cap ; its botanic name from the Greek, *corys*, a helmet.

Three to six feet high, growing in clumps and thickets in dry or moist light soil at the edge of woods or beside walls. Ranges from Maine and Ontario, south to Florida and Kansas. Suckers freely.

*Stems.*—Young shoots russet-brown, densely hispid-pubescent with pinkish hairs, the twig finally becoming smooth ; stem dark brown.

*Leaves.* — Alternate, simple, pinnately veined, three to six inches long, ovate or broadly oval, heart-shaped or rounded at base, irregularly and somewhat doubly serrate, acute or acuminate at apex. When full grown are dark yellow green, nearly smooth above, pale green and finely tomentose beneath. In autumn they turn a dull yellow. Petioles short, terete, glandular-hairy. Stipules large, acute, toothed, fugitive.

*Flowers.* — March, April, before the leaves ; monœcious. Staminate aments borne in the axils of last year's leaves along the stem toward the end ; when mature are slender, cylindrical, tremulous catkins, three to four inches long, terminal or dependent from lateral foot stalks, solitary or rarely clustered. The flowers, solitary in the axil of each bract, consist of four stamens and two bractlets ; filaments are two-cleft, each fork bearing an anther-sac. Pistillate flowers are little star-like tufts of crimson stigmas, projecting above a short scaly bud of many

Hazel-nut, *Corylus americana.*
Leaves 3′ to 6′ long.

Hazel-nut, *Corylus americana.*
Catkins 3′ to 4′ long.

scales; the outer scales broad and edged with hair, the inner lanceolate hairy and fleshy. Ovary incompletely two-celled, adnate to the calyx; style short, stigmas two, threadlike. These inner scales increase in size with the nut and become the husk, or involucre.

*Fruit.*—Nut, ovoid, or oblong, about half an inch high, slightly flattened; pale brown, roughish at base where it adheres to the involucre. Involucre compressed, composed of two nearly distinct, downy, leaf-like bractlets, fringed on their margins, commonly broader than high, more or less exceeding the nut, becoming grayish brown when mature. Kernel sweet. July, August.

The Hazel-nut responds to the first smile of spring in the same way as the alders. The staminate catkins

hang stiff and rigid throughout the winter, but they relax as soon as warmth comes, develop their pollen, fling it upon the wind and fade away.

The fruit of the American Hazel resembles the filbert of commerce; in flavor it is fully equal, many consider it superior. Certainly the size and quality of the nut is such, that were it worth while, by careful cultivation, and by judicious selection of seedlings, a race of fruit-bearing hazels could be produced whose product would equal if it did not surpass that of the European species. But as it is, our hazel-nuts comfort the squirrels, who gallantly resent intrusion upon their preserves, and delight the children who wish to go nutting. Possibly this wild service is sufficient; who shall say that it is not?

Winter Branch of American Hazel-nut. Catkins scattered along the branch, as well as grouped at the end.

The name of this bush has always expressed the feel-

Beaked Hazel-nut, *Corylus rostrata.*
Leaves 2′ to 4′ long.

ing that the fruit wears a helmet. That which finally forms this leafy helmet or involucre around the nut, exists around the young ovary as a little girdle of two tiny scales with fringed margins.

### BEAKED HAZEL-NUT

*Côrylus rostràta.*

Two to six feet high, growing in clumps and in thickets. Ranges from Nova Scotia to British Columbia, south to Georgia and Tennessee, west to Kansas and Oregon. Suckers freely.

*Stems.*—Recent shoots yellowish brown, densely hairy or smooth ; older branches darker brown and rough, stems dark brown.

*Leaves.*—Alternate, simple, pinnately veined, veins depressed above, very prominent beneath, two to four inches long, ovate, oblong-ovate, or obovate, heart-shaped or rounded at base, irregularly and somewhat doubly serrate, acute or acuminate at apex. When full grown are bright green, hairy or smooth above, paler and sparingly hairy or very downy below. In autumn they turn bright yellow. Petioles short, terete, smooth.

*Flowers.*—April, May, before the leaves ; monœcious. Staminate aments very similar to those of *Corylus americana.* Pistillate flowers cluster in a scaly bud and bristle with crimson threadlike stigmas.

*Fruit.*—Nut ovoid, somewhat compressed, pale brown. Involucre composed of two bristly, hairy bractlets united to the summit and lengthened into a tubular beak about twice the length of the nut ; tube minutely grooved, fringed at the summit, and densely hairy. As the nut ripens the involucre becomes a pale yellow brown varying to a rich reddish brown ; kernel sweet.

The marked character of the Beaked Hazel-nut is the involucre which surrounds the nut. It certainly suggests a narrow long-necked bottle with the nut snugly packed inside. As these involucres mature

Low Birch, *Betula pumila.*
Leaves ½′ to 1½′ long.

with the ripening nut, they show a rare scheme of color which varies from yellows through browns to red; and the dense hairs give a velvety look. The nuts are all terminal, but out of a cluster that seem to start even, two or three outstrip the rest and grow,— the others abort, leaving their little bottle necks to show where they began life.

## LOW BIRCH. BOG BIRCH

*Bétula pùmila. Bétula hùmilis.*

*Betula*, an ancient name of uncertain derivation.

A bog shrub two to fifteen feet high, with twigs densely pubescent at first, afterward glabrous. Ranges from Newfoundland to the Northwest Territories, southward to New Jersey, Ohio and Minnesota.

*Leaves.*—Alternate, simple, pinnately veined, veins very prominent beneath, one-half to an inch and a half long, obovate, broadly oval or orbicular, rounded or wedge-shaped at base, coarsely and irregularly dentate, obtuse or slightly acute at apex. They come out of the bud pale green, densely pubescent, brownish; when full grown are thick, dull green, pubescent or glabrous above, pale green, brownish tomentose or glabrous and very reticulately-veined beneath. Autumnal tint clear, bright yellow. Petioles short. Stipules fugacious.

*Flowers.*—May, June, with the leaves. Monœcious; the flowers of both kinds borne in catkins. Staminate flower consists of a four-toothed perianth, subtended by two bractlets and bearing two stamens; filaments short, deeply two-cleft; each fork bearing an anther-sac. Pistillate flowers two or three in the axil of each bract, the bracts deciduous with the fruits; perianth none; ovary sessile, two-celled; styles two, mostly persistent.

*Fruit.*—Strobile, oblong-cylindric, about three-fourths of an inch long, erect, peduncled. Fruiting bract puberulent or ciliate, three-lobed, lateral lobes shorter than the middle one. Nut small, oblong, rather broader than its wings.

Dwarf Birch, *Betula glandulosa.*
Leaves ¾′ to 1′ long.

Our two low birches undoubtedly owe their humble position in an arborescent genus to their environment. One is a denizen of storm-swept mountain tops; the other dwells in the bogs. Both are excellent shrubs in cultivation, clean cut, slender-stemmed, bright-foliaged.

The birch fruit is an exceedingly interesting form. It appears as a cone made up of a large number of three-lobed scales closely packed one above another, all attached to a central axis. Lying above each one, in fact fitting into a little hollow prepared for it, is a small winged nut, which as the cone matures is released from its protecting scale and permitted to sail away as the wind directs. One has to reconstruct one's idea of a nut to make this minute winged seed seem to be one, but so the botanists call it.

## DWARF BIRCH. GLANDULAR BIRCH

*Bétula glandulòsa.*

A shrub, one to four feet high ; twigs brown, glandular-dotted, not pubescent; found in wet meadows and on mountain sides. Ranges from Newfoundland to Alaska, the higher mountains of New England and northern New York, west to Michigan, Minnesota and in the Rocky Mountains to Colorado ; also in Asia.

*Leaves.*—Alternate, simple, pinnately veined, three-fourths to an inch long, orbicular, oval or obovate, rounded or slightly cordate at base, irregularly dentulate-serrate, rounded at apex. When full grown are very reticulate. Thick, bright green, glabrous above, pale and glandular-dotted beneath. Autumnal tint clear bright yellow. Petioles short. Stipules fugacious.

*Flowers.*—June, July. Monœcious. Staminate aments solitary, about half an inch long ; the flowers, about three together in the axil of each bract, consisting of a membranous four-

458

Speckled Alder, *Alnus incana.*

Leaves 3′ to 5′ long.

toothed scale, two stamens, and subtended by two bractlets; filaments short, deeply two-cleft, each fork bearing an anther-sac. Pistillate aments cylindric, erect, peduncled; flowers two or three in the axil of each bract; the bracts three-lobed, lateral lobes divergent, deciduous with the fruit; ovary sessile, two-celled; styles two.

*Fruit.*—Strobile, oblong-cylindric, a half to an inch long, erect, peduncled, obtuse at base and apex. Fruiting bract glabrous, three-lobed, lateral lobes divergent, rather shorter than the middle one. Nut tiny, oblong, usually narrower than its wings.

A little inland on the North Cape, the dwarf birch makes its appearance; when sheltered attaining a length of about a foot with a stem of a quarter to a third of an inch in diameter, and requiring a generation or two to reach these dimensions. It did not raise its top toward the sun, but crouched to the earth, clinging to it like a creeping plant, to escape being torn away by the force of the winds.

—"Land of the Midnight Sun." PAUL B. DU CHAILLU.

## SPECKLED ALDER. HOARY ALDER

*Álnus incàna.*

*Alnus,* an ancient Latin name derived from the Celtic; in allusion to the growth of these plants along streams.

The common northern brook-side alder, abundant at the edge of streams and in swamps; reaches a height of eight to ten feet. Ranges from Newfoundland to Pennsylvania and west to Nebraska.

*Stems.*—Recent shoots and fruit stalks brown and downy, dotted with orange lenticels, which gradually become ashen or grayish brown. Those stems that are deeply shaded are often deep red or dark green. All are speckled with conspicuous light gray lenticels.

*Leaves.*—Alternate, simple, three to five inches long, two to four inches wide, broad-oval, rounded or cordate at base, doubly or irregularly serrate, acute at apex. They come out of the bud very downy; when full grown are bright dark green above, pale, sometimes pubescent and often whitish, below; midvein and primary veins depressed above, ridged below. In autumn they turn a bright, clear yellow. Petiole short, stout.

Upper Spray, Catkins of *Alnus rugosa.*
Lower Spray, Catkins of *Alnus incana.*

## BIRCH FAMILY

*Flowers.*—March, April, before the leaves. Monœcious. Staminate aments are slender, cylindrical, formed in the previous autumn and hang in stiff and terminal clusters of three, four or five together on short, leafless branches or peduncles; when mature they become two or three inches long. They then consist of a central axis bearing brown or purple scales on short stalks; beneath each scale are three similar ones, each containing a three to five-lobed calyx-cup, with three to five stamens from whose anthers issues a cloud of pollen. The pistillate aments are also formed during the previous autumn; are one-fourth to three-eighths of an inch long, clustered usually in threes; when mature they become deep purple, bristling with scarlet styles. The position of these pistillate aments is a distinguishing character of the plant; they look upward.

*Fruit.*—Strobile of woody scales grown together, composed of the pistillate ament enlarged and hardened. Its scales have become woody and each protects a wingless seed-vessel which is one-celled and one-seeded. October.

The Speckled Alder is easily distinguished by the brilliant, polished, reddish green color of its stem-bark, and the size, regularity, impressed reticulations and the downy under-surface of the leaves. The branchlets, at the time of flowering, are dependent, and the long, pendulous, sterile catkins are thus terminal, while the ovate fertile ones are on shorter, lateral foot-stalks just above. This is the reverse of the arrangement of the catkins in the Common Alder in which the fertile aments, being erect, seem terminal, while the sterile ones bend down. The flowers of the alder are among the earliest harbingers of spring.

—George H. Emerson.

The earliest familiar token of the coming season is the expansion of the stiff catkins of the alder into soft drooping tresses. These are so sensitive, that if you pluck them at almost any time during the winter, a few days' sunshine will make them open in a vase of water, and thus they eagerly yield to every moment of April warmth. The blossom of the birch is more delicate, that of the willow more showy, but the alders come first. They cluster and dance everywhere upon the bare bough above the watercourses; the blackness of the buds is softened into rich brown and yellow, and as this graceful creature thus comes waving into the spring, it is pleasant to remember that the Norse Eddas fabled the first woman to have been named Embla, because she was created from an alder-bough.

—Thomas Wentworth Higginson.

The Speckled Alder crowds as near to the water's edge as it is possible to grow and then leans over as if hoping to go farther. In midsummer its dark green foliage fringes the northern watercourses and forms a natural hedge. Its strong matted roots give stability to the soft banks and keep the stream within bounds.

Throughout the winter many of the slender stems bear terminal clusters of stiff, cylindrical, uncompromising catkins which were formed the previous autumn, and which without protection withstand the assaults of frost and snow and ice. These catkins like the flower buds of the Silver Maple respond to the first breath of spring; the stiff fibres relax, the scales open, and clusters of long plumy tassels, royal in their purple and gold, droop from every twig and branchlet. The catkin-scales are a deep brownish purple and the anthers bear immense quantities of pollen which when mature fall in clouds of golden dust.

The fruit looks like a small pine cone; each woody scale protects a woody seed-vessel which in time is released as the little cone opens. The seeds are discharged in the autumn and early winter, but the cones persist until the following summer.

Lenticels appear more or less abundantly upon all exogenous woody stems; upon many quite as abundantly as upon the *Alnus incana*, but in comparison with *Alnus rugosa* it bears a great many, whence the common name Speckled Alder.

In very young shoots of shrubs and trees there are stomata or breathing pores which occur abundantly in the epidermis, serving for the admission of air and the escape of moisture; while the green layer of the bark answers the same purpose that is served by the green pulp of the leaf. As the shoot matures, the stomata are succeeded by lenticels or spongy places, which scattered over the external surface of the bark serve to admit air to the interior of the stem. They appear at first as roundish spots of very small size, but as the shoot on which they occur increases in diameter the lenticels enlarge.

Gardeners think well of the Speckled Alder. It thrives in wet places, its leaves push out early, making it attractive when other shrubs are bare. Alders transplant well, are natural adjuncts to a slow-flowing stream, and appropriate companions for the willows.

## SMOOTH ALDER

*Álnus rugòsa. Álnus serrulàta.*

The common alder of the southern states ; often found grow-ing with the northern form, frequently forming thickets at the edge of streams and in swamps ; usually six to twelve feet high. Roots large, strong, throwing up many suckers ; bark astringent. Ranges from Massachusetts to Florida, westward to southern Minnesota and Texas.

*Stems.*—When young, brownish green, smooth or downy ; older stems grayish green or dark green.

*Leaves.*—Alternate, simple, two and one-half to four and one-half inches long, broad, oval or obovate, rounded or wedge-shaped at base, minutely serrulate and undulate, rounded or with a blunt point at apex. They come out of the bud pale green and downy ; when full grown are thick, dark green, gla-brous and shining above, paler green, and usually pubescent on the veins beneath. Small, resinous dots appear on young leaves. Midvein and primary veins depressed above, ridged beneath ; downy when leaves are young, afterward downy at the axils only. The autumnal tint is yellow touched with red. Stipules broad-

Smooth Alder, *Alnus rugosa*
Leaves 2½′ to 4½′ long.

oval, rounded and enclose the unexpanded leaf. Petioles short, scaly, dotted.

*Flowers.*—March, April, before the leaves. Monœcious. The staminate aments are slender, cylindrical; formed in the previous autumn, and hang stiff, in terminal clusters of three, four or five together on short leafless branches or peduncles. When mature they become drooping tassels loaded with pollen. They consist of a central axis, which bears brown or purple, heart-shaped or rhomboidal scales on short stalks. Beneath each scale are three smaller ones, each containing a three to five-lobed calyx-cup, with three to five stamens from whose anthers issues a cloud of pollen. The pistillate aments are also formed during the previous autumn ; are one-fourth to three-eighths of an inch long, clustered usually in threes ; when mature they become deep purple bristling with scarlet styles. The pistillate aments look forward and downward.

*Fruit.*—Strobile of woody scales grown together, composed of the pistillate ament enlarged and hardened. Its scales have become woody, and each protects a wingless seed-vessel which is one-celled and one-seeded. October.

The two Alders, *Alnus incana* and *Alnus rugosa*, are very much alike in habit ; they enter upon the heritage of the spring-time like two Dromios,—not one before the other. The change that the first warm days in early spring produce in the Alder bushes is very gratifying to one who is listening for the call of the robin and the song of the bluebird. It gives an added appreciation of the power of sunshine.

Through all the black days of winter, assailed by ice and snow and cutting winds, the stiff, ungainly catkins have held their place untouched and unchanged ; but when " The hounds of spring are on winter's traces," and the March sun has warmed the earth a little, the dark, stiff cylinders begin to soften and lengthen,— gradually they lose the purple and take on the yellow, the color of many stamens and much pollen. The su-

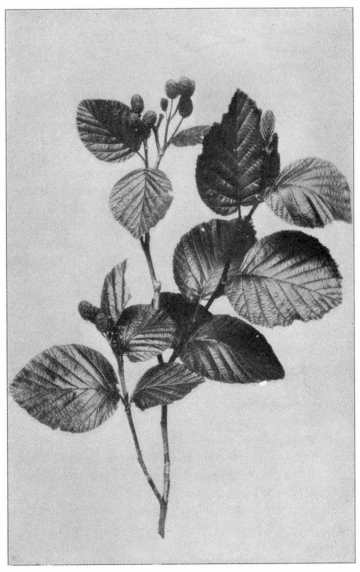

Mountain Alder, *Alnus alnobetula.*

Leaves 2′ to 5′ long.

preme moment is brief; for a day or two they are the perfection of grace and beauty, then the axis weakens and becomes lax; they cast their pollen to the winds and pass away.

### GREEN OR MOUNTAIN ALDER

*Álnus alnobétula. Álnus víridis.*

A shrub of northern habitat, ranging from Newfoundland to Alaska, southward to Michigan and New York, and down to the Carolinas along the Alleghany mountains. It attains a height of six feet; the young foliage is glutinous and more or less pubescent.

The leaves are broadly oval or ovate, two to five inches long, minutely incised-serrulate, rounded or slightly heart-shaped at base, acute or obtuse at apex. When mature dark green and glabrous above, paler and pubescent on the veins beneath. The next year's buds are found well grown in the axils of the leaves in July, are three-eighths of an inch long, reddish, slender, pointed,—quite a marked summer character of the bush.

For an alder it is a late bloomer, the catkins expanding with the leaves. The staminate are very large and handsome and quite abundant. Like all our alders the sterile catkins are exposed during the winter; but the small fertile ones are protected within large brown buds, thus differing from the two better known species, which have all the catkins exposed during the winter. The fruiting cones are one-half to five-eighths of an inch long; the nut is winged. The bush gives the impression of lush, strong growth; possibly it is no greener than its neighbors.

# SALICÀCEÆ—WILLOW FAMILY

## THE WILLOW

*Sàlix.*

" The role that the willow plays in the north temperate zone
is to a certain extent analogous to that of the Eucalyptus in sub-
tropical regions in that it flourishes in wet ground and absorbs
and transpires immense quantities of water.   But while most of the
species occur spontaneously in wet ground or along the banks of
streams, the willow may be cultivated in various locations."
                          —" Cyclopedia of American Horticulture."

*Salix* is a genus of diœcious trees and shrubs, characterized by simple leaves, much longer than broad ;
buds with a single bud scale ; flowers in lax scaly catkins ; each flower subtended by a single entire scale
and nearly or quite destitute of a perianth.   The staminate flowers have one, two, or three to six stamens ;
the pistillate flowers consist of a single pistil, composed
of two carpels and two more or less divided stigmas.
At maturity the pistil opens, setting free the small
seeds which are furnished with long silky down.

The willow hybridizes naturally, and it is this which
makes the determination of the different species so
difficult.   The most that an amateur can hope to do is
to know the marked types.   Yet we at least can know

Pussy Willow, *Salix discolor*.

Catkins on the stem at the left are pistillate; those on the stems at the right are staminate

Balsam Willow, *Salix balsamifera.*

Leaves 2′ to 4′ long.

the shrubs that follow the watercourses, that shine and gleam in the winter sunshine; telling by their brilliancy in February that spring is coming. One species, the Pussy Willow, meets the goddess half way, with its furry catkins creeping out from under their protecting scales.

In order really to know a willow, it should be seen leafless, when bursting into bloom, in full leaf, and in fruit; and as each species is diœcious, both pistillate and staminate forms should be studied. This can be done satisfactorily only in plantations definitely arranged for the purpose.

## BALSAM WILLOW

*Sàlix balsamìfera.*

An irregularly branching shrub four to ten feet high, often growing in clumps; found in open swamps and low lands. Ranges across the continent from Labrador to Manitoba, southward to Maine and Minnesota; has been found in the White Mountains.

*Stems.*—Bark of old stems smooth, dull gray, branches olive; recent twigs reddish brown, shining.

*Leaves.*—Alternate, simple, very reticulate-veined, two to four inches long, elliptic, ovate or obovate, rounded or heart-shaped at base, glandular-serrate, acute or obtuse at apex. When full grown are dark green, glabrous above, pale green or glaucous beneath. Petioles long and slender. Stipules minute or none.

*Flowers.*—May. Catkins borne on slender leafy peduncles, expanding with the leaves. The staminate densely-flowered, silky, cylindric, about an inch long; scales rosy, anthers at first reddish, becoming deep yellow. The pistillate catkin in fruit, becomes very lax, two to three inches long. Fruiting capsule very narrow, acute, not quite a quarter of an inch long.

Broad-leaved Willow, *Salix glaucophylla.*
Leaves 3′ to 4′ long.

With the fertile capsules opening and coalescing into huge soft balls of whitest wool almost hiding the beautiful red and maroon leaves of the growing tips, it (*Salix balsamifera*) is certainly the handsomest willow I ever saw.

—Torrey Botanic Club.

The Balsam Willow assumes its finest form in open swampy grounds, where it is exposed to the sun on all sides; under these conditions it forms large broad clumps. When in flower, it is one of the most beautiful of willows.

### BROAD-LEAVED WILLOW

*Sàlix glaucophýlla.*

Two to six feet high, found on the sandy shores of the Great Lakes. Ranges from Illinois and Michigan to Wisconsin; occasionally found somewhat back from the shore.

*Stems.*—Light gray; shoots and twigs smooth and yellowish.

*Leaves.*—Alternate, simple, three to four inches long, nearly two inches wide, ovate, obovate or oblong-lanceolate, rounded or acute at base, serrulate with gland-tipped teeth, short acuminate at apex; when full grown dark green and shining above, glaucous beneath. Petioles stout, a quarter to half an inch long. Stipules large, persistent, auriculate, dentate.

*Flowers.*—April. Catkins expanding before the leaves; very silky, leafy-bracted at base. Staminate about two inches long; pistillate often three inches long in fruit. Bracts densely white, downy, persistent. Fruiting capsules long-beaked from an ovoid base, acute, about a quarter of an inch long.

*Salix glaucophylla* lives by choice on the sand ridges and dunes of the Great Lakes, and is especially abundant on the shore of Lake Michigan. Every plant that lives among shifting sands develops its own means of self-protection; and this is usually either a peculiarly fibrous root or an extremely vital stem. This willow depends largely upon its stem, which takes root

Heart-leaved Willow, *Salix cordata.*

readily at the nodes and quickly sends shoots into the air while the roots take hold of the sand. In this way extensive clumps are formed which crown the low hills.

## HEART-LEAVED WILLOW. DIAMOND WILLOW

*Sàlix cordàta.*

Five to twelve feet high, growing in clumps in wet soil and along the watercourses. Range from New Brunswick to British Columbia, south to Virginia, Missouri and California. Hybridizes freely.

*Stems.*—Brown or on older stems ashy gray or yellowish brown. Branches greenish brown, or bright green or bronze yellow, smooth ; recent shoots yellowish, or pale green, or downy white.

*Leaves.*—Alternate, simple, oblong, lanceolate, narrowed, obtuse or heart-shaped at base, sharply serrulate with glandular teeth, acuminate at apex. They come out of the bud conduplicate, downy ; when full grown, green on both sides or paler beneath. Petioles half to three-fourths of an inch long. Stipules oblique, serrulate, usually large and persistent.

*Flowers.*—April, May. Catkins expanding before the leaves. Staminate about three-fourths of an inch long, about three stamens to a flower ; the pistillate one to two inches long in fruit. Fruiting capsule narrowly-ovoid, acute.

This shrub of the watercourses grows in characteristic clumps which are formed by the development of sprouts from the original plant. In the larger clumps the first or oldest stem is usually dead or dying ; its vitality sapped by the gradual formation of the stems about it. These stems are smooth and flexible, but tough as well, and are sometimes used in basket work.

The name Diamond Willow, which seems to be local to the west, is due to the peculiar way in which the bark cracks on the older stems.

The plant loves water and prefers locations that are frequently submerged. The roots form large tangled masses on the sides of streams, and are much larger than the stems proceeding from them.

## FURRY WILLOW

*Sàlix adenophýlla.*

Straggling shrub, three to seven feet high, found in the sand of lake shores and river banks. Ranges from Labrador to Ontario, southward to Pennsylvania and Illinois. Hybridizes with *Salix cordata.*

*Leaves.* — Alternate, simple, one to two inches long, ovate, heart-shaped or rounded at base, finely serrulate with gland-tipped teeth, acute, or short acuminate, or the lower obtuse at apex. When young densely silky tomentose, the silky hairs falling away from the leaves when old. Petioles stout, short, dilated at the base, densely silky. Stipules ovate-cordate, obtuse serrulate, persistent, densely silky.

*Flowers.*—April, May. Catkins expanding with the leaves, leafy-bracted at base, densely flowered. Staminate less than an inch long ; pistillate about two inches long in fruit. Fruiting capsule small, ovoid-conic, acute.

The Furry Willow like the Broad-leaved Willow loves the sands. Its common name is not misapplied, for the growing shoot is densely covered — twigs, petioles, stipules, and opening leaves—with a furry white coat of woolly hairs which give a grayish green aspect to the bush. In order to hold its own in adverse conditions, its stems are endowed with an intense vitality, and where the sand drifts over and buries one, it there takes root and sends up other stems and so forms clumps which in time cover the barren waste.

The economic value of those plants of the shore that

bind down the moving sand is very great; for the protection of valuable property from the encroachment of shifting dunes is becoming an important problem in many parts of our country. The regions most affected are the Atlantic and Pacific coasts, the lake district of Michigan, and the Columbia river district of Washington and Oregon. Very successful work in holding the sand by grass and shrub planting has already been done by the State of Massachusetts on a portion of Cape Cod known as the Province Lands.

### BOG WILLOW

*Sàlix myrtilloìdes.*

Erect, slender, glabrous, twigs pale brown, attains the height of one to three feet, found in bogs. Ranges from New Brunswick and Quebec to British Columbia, south to New Jersey and Iowa; also in northern Europe.

*Leaves.*—Alternate, simple, an inch to an inch and a half long, oblong, elliptic or somewhat obovate, mostly narrowed at the base, entire, slightly revolute, obtuse or acute at the apex, when full grown bright green above, pale or glaucous beneath. Petioles short.

*Flowers.*—April, May. Catkins expanding with the leaves, leafy-bracted at the base, rather dense. The staminate rather less than an inch long; the pistillate rather more. Fruiting capsule oblong-conic, obtuse, glabrous, about one-fourth of an inch long.

### PRAIRIE WILLOW

*Sàlix hùmilis.*

Upland grayish willow, three to eight feet high, varying much in size and shape of leaves; found on dry soil. Ranges from Nova Scotia to Ontario, south to North Carolina and Tennessee, and west to Nebraska. Hybridizes with *Salix discolor*.

Bog Willow, *Salix myrtilloides.*
Leaves 1′ to 1½′ long.

Prairie Willow, *Salix humilis.*

Leaves 2' to 4' long.

Dwarf Gray Willow, *Salix tristis.*
Leaves ¾′ to 2′ long.

*Leaves.*—Alternate, simple, two to four inches long, lanceolate or oblong-lanceolate, the lowest obovate, acute at both ends, or obtuse at the apex, sparingly denticulate, and slightly revolute. When full grown dark green, dull, puberulent or glabrous above, glaucous and somewhat downy beneath. Petioles short. Stipules obliquely lanceolate or ovate.

*Flowers.*—April, May. Catkins unfolding much before the leaves, sessile, short, dense, recurved. Fruiting capsule narrowly conic.

## SAGE WILLOW. DWARF GRAY WILLOW

*Sàlix trìstis.*

A shrub with slender tufted stems, one to two feet high, found in dry soils. Ranges from Maine to Minnesota, southward to Florida and Tennessee.

*Leaves.*—Simple, alternate, three-fourths to two inches long, three-eighths to half an inch wide, oblanceolate or linear-oblong, wedge-shaped or rounded at base, obscurely undulate and revolute, acute or obtuse at apex. When full grown thick, very reticulate, yellow-green above, densely woolly, pubescent beneath. Petioles short. Stipules minute, deciduous.

*Flowers.*—March, April. Catkins expanding with the leaves, small, globular or oval, sessile, densely flowered; bracts persistent. Fruiting capsule about a quarter of an inch long.

The Dwarf Gray Willow obtains its common name from the grayish or olive green effect which the white pubescence of the under surface of the leaves gives to the bush. The slender stems are erect and the leaves stand up well so that much of the under surface is seen. This willow is rather common and is to be looked for on sandy plains and on the borders of hillside thickets.

Hoary Willow, *Salix candida.*

Leaves 2′ to 4′ long.

## HOARY WILLOW

*Sàlix cándida.*

A dwarf whitish shrub, two to five feet high, the older twigs red or purple, the younger densely white-tomentose; found in bogs.  Ranges from Labrador to the Northwest Territories, southward to New Jersey, Iowa and Montana.

*Leaves.*—Alternate, simple, very reticulate-veined, two to four inches long, narrow-oblong or oblong-lanceolate, acute at both ends, or sometimes obtuse at apex, margin obscurely repand-denticulate or entire, slightly revolute; midvein white above, very prominent beneath.  When young densely covered above and beneath with white tomentum; when full grown are thick, green, loosely tomentose or glabrate above, densely tomentose beneath.  Petioles short.  Stipules ovate, very revolute, semi-persistent, green above, white tomentose beneath, about equalling the petioles in length.

*Flowers.*—May.  Catkins expanding before the leaves, densely-flowered, cylindric; the staminate about an inch long; the pistillate one to two inches long in fruit; bracts hairy, persistent.  Fruiting capsule ovoid-conic, acute, one-fourth of an inch long.

On its native bogs the Hoary Willow appears as a sprawling, straggling bush, and in the garden where it readily makes itself at home it never becomes attractive in habit; yet it is always conspicuous, for its leaves as well as the young shoots are densely covered with a white weblike wool, which marks it among its companions.  The blossoms are extremely beautiful, as what color they have is emphasized by the white down about them.  The staminate catkins are at first tipped by red anthers which give a rosy color to the whole; later as the pollen escapes they become bright yellow. The pistillate catkins are hoary at first, later the pistils are tipped by dark red stigmas.  Its flowers and its foliage entitle it to a place in any garden.

Silky Willow, *Salix sericea.*
Leaves 2′ to 4′ long.

## SILKY WILLOW

*Sàlix serìcea.*

A tall willow with slender, purplish, slightly downy twigs, found in swamps and along streams.  Ranges from Maine to Michigan and southward to Virginia.

*Leaves.*—Alternate, simple, two to four inches long, oblong or lanceolate, narrowed or obtuse at base, serrate with glandular teeth, acuminate at apex.  The young leaves are densely silky-pubescent, when full grown they become glabrous, dark green above, paler and somewhat glaucous beneath.  Petioles short, sometimes glandular.  Stipules narrow, deciduous.

*Flowers.*—May.  Catkins expanding before the leaves, sessile, usually with a few leafy bracts at the base, densely flowered. The staminate about an inch long; the pistillate in fruit nearly two inches.  Fruiting capsule small, ovoid-oblong, obtuse, pubescent.

*Salix petiolaris,* the Slender Willow, is very similar in general appearance to *Salix sericea,* only it is of a more delicate type.  Its home is the swamps, its range more northern and western.  The flowers appear in May.

Slender Willow, *Salix petiolaris.*

Leaves 2′ to 4′ long.

# EMPETRÀCEÆ—CROWBERRY FAMILY

## BLACK CROWBERRY. HEATHBERRY

### *Émpetrum nìgrum.*

*Empetrum*, upon a rock; an ancient Greek name, referring to the growth of these plants in rocky places.

A low, evergreen, much branched shrub, forming dense masses
in rocky places; branches closely beset with oblong-linear leaves.
Found on the high mountains of New England and New York,
on the northern shore of Lake Superior, on the banks of the
Saguenay, along the international boundary to British Columbia
and in Alaska. Bark reddish brown; that of branches rough-
ened with the remains of petioles.

*Leaves.*—Simple, thickly scattered or whorled, three-eighths
to one-fourth of an inch long, oblong-linear, entire, edges so
revolute that they meet at the back; bright green. The leaves
are jointed to short pulvini, channelled on the lower side by the
revolute margins.

*Flowers.*—Summer; diœcious, inconspicuous, solitary in the
axils of the upper leaves, purplish. Sepals and petals mostly
three. Staminate flowers with three stamens, the anthers introrse. Pistillate flowers with a globose, six to nine-celled ovary
and a short thick style with six to nine-toothed segments.

*Fruit.*—Berry-like drupe, globular, black, seated in the calyx
and crowned with remnants of the stigma. Flesh juicy, slightly
acid, not unpleasant, containing six to nine seed-like nutlets.
Eaten by birds.

The Black Crowberry is a subarctic plant, found in
America, Europe, and Asia, which seeks the cold thin

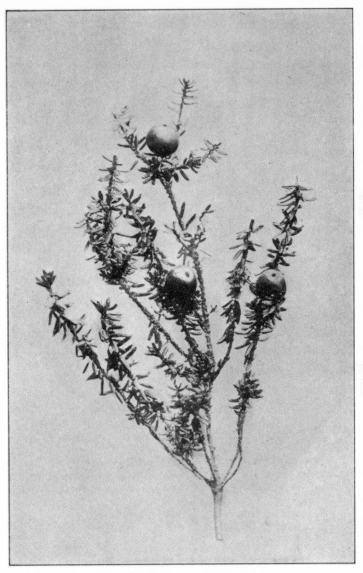

Black Crowberry, *Empetrum nigrum.*

Leaves ⅜′ to ¼′ long.

air of mountain tops and is not very particular as to wet or dry if only its home is cool enough. It lifts its branches three to four inches. It curves the edges of its tiny leaves backward until they meet, in order to lessen evaporation. Although it lives amid moisture, it must economize its store because so much of the time the temperature is below freezing, when no leafy plant can work. Linnæus records that it lives on the mountains of Lapland, where other plants perish with the cold. Just over the mountains from Sitka it is found in great abundance ; also in Scotland it abounds, and is there the badge of the clan McLean. Cattle do not browse upon its foliage. The berries are rather pleasant to the taste; are eaten by man and eagerly sought by the arctic birds. The plant will grow in northern gardens, but requires a moist, boggy soil and a shaded situation. The seeds are slow to germinate, and the seedlings are slow in growth.

Among its many local names are Crakeberry, Crow-pea, Black-berried Heath, Wire Ling, and the Canadians call the berries Camerines.

In a certain way an arctic plant appeals to the imagination more than other plants. It has by variation and natural selection, through ages unmeasured and immeasurable, adapted itself to the harshest climate that this earth produces ; and looking out toward the limit of everlasting snow, it apparently calls life good and the earth enjoyable. Most of the distinctively arctic plants encircle the globe with little or no variation in form. There seems to be no distinct Asia, Europe, or America, along those higher latitudes ; all are alike in their pitiless cold.

Conrad's Broom Crowberry, *Corema conradii.*

Leaves $\frac{3}{16}'$ to $\frac{1}{4}'$ long.

## CONRAD'S BROOM CROWBERRY

*Corèma conrâdii.*

*Corema,* broom, in allusion to the bushy habit.

Low, evergreen, much branched, densely leafy; growing in large patches on rocky or sandy soil. Ranges from Newfoundland to New Jersey, near the coast; has been reported on the Shawangunk mountains in Ulster County, New York.

*Leaves.*—Crowded, narrowly-linear, three-sixteenths to one-fourth of an inch long. Thickened, obtuse, bright green, puberulent when young, glabrous when mature. Leaves are jointed to short pulvini, and channelled on the lower side by the meeting of the revolute margins.

*Flowers.*—April, May. Diœcious, small, borne in terminal heads. Corolla none. Staminate flowers with three or four long exserted purple stamens with brown anthers, occasionally with a rudimentary or a perfect pistil. The pistillate flowers have a two to five-celled ovary, a slender two to five-cleft style, and are almost concealed by the upper leaves.

*Fruit.*—A very small, globose drupe, nearly dry, usually with three nutlets.

This is one of the rarest of North American shrubs; as a matter of fact it does not look very much like a shrub, but wanders over the ground as if it were a Christmas-green; and in the regions where it abides will often densely cover vast sandy stretches.

The leaf is apparently linear, but what has really happened is that each half of the leaf has turned itself backward until the opposite edges have met, and the channel at the back shows the line of union. The well known Labrador Tea turns the edges of its leaves backward, but they do not meet; in the Crowberries the edges meet.

# TAXÀCEÆ—YEW FAMILY

## AMERICAN YEW. GROUND HEMLOCK

*Táxus canadénsis.*

*Taxus*, said to be derived from *taxon*, the Greek word for bow ; on account of the use made of the wood of the European species.

Low, straggling, evergreen bush, one to four feet high, with wide-spreading branches, common in northern woods, often covering large areas of low, moist, shaded land. Ranges from Newfoundland to Lake Winnipeg and southward to Virginia and Iowa.

*Leaves.* — Evergreen, alternate, linear, sharp-pointed ; disposed in a subspiral and appearing two-ranked by the twisting of the short compressed petioles. Dark green above, somewhat paler beneath.

*Flowers.*—Diœcious or monœcious, solitary, axillary. Staminate-flowers have four to eight stamens collected into a globular head. Pistillate flower consists of an erect ovule on a ring-like disk, which enlarges as the fruit matures and becomes a bright red fleshy cup, and nearly encloses the ripe seed.

*Fruit.*—Nut-like seed ; nearly enclosed in a red, pulpy, berry-like cup.

In various parts of the western counties of Massachusetts occurs a humble, almost prostrate evergreen, conspicuous for the rich and deep green of its foliage. It is the American Yew.

—GEORGE H. EMERSON.

The Yew at first sight looks like a seedling hemlock that perhaps has not fared quite well, and is inclined to

493

American Yew, *Taxus canadensis*.

straggle and sprawl. Closer observation, however, shows a larger, stronger leaf of darker green, with its under surface a decided yellow green where the hemlock is glaucous or a pale blue green. Then, too, the Yew leaves break ranks much oftener than those of the hemlock.

In midsummer one may find, scattered and solitary, sometimes at the end of a branch and sometimes at the side, a beautiful translucent red berry, the size of a currant or a trifle larger. When one examines this red berry it is found to have a cylindrical opening down to its very heart, an opening an eighth of an inch across: and at its heart, surrounded by all this red pulpy protection, is a dark brown bony seed. In taste this berry is sweetish and rather insipid.

This little bush can be made very useful in covering moist ground which is well shaded. To plant it in sunny locations is a mistake, it languishes if it does not die.

### EUROPEAN YEW

*Táxus baccàta.*

The Yew-tree of the poet and the historian is *Taxus baccata*, a plant of wide distribution, found throughout Europe, save in the extreme north, and also native to western Asia. It is not native in America, nor has the type ever really flourished here, though hybrids are abundant and fairly hardy. A few well grown Yew-trees are reported in New York, Philadelphia, and Baltimore where they were planted fully one hundred years ago; but the climate of New England is too severe for them, and they will grow there only if well

European Yew, *Taxus baccata.*

protected; which being translated means that they will not grow satisfactorily at all.

In England the tree usually attains the height of thirty to forty feet with low spreading branches.

The English custom of planting Yews in churchyards has never been satisfactorily explained, nor is it understood why the trees should be so closely connected with superstitions relating to ghosts and fairies. Possibly both may be of druidical origin. The fact that the leaves are poisonous may account for some of it; certainly the belief that the tree was noxious was very widespread.

Shakespeare did not omit the Yew in his pictures of English life, for the Clown in "Twelfth Night" lamenting the indifference of his lady-love sings,—

> My shroud of white, stuck all with yew,
> O, prepare it !

and in "Macbeth" among the contents of the witches' caldron are,—

> * * * slips of yew
> Slivered in the moon's eclipse.

In "Richard II." Scroop says to the fallen king,—

> Thy very beadsmen learn to bend their bows
> Of double-fatal yew against thy state.

Two garden forms of *Taxus baccata* are extensively planted under the names of Irish Yew, *Taxus baccata fastigiata*, and Japanese Yew, *Taxus baccata adpressa*. Other forms appear, but these two are the most distinct and the most interesting.

The Irish Yew is distinguished by its erect branches, which produce a narrow, compact, cylindrical form, sometimes broadened at the apex in old age. The leaves are not two-ranked, but are spirally arranged, of large size and very dark green. The fruit is oblong, not spherical. All the individuals of this variety are pistillate. The original plant was found during the last century on the mountains of County Fermanagh, Ireland, and planted in the garden at Florence Court, a seat of the Earl of Enniskillen. It is a very beautiful plant, particularly in autumn, when the dark green branches are studded with scarlet berries.

The Japanese Yew was long believed to be of eastern origin, but is now generally supposed to be a seedling of *Taxus baccata*. It is, however, fair to say that all horticulturists do not assent to this opinion. It is characterized by its numerous spreading branches and its very short, broad leaves. It, too, is pistillate and is rather hardier than other allied forms. Varieties with yellow and with variegated leaves have also been developed.

# GLOSSARY OF BOTANICAL TERMS

ACHENE.—A dry one-seeded indehiscent fruit with the pericarp fitting close-ly around the seed.

ACUMINATE.—Gradually tapering to the apex.

ACUTE.—Sharp pointed.

ADNATE.—An organ adhering to a contiguous differing one.

ADVENTIVE.—Not indigenous, but apparently becoming naturalized.

ALTERNATE.—Applied to that form of leaf arrangement in which only one leaf occurs at a node.

AMENT.—A spike of imperfect flowers subtended by scarious bracts, as in willows. Used interchangeably with catkin.

ANTHER.—The part of the stamen which contains the pollen.

APETALOUS.—Without a corolla.

APPRESSED.—Lying close and flat against.

ARBORESCENT.—Tree-like in size and habit of growth.

ARIL.—A fleshy organ growing at the point of attachment of a seed to the pericarp.

ASCENDING.—Growing obliquely upward, or upcurved.

AWL-SHAPED.—Narrow upward from the base to a slender or rigid point.

AWN.—A slender bristle-like organ.

AXIL.—The point on the stem immediately above the base of the leaf.

AXIS.—The central line of any organ or support of a group of organs; a stem.

AXILLARY.—Borne at, or pertaining to, an axil.

BACCATE.—Berry-like; pulpy.

BEAKED.—Ending in a prolonged tip.

BERRY.—A fruit whose pericarp is wholly pulpy.

BIENNIAL.—Of two years' duration.

BIPINNATE.—Twice pinnate.

BLADE.—The flat expanded part of a leaf.

BRACT.—A leaf, usually small, subtending a flower or flower-cluster.

BRACTEATE.—Having bracts.

BRACTLET.—A secondary bract, borne on a pedicel, or immediately beneath a flower; sometimes applied to minute bracts.

BUD.—The rudimentary state of a stem or branch; an unexpanded flower.

BUSH.—A low and much branched shrub. Used interchangeably with shrub.

CÆSPITOSE.—Growing in tufts.

CALYX.—The outer whorl of floral envelopes.

CAMPANULATE.—Bell-shaped.

CANESCENT.—With gray, or hoary, fine pubescence.

CAPITATE.—Shaped like a head.

CAPSULE.—A dry fruit of two carpels or more, usually opening by valves or teeth.

CARPEL.—A simple pistil, or one member of a compound pistil.

CATKIN.—An ament.

CELL.—A cavity of an anther or ovary.

CILIATE.—Provided with marginal hairs.

CLEFT.—Cut about halfway to the midvein.

COHERE.—The union of one organ with another.

COMPOUND.—Composed of two or more similar parts united into a whole.

CONDUPLICATE.—Folded lengthwise.

COMPOUND-LEAF.—One divided into separate leaflets.

CONNATE.—Similar organs more or less united.

CONNECTIVE.—The end of the filament between the anther-sacs.

CONVOLUTE.—Rolled around or rolled up longitudinally.

CORDATE.—Heart-shaped.

CORIACEOUS.—Leathery in texture.

COROLLA.—The inner whorl of floral envelopes.

CORYMB.—A convex or flat-topped flower-cluster, of the racemose type; the outer flowers unfold first.

CORYMBOSE.—Corymb-like.

CRENATE.—Scalloped; with rounded teeth.

CRENULATE.—Diminutive of crenate.

CROSS-FERTILIZATION.—When the stigma of one flower receives the pollen of a different flower.

CUNEATE.—Wedge-shaped.

CUSPIDATE.—Sharp pointed.

CYME.—A convex or flat flower cluster in which the central flowers unfold first.

CYMOSE.—Cyme-like; arranged in cymes.

DECIDUOUS.—Falling away at the close of the growing period.

DECUMBENT.—Stems or branches in an inclined position, but the end ascending.

DECURRENT.—Applied to the prolongation of an organ, or part of an organ running along the sides of another.

DEHISCENT.—Opening to emit the contents.

DELTOID.—Broadly triangular, like the Greek letter *delta*.

DENTATE.—Toothed, especially with outwardly projecting teeth.

DENTICULATE.—Diminutive of dentate.

DETERMINATE.—Limited or defined.

DIFFUSE.—Loosely spreading.

DIŒCIOUS.—Bearing staminate flowers on one plant and pistillate ones on another of the same species.

DISK.—An enlargement or prolongation of the receptacle of a flower around the base of the pistil.

DISTINCT.—Separate from each other.

DRUPE.—A simple fruit, usually indehiscent, with fleshy exocarp and bony endocarp.

DRUPELET.—Diminutive of drupe.

ECHINATE.—Prickly.

ELLIPTIC.—With the outline of an ellipse ; oval.

EMARGINATE.—Notched at the apex.

ENDOCARP.—The inner layer of the pericarp.

ENTIRE.—Without divisions, lobes or teeth. Used largely with regard to margins of leaves, petals and sepals.

EPIGYNOUS.—Adnate to or borne on the upper part of the ovary.

EROSE.—Irregularly margined, as if gnawed.

EVERGREEN.—Bearing green leaves throughout the year.

EXFOLIATING.—Peeling off in layers.

EXOCARP.—The outer layer of the pericarp.

EXSERTED.—Prolonged past surrounding organs.

EXSTRORSE.—Facing outward.

FALCATE.—Scythe-shaped.

FERTILE.—Capable of producing fruit.

FERTILIZATION.—The union which takes place when the contents of the pollen cell enters the ovule.

FILAMENT.—The stalk of an anther, the two forming a stamen ; any thread-like body.

FOLLICLE.—A fruit consisting of a simple carpel opening by the ventral suture.

FRUIT.—The seed-bearing product of a plant, simple, compound, or aggregated, of whatever form.

FUGACIOUS.—Falling soon after development.

FUGITIVE.—Plants not native, but occurring here and there without direct evidence of being established.

# GLOSSARY OF BOTANICAL TERMS

GAMOPETALOUS.—With petals more or less united.

GAMOSEPALOUS.—With sepals more or less united.

GENUS, *pl.* GENERA.—When several species resemble each other so distinctly that their general characters indicate relationship, the group is called a genus.

GIBBOUS.—Enlarged or swollen on one side.

GLABRATE.—Nearly, or without hairs.

GLABROUS.—Devoid of hairs.

GLAND.—A secreting cell or group of cells; any protuberance or appendage having the appearance of such an organ.

GLANDULAR.—Bearing glands or gland-like.

GLAUCOUS.—Covered with a bluish-white or white bloom; hoary.

GLOBOSE.—Globular, spherical or nearly so.

HABIT.—The general appearance of a plant.

HABITAT.—A plant's natural place of growth.

HEART-SHAPED.—As applied to leaves it means a sinus more or less deep where the petiole meets the blade.

HEAD.—A dense round cluster of sessile or nearly sessile flowers.

HIRSUTE.—With rather coarse stiff hairs.

HISPID.—With stiff bristly hairs.

HISPIDULOUS.—Diminutive of hispid.

HOARY.—Grayish-white with fine close pubescence.

HYBRID.—A cross between two species.

HYPOGYNOUS.—Situated on the receptacle, beneath the ovary and free from it and from the calyx.

IMBRICATE.—Overlapping.

INCISED.—Cut into sharp lobes.

INCLUDED.—Not projecting beyond surrounding parts.

INDEFINITE.—In regard to stamens; inconstant in number or very numerous.

INDIGENOUS.—Native and original to the country.

INDEHISCENT.—Not opening to emit the contents.

INFERIOR.—Lower or below. Inferior ovary, one that is adnate to the calyx.

INFLATED.—Bladdery.

INFLORESCENCE.—The flowering part of a plant, and especially its mode of arrangement.

INFRA.—In composition, below; *infrastipular*, below the stipules.

INSERTED.—Attached to or growing out of.

INTER OR INTRA.—In composition, between.

INTERNODE.—Portion of stem or branch between two successive nodes.

INTRORSE.—Facing inward; applied to stamens that face toward the pistil.

INVOLUCRE.—A whorl of bracts, subtending a flower or flower cluster.

INVOLUTE.—Rolled inward.

IRREGULAR (FLOWER).—Showing inequality in the size, form or union of its similar parts.

KEEL.—A central dorsal ridge; the two anterior united petals of a papilionaceous flower.

LANCEOLATE.—Considerably longer than broad, tapering upward from the middle or below.

LEAFLET.—One of the divisions of a compound leaf.

LEGUME.—A simple dry fruit, dehiscent along both sutures; is the characteristic fruit of the Pea Family.

LIMB.—The expanded part of a petal, sepal or gamopetalous corolla.

LINEAR.—Elongated, narrow with sides nearly parallel.

LIP.—Each of the upper and lower divisions of a bilabiate corolla or calyx.

LOBE.—Any segment of an organ.

LOBED.—Divided into lobes.

MESOCARP.—The middle layer of a pericarp.

MIDVEIN.—The central vein or rib of a leaf or other organ.

MONADELPHOUS.—Applied to stamens united by their filaments into a tube or column.

MONŒCIOUS.—With stamens and pistils in separate flowers on the same plant.

MUCRONATE.—With a short, sharp, abrupt tip.

NAKED.—Lacking organs or parts which are normally present in related species.

NATURALIZED.—Plants not indigenous to the region, but so firmly established as to have become part of the flora.

NODE.—The place upon a stem which normally bears a leaf or a whorl of leaves.

NUT.—An indehiscent one-seeded fruit with a hard or bony pericarp.

NUTLET.—Diminutive of nut.

OBCONIC.—Inversely cone-shaped.

OBCORDATE.—Inversely heart-shaped.

OBLANCEOLATE.—Inversely lanceolate.

OBLONG.—Considerably longer than broad and with nearly parallel sides.

OBOVATE.—Inversely ovate.

OBTUSE.—Blunt or rounded at the end.

ORBICULAR.—Approximately circular.

OVAL.—Broadly elliptical.

OVARY.—The ovule-bearing part of the pistil.

OVATE.—In outline like a longitudinal section of a hen's egg.

OVULE.—The rudimentary seed.

# GLOSSARY OF BOTANICAL TERMS

PALMATE.—Diverging radiately like the fingers.

PANICLE.—A compound flower-cluster of the racemose type.

PANICULATE.—Borne in or resembling a panicle.

PAPILIONACEOUS.—Term applied to the irregular flowers of the Pea Family.

PAPPUS.—Down, as that on the seeds of some plants.

PARASITIC.—Growing upon other plants and absorbing their juices.

PEDICEL.—The stem of a flower in a flower cluster.

PEDUNCLE.—Stem of a flower, or of a flower cluster.

PERFECT.—Flowers with both stamens and pistils.

PERIANTH.—The floral envelopes,—sepals and petals, considered collectively.

PERICARP.—The walls of the ripened ovary, the part of the fruit that encloses the seeds.

PERIGYNOUS.—Borne on the perianth, around the ovary.

PERSISTENT.—Organs remaining attached to those bearing them, after the growing period.

PETAL.—One of the leaves of the corolla.

PETALOID.—Similar to petals.

PETIOLE.—The stem of the leaf.

PINNA, *pl.* PINNÆ.—A primary division of a pinnately compound leaf.

PINNATE.—Leaves divided into leaflets or segments on each side of a common axis.

PISTIL.—The seed-bearing organ of the flower, consisting of the ovary, stigma, and style when present.

PISTILLATE.—With pistils, usually in the sense of without stamens.

PLICATE.—Folded into plaits like a fan.

POD.—Any dry and dehiscent fruit.

POLLEN.—The fertilizing grains contained in the anther.

POLYGAMOUS.—Applied to plants which produce staminate, pistillate and perfect flowers all on the same plant.

POME.—The fleshy fruit of the Apple Family.

PRICKLE.—A slender sharp outgrowth from the bark of a plant

PROCUMBENT.—Trailing or lying on the ground.

PUBESCENT.—Downy, covered with soft hairs.

PUNCTATE.—With translucent dots or pits.

PYRIFORM.—Pear-shaped.

RACEME.—A simple inflorescence of pedicelled flowers upon a common, more or less elongated axis.

RACEMOSE.—Resembling a raceme.

RACHIS.—The axis of a compound leaf or of a spike or raceme.

RADIANT.—With the marginal flowers enlarged.

RECEPTACLE.—The end of the flower stalk bearing the floral organs.

# GLOSSARY OF BOTANICAL TERMS

REFLEXED.—Bent backward abruptly.

REGULAR.—Uniform in shape or structure.

REPAND.—With slightly uneven and somewhat sinuate margin.

RETICULATE.—In the form of a network.

RETRORSE.—Facing outward; applied to stamens that face away from the pistil.

REVOLUTE.—Rolled backwards.

ROOT.—The underground part of a plant which supplies it with nourishment.

ROSTRATE.—Having a beak.

ROTATE.—With a flat, circular, corolla limb.

SALVER-SHAPED.—Having a slender tube abruptly expanded into a flat limb or border.

SAMARA.—An indehiscent winged fruit.

SEED.—The ripened ovule.

SECUND.—Borne along one side of an axis.

SEGMENT.—A division of a leaf or fruit.

SEPAL.—One of the leaves of a calyx.

SERRATE.—With teeth projecting forward.

SERRULATE.—Diminutive of serrate.

SESSILE.—Without a stalk.

SILKY.—Covered with close-pressed, soft and straight pubescence.

SIMPLE.—As applied to leaves; in one piece, undivided.

SINUATE.—With wavy margins.

SINUS.—The cleft between two lobes.

SMOOTH.—Without irregularities; destitute of hairs.

SPORT.—A sudden variation from the normal type of structure.

SPECIES.—A group of individuals which possess in common such a number of constant characters that they may be considered to be descended from a common ancestral form.

SPIKE.—An elongated flower cluster.

SPINE.—A sharp woody or rigid outgrowth from the stem.

SPRAY.—The ultimate division of a branch.

STAMEN.—The organ of the flower that bears the pollen.

STANDARD.—The upper dilated petal of a papilionaceous corolla.

STELLATE.—Star-like.

STERILE.—Unproductive; as a flower without pistil or stamen without anther.

STIGMA.—The summit or side of the pistil to which the pollen grains become attached.

STIPULATE.—With stipules.

STIPULE.—Appendages at the base of a petiole, often adnate to it.

STOLON.—A runner ; or any basal branch that is disposed to root.

STOMATA, *pl.*—The transpiring orifices in the epidermis of plants.

STRIATE.—Marked with fine longitudinal lines or ridges.

STROBILE.—A compact flower cluster with large scales, concealing the flowers. When this cluster matures and contains seeds, it is still called a strobile.

STYLE.—The attenuated portion of the pistil connecting the stigma and the ovary.

SUTURE.—A line of splitting or opening.

TERETE.—Circular in cross section.

THROAT.—The part between the proper tube and the limb of a gamopetalous corolla.

THYRSE, OR THYRSUS.—A compact panicle.

TOMENTOSE.—Covered with tomentum.

TOMENTUM.—Dense, matted wool-like hairs.

TRUNCATE.—Ending abruptly as if cut off.

UMBEL.—A flower-cluster, flat or convex, with all the pedicels arising from the same point.

UMBELLATE.—Borne in umbels ; resembling an umbel.

UNDULATE.—With wavy margins.

VALVATE.—Meeting by the margins ; not overlapping.

VEIN.—One of the branches of the woody portion of leaves or other organs.

VEINLET.—A branch of a vein.

VENATION.—Arrangement of veins.

VERNATION.—The arrangement of leaves in the bud.

VERSATILE.—Applied to an anther attached at or near its middle to the filament.

VILLOUS.—Covered with long, soft, shaggy hairs.

WHORL.—A group of three or more similar organs at a node.

WING.—Any thin expansion bordering or surrounding an organ. The lateral petal of a papilionaceous corolla.

WOOLLY.—Clothed with long and matted hairs.

# GLOSSARY OF LATIN SPECIFIC EPITHETS

THIS glossary provides explanations of all the Latin specific epithets used in this book except those which are latinizations of persons' names. Adjectives are listed under the masculine ending only. For an explanation of the grammatical nature of the specific epithets, see the Appendix of Nomenclatural Changes, p. 513.

acerifolius—maple-leaved
acuminatus—gradually tapering to the apex
adenophyllus—glandular-leaved
adpressus—pressed together
africanus—African
albus—white
allegheniensis—growing in the Alleghanies
alnifolius—alder-leaved
alnobetula—alder-birch
alpinus—alpine
altamaha—named for the Alatamaha (Altamaha) River in Georgia
alternifolius—alternate-leaved
americanus—American
amomum—an old generic name, now applied to a genus of tropical gingers
amygdalus—almond

anagyroides—resembling *Anagyris* (a certain legume)
angustifolius—narrow-leaved
apiifolius—celery-leaved.
aquifolius—holly-leaved
arboreus—tree-like
arborescens—becoming tree-like
arbutifolius—arbutus-leaved
argenteus—silvery
argutus—sharp
arkansanus—belonging to Arkansas
aromaticus—aromatic
asperifolius—rough-leaved
asplenifolius—leaf like that of a fern
atrococcus—black-berried
atropurpureus—dark-purple
aureus—golden

baccatus—berry-like

balsamifer—bearing balsam
blandus—smooth, charming
botryapium—grape-pear
brachycera—short-horned
buxifolius—box-leaved

cæspitosus (cespitosus) — tufted, growing in mats
calendulaceus—yellow
calyculatus—having bracts around the calyx, imitating an outer calyx
canadensis—Canadian
candidus—white, hoary
candidissimus—most white
canescens—downy with white hairs
caninus—canine
carolinensis—Carolinian
carolinus—Carolinian
cassinoides—resembling *Ilex cassine*, a kind of holly known as "yaupon."
catharticus—purging
cerifer—producing wax
ciliatus—marginally fringed with hairs
circinatus—coiled
cneorum—ancient generic name
coccineus—scarlet
cœruleus—blue
colchicus—from Colchis
commutatus—changeable
concinnus—neat
conspicuus—observed, showy
copallinus—producing gum-copal
cordatus—heart-shaped
cornutus—horned
coronarius—wearing a crown
corymbosus—corymbed
cotinoides—resembling *Cotinus*

crispus—crisped; from the leaf margin
crux-andreæ—St. Andrew's-cross
cuneatus—wedge-shaped
cynosbati—dogberry

densiflorus—densely-flowered
denudatus—naked, denuded, i. e., glabrous
dentatus—toothed
discolor—two-colored
dumosus—found in thickets, bushy

editorum—of the highlands
edulis—edible
ericoides—heath-like

fascicularis—tufted, or in fascicles
fastigiatus—with branches erect and parallel
fertilis—fruitful
flagellaris—like a whiplash
flavescens—yellow
floridus—flowering
floribundus—with abundant flowers
frangula—an old generic name, referring to the brittleness of the plant
frondosus—leafy
fruticosus—bushy

gale—myrtle bush
gallicus—French
glaber—without hairs
glandulosus—glandular
glaucus—whitish
glaucophyllus—white-leaved
glaucophylloides—resembling *Salix glaucophylla*
gracilis—slender

grandiflorus—great-flowered
grœnlandicus—of Greenland
grossularia—old generic name of
    the gooseberry

halimifolius—halimus-leaved
hirtellus—bristly
hirtus—rough
hispidulus—with minute hairs
hispidus—with rigid hairs
humilis—low
hypericoides—hypericum-like
hypnoides—narcotic

idaeus—of Mt. Ida
incanus—hoary
indicus—Indian, i. e., of the East
    Indies
inodorus—odorless
involucratus—involucred

japonicus—Japanese

laciniatus—cut into pointed lobes
lacustris—by a lake
lævifolius—smooth-leaved
lævigatus—smooth
lagenarius—bottle-like
lanceolatus—lance-shaped
lantanus—an old generic name,
    meaning flexible
lantanoides—lantana-like
latifolius—broad-leaved
ligustrinus—flexible, privet-leaved
liliflorus—lily-flowered
longipes—long-stemmed
lonicera—resembling honey-
    suckle, *Lonicera*
lucidus—shining
luteus—yellow

macrostachyus—great-spiked

marianus—of Maryland
maritimus—growing by the sea
maximus—greatest
melanocarpus—black-fruited
microcarpus—small-fruited
microphyllus—small-leaved
mollis—soft
montanus—of the mountains
mucronatus—bristle-pointed
myrtilloides—myrtle-like

nanus—dwarf
niger—black
nigrobaccus—blackberry
nitidus—shining
nudus—bare, naked
nudiflorus—flowers without
    leaves

occidentalis—western
oblongifolius—oblong-leaved
obovatus—obovate
odoratus—fragrant
oligocarpus—few-fruited
opulifolius—opulus-leaved
opulus—an old generic name for
    some viburnums
orbiculatus—round
ovatus—ovate
oxyacanthoides—like *Oxyacan-*
    *thus* (hawthorn); literally,
    sharp-spined
oxycoccos—sour-berry

pallidus—pale
palustris—growing in the marsh
paniculatus—bearing panicles
parviflorus—small-flowered
parvifolius—small-leaved
paucifolius—few-leaved
pedicellaris—having pedicels
pensylvanicus—Pennsylvanian

pentagynus—five-fruited
peregrinus—spreading, wandering
petiolaris—petiolate
pilosus—downy, with silky hairs
plenus—full, i. e., double-flowered
polifolius—with leaves like *Polium* (a mint)
ponticus—of Pontus (in Asia Minor)
procumbens—trailing
prolificus—prolific
prostratus—prostrate
prunifolius—plum-leaved
pubens—with hairs
pubescens—with hairs
pumilus—low, dwarf
purpureus—purple
pyracantha—fire-thorn
pyrifolius—with leaves of the pear

racemosus—bearing racemes
radicans—striking root
recognitus—restudied
repens—creeping
resinosus—resinous
rigidus—stiff
roseus—rose-colored
rostratus—beaked
rotundifolius—round-leaved
rubiginosus—rusty
ruber—red
rugosus—wrinkled

salicifolius—willow-leaved
sanguineus—bloody
sativus—planted
scaber—rough to the touch
sericeus—silky
serotinus—late

serpyllifolius—wild-thyme-leaved
serrulatus—serrate or serrulate
setiger—bristly
simplicissimus—most simple, i. e., unbranched
spathulatus—spatula-like
spicatus—with spikes, i. e., with spikes of flowers
spinosus—spiny
stamineus—with prominent stamens
stans—erect, standing firm
stellatus—star-like
sterilis—sterile
stolonifer—producing stolons
strictus—very straight
strigosus—with appressed, stiff hairs
suberectus—suberect, i. e., somewhat erect
subsericeus—somewhat silky
suspensus—drooping
susquehanæ—of the Susquehanna region
symphoricarpos—snowberry
syrticola—sand-dweller

tataricus—Tartarian
taxifolius—yew-leaved
tenellus—delicate
tetrandrus—with four stamens
tinctorius—capable of coloring
tomentosus—woolly, covered with tomentum
toxicodendron—an old generic name; literally, poison-tree
trifoliatus—three-leaved
trifidus—three-cleft
trilobatus—three-lobed
trilobus—three-lobed
tripetalus—three-petaled
tristis—sad

typhinus—like a cat-tail

uliginosus—growing in swamps or wet places
umbellatus—bearing umbels
uva-crispa—old name for the gooseberry (berry with curled or crisped hair [on the leaves])
uva-ursi—an old generic name; literally, bear-berry

vacillans—unstable, unsteady
venenatus—poisonous

vernix—varnish
verticillatus—whorled
villosus—downy
virginianus—Virginian
virginicus—Virginian
viridis—green
viscosus—clammy
vitis-idaea—an old generic name for the bilberry; literally, grape vine of Mt. Ida
vulgaris—common

xylosteum—an old generic name; literally, bone-wood

# APPENDIX

## NOMENCLATURAL CHANGES

*Compiled by Edward G. Voss*

WE are all aware of, and often puzzled by, the changes which sometimes occur in the supposedly stable scientific names for plants. In introducing a table which shows current names for the plants described by Harriet L. Keeler in *Our Northern Shrubs*, it should be helpful to explain some of the reasons why names change as well as how this table was developed.

It might be well at the beginning to remind the reader that the scientific name of a species consists of two words: the first is the name of the *genus* to which the plant belongs and the second is the *specific epithet*. While the generic name in such a binomial is always a noun (and is singular), the specific epithet may be another noun in apposition (e. g., as in *Magnolia kobus*, *Ribes grossularia*); a noun in the Latin genitive (possessive) case, either singular or plural (e. g., in *Spiraea vanhouttei*, *Rubus randii*, *Leucothoë editorum*); or—most frequently—an adjective, in which case it must agree with the generic name according to rules for Latin declension (e. g., *Rubus odoratus*, *Magnolia acuminata*, *Hypericum prolificum*, *Calluna vulgaris*, *Ligustrum vulgare*). For a glossary of specific epithets, see pages 507–511.

Since the publication of Miss Keeler's book in 1903, many of the shrubs have come to be known under names differing from those used by her. Major agreements on internationally accepted rules of nomenclature for scientific names were reached at the Third International Botanical Congress, held in Vienna in 1905—two years after this book. The present International Code of Botanical Nomenclature has resulted from additional modification of the rules, most notably in 1930 and 1950. Although changes in the Code have now become less numerous and far-reaching than formerly, amendments and refinements have been made at all International Botanical Congresses, the most recent of which was in 1964.

Changes in scientific names may, therefore, result from changes in the International Code itself, as botanists have worked toward greater uniformity and stability in applying the basic principles: (1) that each kind of plant, when classified in a particular way, may have only one correct scientific name; (2) that this name must be the earliest (beginning with Linnaeus) for which a description was published under certain rules regarding proper publication and formation of names; (3) that identical names may not be used for different kinds of plants; and (4) that each name is ideally standardized by designation of a particular representative or *type* to which the name always applies and by which application of the name can be interpreted (e. g., if two names applied to two different species are treated as synonyms, it is basically because the *types* of the two names are judged to belong to the same species).

This appendix is not the place for a further discussion or elaboration of the Code of Nomenclature, but it should be pointed out that such rules exist—developed to some degree of refinement—and that therefore names change when it is discovered that they have been incorrectly applied or misinterpreted (as determined by their types), that a valid name was published earlier than one in current use, or that some other rule was violated by a certain usage. Ultimately, nomenclatural changes of these sorts should become much reduced in number as stability is reached; indeed, modern manuals are much more in agreement regarding the names they use than are many of their predecessors.

Another reason for some changes of name is that they follow changes in scientific understanding of the plants themselves. Improvements in classification which result from increased knowledge about the relationships among plants—and consequent changes of name if required—will always occur as long as botany is an active and growing science. The International Code can specify the procedures for coining new names and for rejecting or applying old ones, but it cannot legislate such things as the judgment of a taxonomist concerning the breadth of variation allowable within a species, or the desirability of recognizing a certain plant as different enough to require treatment as a distinct entity, with a distinct name. Competent taxonomists may not always be in agreement on the classification of some plants. For example, whether the characteristics which distinguish the choke-berries (treated by Keeler in the genus *Aronia*) from the pear (genus *Pyrus*) are of sufficient magnitude to justify segregation into a different genus is a matter of taxonomic judgment. If the red chokeberry is classified in the genus *Pyrus*, its correct name is *Pyrus arbutifolia*; if it is classified in a separate genus for the choke-berries, its correct name is *Aronia arbutifolia*.

Another example of judgment often involves whether American plants are significantly different from their European relatives. Miss Keeler treated the highbush-cranberry under the name *Viburnum opulus*, applying it to both European and North American plants; and she applied the name *Lonicera coerulea* to a fly honeysuckle of both North America and the Old World. Botanists who recognize the American plants of these groups to be specifically distinct from the Old World ones use the names *Viburnum trilobum* and *Lonicera villosa*, respectively. In cases such as these, the list which follows calls attention to the broader concept in the original book by listing the name for the American plant and explaining "(American plants)." On the other hand, there are cases such as the mountain cranberry, *Vaccinium vitis-idaea*, of which American plants are now generally recognized as differing from the European only at the level of a "variety" (*Vaccinium vitis-idaea* var. *minus*); the same binomial, however, applies to the species in the inclusive sense and hence it has not seemed necessary in the list below to give only the American variety.

Several provisions, helpful in achieving uniformity in treatment of scientific names, were added to the International Code in 1950 and have been followed in the list below even when they require slight deviations from the style of the manuals generally followed in the list (both of which were in press before 1950):

(1) Specific and varietal epithets in the genitive, when based on the name of a man, uniformly end in *i* following another vowel, *y*, or *er*; and in *ii* following any other consonant.

(2) All specific and varietal epithets begin with a small

initial letter. (The Code allows one, if he wishes, to capitalize an epithet which is based on a person's name or which is an old plant name in apposition, but the recommendation is to do as Keeler did—to decapitalize all such epithets.)

(3) The variety of a species which includes the type of that species is designated by repetition of the specific epithet (e. g., *Rhus radicans* var. *radicans*); it can thus be easily contrasted with the one or more other varieties (e. g., *Rhus radicans* var. *rydbergii*) which together comprise the species. This means that when no variety is indicated, typical or otherwise, no restriction to any one variety is necessarily implied in the use of a binomial name.

It should also be noted that it is not acceptable style to give the name of a subspecies, variety, or form as a three-word name without indicating the rank; for these three categories are all recognized, ranked in the order given, in botanical nomenclature and are not equivalent. Thus, we must say, for example, *Hydrangea paniculata* var. *grandiflora* or *Rhus glabra* f. *laciniata*, not "*Hydrangea paniculata grandiflora*" or "*Rhus glabra laciniata*."

In the original edition, authorities were not given for the scientific names used, and they are not indicated here. Some of the shrubs are of known or presumed hybrid origin, but the hybrid sign [×] is omitted. The marks indicating the accented syllable are not included in the list below.

This list is concerned only with scientific names for the plants treated. No attempt has been made to verify the accuracy of identification of the plants in the photographs or of facts stated about them. During the past 65 years, botanists have learned a great deal about the distribution and distinguishing characters of these shrubs, but obsolete statements on these matters are not altered. The alert reader will detect occasional statements which would be inadmissible in the light of modern scientific knowledge; for example, there is no "effluvium exhaled by" poison sumac "under a hot sun"—or under any other conditions, for actual physical contact with the non-volatile poisonous oil is required to produce dermatitis in sensitive persons.

The list below is based on the eighth edition of *Gray's Manual of Botany*, written by M. L. Fernald and published in 1950 (American Book Co.). Names of cultivated species, including many which grow naturally beyond the northeastern region covered by *Gray's Manual* but included by Miss Keeler, follow L. H. Bailey's *Manual of Cultivated Plants*, revised edition, published in 1949 (Macmillan Co.). In the very few instances where different names for the same plant are used in these two manuals, there is generally a brief explanatory note or both names are given. Many additional works, including monographs of certain groups, were consulted to aid in interpreting what plant was being treated by Keeler, who had available the sixth edition of *Gray's Manual* and contemporary works. In a very few cases, species are in neither of the basic manuals, Fernald or Bailey; for these, Bailey's monograph of *Rubus* (Gentes Herbarum, Vol. 5, 1941–1945) was followed for the blackberries and the Royal Horticultural Society *Dictionary of Gardening*, second edition (1956), was used for cultivated plants. The latter work also confirmed practically every disposition of a name in Bailey's manual.

In the left column appear the names used by Miss Keeler, in the same order as she treated the plants. Shrubs presently known under the same name as that indicated by Miss Keeler are not listed. As an aid in locating names, all family names are included, with the number of the page on which the treatment of each begins. A few species not considered shrubs and merely mentioned in passing, often under unrelated species, are not listed. In the several instances when Miss Keeler gave more than one scientific name for a species, the additional names are listed in parentheses in the left column.

In the right column appear the equivalent names in current use, as described in the preceding paragraphs. Sometimes these names are purely nomenclatural synonyms, the change being required solely by one or more provisions of the International Code. Sometimes the newer names result at least in part from some taxonomic judgment as to the application of a name; when these are rather generally accepted, as illustrated by the manuals cited, no distinction is made in this list between strictly nomenclatural synonyms and those which involve interpretations of plant classification. However, occasionally it has been necessary to make a more critical judgment as to the plant described by Miss Keeler and the best current name to use for it, when a strict synonym for the name she used would not apply to the plant she apparently had in mind (as interpreted, for example, on the basis of her description or statement of distribution). In these cases, a † (dagger) appears by the name to indicate that more than the usual amount of taxonomic judgment is involved and that the synonymy indicated is therefore not so straightforward.

Some errors in interpreting equivalents may have occurred, but it is hoped that the table below will be useful to the reader in supplying up-to-date names and in promoting good usage.

| ORIGINAL NOMENCLATURE | PAGE | CURRENT NOMENCLATURE |
|---|---|---|
| RANUNCULACEAE<br>*Xanthorrhiza apiifolia* | 3 | RANUNCULACEAE<br>*Xanthorhiza simplicissima* |
| MAGNOLIACEAE<br>*Magnolia conspicua*<br>*Magnolia obovata (M. purpurea; M. discolor)*<br>*Magnolia lennei* | 6 | MAGNOLIACEAE<br>*M. denudata*<br>*M. liliflora*<br><br>*M. soulangeana* var. *lennei* |
| BERBERIDACEAE<br>*Berberis aquifolium*<br>*(Mahonia aquifolia)* | 12 | BERBERIDACEAE<br>*Mahonia aquifolium* |
| CISTACEAE | 19 | CISTACEAE |
| HYPERICACEAE<br><br><br>*Hypericum prolificum* | 23 | GUTTIFERAE (Fernald),<br>HYPERICACEAE (Bailey)<br>*H. prolificum* (Although the name *H. spathulatum* is adopted in Fernald, that name has been shown to be incorrect and it is seldom used in other works.) |
| *Ascyrum hypericoides (A. crux-andreae)* | | *A. hypericoides* |
| THEACEAE<br>*Stuartia pentagyna*<br>*Gordonia pubescens (G. altamaha)* | 31 | THEACEAE<br>*Stewartia ovata*<br>*Franklinia alatamaha* (Some authors use the variant spelling *altamaha*.) |
| MALVACEAE | 36 | MALVACEAE |
| TAMARISCEAE<br>*Tamarix parvifolia (T. tetrandra, T. africana)* | 39 | TAMARICACEAE<br>†*T. parviflora* (The taxonomy of this genus has been the source of much confusion, and several of the names have been misapplied. One should consult |

# APPENDIX: NOMENCLATURAL CHANGES

| ORIGINAL NOMENCLATURE | PAGE | CURRENT NOMENCLATURE |
|---|---|---|
| | | Baileya, Vol. 15, pp. 19–25 (1967) for an up-to-date treatment of the introduced and naturalized species.) |
| *Tamarix indica* | | *T. gallica* var. *indica* |
| RUTACEAE<br>*Xanthoxylum americanum* | 43 | RUTACEAE<br>*Zanthoxylum americanum*<br>(Fernald and some other authors use the variant spelling *Xanthoxylum*.) |
| ILICINEAE [*Ilicaceae*]<br>*Ilicoides mucronata*<br>(*Nemopanthes fascicularis*) | 48 | AQUIFOLIACEAE<br>*Nemopanthus mucronatus* |
| CELASTRACEAE | 58 | CELASTRACEAE |
| RHAMNACEAE | 62 | RHAMNACEAE |
| HIPPOCASTANACEAE<br>*Aesculus parviflora* (*A. macrostachya*) | 71 | HIPPOCASTANACEAE<br>*A. parviflora* |
| STAPHYLEACEAE | 74 | STAPHYLEACEAE |
| ANACARDIACEAE<br>*Rhus hirta*<br>*Rhus glabra laciniata*<br>*Rhus vernix* (*R. venenata*)<br>*Rhus radicans* (*R. toxicodendron*)<br>*Rhus microcarpa* (*R. toxicodendron*)<br>*Rhus aromatica* (*R. canadensis*)<br>*Rhus trilobata*<br><br>*Cotinus cotinus*<br>*Cotinus cotinoides* | 78 | ANACARDIACEAE<br>*R. typhina*<br>*R. glabra* f. *laciniata*<br>*R. vernix*<br>*R. radicans* var. *radicans*<br><br>†*R. radicans* var. *rydbergii*<br><br>*R. aromatica*<br><br>†*R. aromatica* var. *serotina* and *R. trilobata*<br>*C. coggygria*<br>*C. obovatus* (Fernald), *C. americanus* (Bailey) |
| PAPILIONACEAE<br>*Laburnum vulgare* | 94 | LEGUMINOSAE<br>*L. anagyroides* |

# APPENDIX: NOMENCLATURAL CHANGES

| ORIGINAL NOMENCLATURE | PAGE | CURRENT NOMENCLATURE |
|---|---|---|
| DRUPACEAE | 107 | ROSACEAE (in part) |
| *Prunus cuneata* | | *P. susquehanae* |
| *Prunus japonica* (*P. nana, P. amygdalus*) | | *P. japonica, P. tenella,* and *P. amygdalus* (Treated as three distinct species by Bailey.) |
| ROSACEAE | 118 | ROSACEAE (in part) |
| *Spiraea salicifolia* | | †*S. alba* |
| *Spiraea triloba* | | *S. trilobata* |
| *Opulaster opulifolius* (*Physocarpus opulifolius*) | | *Physocarpus opulifolius* |
| *Exochorda grandiflora* | | *E. racemosa* |
| *Rubus strigosus* | | *R. strigosus* (By Fernald treated as *R. idaeus* var. *strigosus* and other varieties.) |
| *Rubus idaeus* | | *R. idaeus* (*R. idaeus* var. *idaeus* as classified by Fernald.) |
| *Rubus nigrobaccus* (*R. villosus*) | | *R. allegheniensis* |
| *Rubus suberectus* | | *R. canadensis* |
| *Rubus nigrobaccus sativus* | | *R. allegheniensis* |
| *Rubus randii* | | *R. canadensis* |
| *Rubus argutus* (*R. frondosus*) | | *R. argutus* and *R. frondosus* (Now treated as two distinct species.) |
| *Rubus canadensis* (*R. millspaughii*) | | *R. canadensis* |
| *Rubus allegheniensis* (*R. villosus* var. *montanus*) | | *R. allegheniensis* |
| *Rubus procumbens* (*R. canadensis*) | | *R. flagellaris* |
| *Rosa carolina* | | *R. palustris* |
| *Rosa humilis* | | *R. carolina* |
| *Rosa lucida* | | *R. virginiana* |
| *Rosa rubiginosa* | | *R. eglanteria* |
| POMACEAE | 187 | ROSACEAE (in part) |
| *Aronia arbutifolia* | | *Pyrus arbutifolia* (Fernald), *Aronia arbutifolia* (Bailey) |

# APPENDIX: NOMENCLATURAL CHANGES

| ORIGINAL NOMENCLATURE | PAGE | CURRENT NOMENCLATURE |
|---|---|---|
| *Aronia atropurpurea* | | *Pyrus floribunda* (Fernald), *Aronia prunifolia* (Bailey) |
| *Aronia nigra* | | *Pyrus melanocarpa* (Fernald), *Aronia melanocarpa* (Bailey) |
| *Amelanchier botryapium* | | †*A. arborea* |
| *Amelanchier spicata* | | †*A. stolonifera* |
| *Amelanchier rotundifolia* | | †*A. sanguinea* |
| *Amelanchier oligocarpa* | | *A. bartramiana* |
| *Cotoneaster pyracantha* (*Pyracantha coccinea*) | | *Cotoneaster pyracantha* (Fernald), *Pyracantha coccinea* (Bailey) |
| *Pyrus japonica* (*Cydonia japonica*) | | *Chaenomeles lagenaria* |
| CALYCANTHACEAE | 203 | CALYCANTHACEAE |
| *Butneria florida* (*Calycanthus floridus*) | | *Calycanthus floridus* |
| *Butneria fertilis* | | *Calycanthus fertilis* |
| HYDRANGEACEAE | 208 | SAXIFRAGACEAE (in part) |
| *Hydrangea paniculata grandiflora* | | *H. paniculata* var. *grandiflora* |
| *Philadelphus grandiflorus* | | *P. inodorus* var. *grandiflorus* (Fernald), *P. grandiflorus* (Bailey) |
| SAXIFRAGACEAE | 217 | SAXIFRAGACEAE (in part) |
| *Deutzia candidissima* | | *D. scabra* var. *candidissima* |
| *Deutzia purpurea plena* | | *D. scabra* var. *plena* |
| ITEACEAE | 221 | SAXIFRAGACEAE (in part) |
| GROSSULARIACEAE | 224 | SAXIFRAGACEAE (in part) |
| *Ribes uva-crispa* (*R. grossularia*) | | *R. grossularia* |
| *Ribes oxyacanthoides* | | †*R. hirtellum* |
| *Ribes prostratum* | | *R. glandulosum* |
| *Ribes rubrum* | | †*R. sativum* (Not native in North America; the wild plants referred to by Keeler are *R. triste*.) |

# APPENDIX: NOMENCLATURAL CHANGES

| ORIGINAL NOMENCLATURE | PAGE | CURRENT NOMENCLATURE |
|---|---|---|
| *Ribes floridum* (*R. american-um*) | | *R. americanum* |
| *Ribes aureum* | | *R. odoratum* and *R. aureum* (Now treated as two distinct species.) |
| HAMAMELIDACEAE | 238 | HAMAMELIDACEAE |
| CORNACEAE | 241 | CORNACEAE |
| *Cornus circinata* | | *C. rugosa* |
| *Cornus amomum* (*C. sericea*) | | *C. amomum* |
| *Cornus asperifolia* | | *C. drummondii* |
| *Cornus stolonifera* | | *C. stolonifera* var. *stolonifera* (Fernald), *C. stolonifera* (Bailey) |
| *Cornus candidissima* (*C. paniculata*) | | *Cornus racemosa* |
| *Cornus baileyi* | | *C. stolonifera* var. *baileyi* (Fernald), *C. baileyi* (Bailey) |
| *Cornus alba* (*C. sanguinea*) | | *C. alba* |
| CAPRIFOLIACEAE | 262 | CAPRIFOLIACEAE |
| *Sambucus pubens* (*S. racemosa*) | | *S. pubens* |
| *Viburnum alnifolium* (*V. lantanoides*) | | *V. alnifolium* |
| *Viburnum opulus* | | †*V. trilobum* (American plants.) |
| *Viburnum opulus sterilis* | | *V. opulus* var. *roseum* |
| *Viburnum paucifolium* | | *V. edule* |
| *Viburnum pubescens* | | †*V. rafinesquianum* |
| *Viburnum dentatum* | | †*V. recognitum* (Fernald), †*V. dentatum* (Bailey?) |
| *Viburnum molle* | | †*V. dentatum* (Fernald), †*V. pubescens* (Bailey, in part?) |
| *Symphoricarpos racemosus* | | *S. albus* |
| *Symphoricarpos symphoricarpos* (*S. vulgaris*) | | *S. orbiculatus* |
| *Lonicera coerulea* | | *L. villosa* (American plants.) |
| *Lonicera canadensis* (*L. ciliata*) | | *L. canadensis* |

# APPENDIX: NOMENCLATURAL CHANGES

| ORIGINAL NOMENCLATURE | PAGE | CURRENT NOMENCLATURE |
|---|---|---|
| *Lonicera tartarica* | | *L. tatarica* |
| *Diervilla trifida* (*D. diervilla*) | | *D. lonicera* |
| *Diervilla rosea* | | *Weigela florida* |
| RUBIACEAE | 308 | RUBIACEAE |
| COMPOSITAE | 311 | COMPOSITAE |
| VACCINIACEAE | 315 | ERICACEAE (in part) |
| *Gaylussacia resinosa* | | *G. baccata* |
| *Vaccinium pennsylvanicum* | | *V. angustifolium* var. *laevifolium* |
| *Vaccinium canadense* | | *V. myrtilloides* |
| *Vaccinium pennsylvanicum angustifolium* | | *V. angustifolium* var. *angustifolium* |
| *Vaccinium pennsylvanicum nigrum* | | *V. angustifolium* var. *nigrum* |
| *Vaccinium corymbosum atrococcum* | | *V. atrococcum* |
| *Vaccinium corymbosum pallidum* | | *V. corybosum* var. *glabrum* |
| *Vaccinium caespitosum* | | *V. cespitosum* |
| *Vitis-Idaea vitis-idaea* (*Vaccinium vitis-idaea*) | | *Vaccinium vitis-idaea* |
| *Polycodium stamineum* (*Vaccinium stamineum*) | | *Vaccinium stamineum* |
| *Chiogenes serpyllifolia* (*Chiogenes hispidula*) | | *Gaultheria hispidula* (Fernald), *Chiogenes hispidula* (Bailey) |
| *Oxycoccus macrocarpus* | | *Vaccinium macrocarpon* |
| *Oxycoccus oxycoccus* | | *Vaccinium oxycoccos* |
| ERICACEAE | 343 | ERICACEAE (in part) |
| *Ledum groenlandicum* (*L. latifolium*) | | *L. groenlandicum* |
| *Azalea nudiflora* | | *Rhododendron nudiflorum* |
| *Azalea canescens* | | †*Rhododendron roseum* (Fernald), †*Rhododendron nudiflorum* var. *roseum* (Bailey) |
| *Azalea lutea* (*Azalea calendulacea*) | | *Rhododendron calendulaceum* |

525

# APPENDIX: NOMENCLATURAL CHANGES

| ORIGINAL NOMENCLATURE | PAGE | CURRENT NOMENCLATURE |
|---|---|---|
| *Azalea arborescens* | | *Rhododendron arborescens* |
| *Azalea viscosa* | | *Rhododendron viscosum* |
| *Azalea pontica* | | *Rhododendron ponticum* |
| *Azalea mollis* | | *Rhododendron molle* |
| *Rhodora canadensis* | | *Rhododendron canadense* |
| *Dendrium buxifolium* (*Leiophyllum buxifolium*) | | *Leiophyllum buxifolium* |
| *Chamaecistus procumbens* | | *Loiseleuria procumbens* |
| *Kalmia glauca* | | *K. polifolia* |
| *Phyllodoce coerulea* (*Bryanthus taxifolius*) | | *Phyllodoce caerulea* |
| *Leucothoë catesbaei* | | *L. editorum* (Fernald), *L. catesbaei* (Bailey) |
| *Andromeda polifolia* | | †*A. glaucophylla* (Eastern American plants.) |
| *Pieris mariana* | | *Lyonia mariana* |
| *Xolisma ligustrina* (*Lyonia ligustrina, Andromeda ligustrina*) | | *Lyonia ligustrina* |
| *Chamaedaphne calyculata* (*Andromeda calyculata, Cassandra calyculata*) | | *Chamaedaphne calyculata* (Although all current manuals use this name, it has recently been shown that *Cassandra calyculata* is correct.) |
| *Mairania alpina* | | *Arctostaphylos alpina* |
| CLETHRACEAE | 402 | CLETHRACEAE |
| OLEACEAE | 406 | OLEACEAE |
| *Syringa Josikaea* | | *S. josikaea* |
| *Forsythia seiboldi* | | *F. suspensa* var. *sieboldii* |
| *Forsythia fortunei* | | *F. suspensa* var. *fortunei* |
| LAURACEAE | 415 | LAURACEAE |
| *Benzoin benzoin* (*Lindera benzoin*) | | *Lindera benzoin* |
| THYMELEACEAE | 419 | THYMELAEACEAE |
| ELAEAGNACEAE | 427 | ELAEAGNACEAE |
| *Elaeagnus argentea* | | *E. commutata* |
| *Elaeagnus longipes* | | *E. multiflora* |

# APPENDIX: NOMENCLATURAL CHANGES

| ORIGINAL NOMENCLATURE | PAGE | CURRENT NOMENCLATUKE |
|---|---|---|
| *Lepargyraea argentea* (*Shepherdia argentea*) | | *Shepherdia argentea* |
| *Lepargyraea canadensis* (*Shepherdia canadensis*) | | *Shepherdia canadensis* |
| LORANTHACEAE | 434 | LORANTHACEAE |
| MYRICACEAE | 437 | MYRICACEAE |
| *Myrica carolinensis* (*Merica cerifera*) | | *Myrica pensylvanica* |
| *Comptonia peregrina* (*Myrica asplenifolia*) | | *Comptonia peregrina* |
| FAGACEAE | 446 | FAGACEAE |
| BETULACEAE | 449 | CORYLACEAE (Although this name is used in most current manuals, the name Betulaceae has been conserved by an International Botanical Congress and must now be used when the family is delimited in the broad sense to include both *Betula* and *Corylus*.) |
| *Corylus rostrata* | | *C. cornuta* |
| *Betula pumila* (*B. humilis*) | | *B. pumila* var. *pumila* |
| *Betula glandulosa* | | †*B. glandulosa;* probably also *B. pumila* var. *glandulifera* |
| *Alnus incana* | | *A. rugosa* |
| *Alnus rugosa* (*A. serrulata*) | | *A. serrulata* |
| *Alnus alnobetula* (*A. viridis*) | | *A. crispa* |
| SALICACEAE | 469 | SALICACEAE |
| *Salix balsamifera* | | *S. pyrifolia* |
| *Salix glaucophylla* | | *S. glaucophylloides* var. *glaucophylla* |
| *Salix cordata* | | †*S. rigida* |
| *Salix adenophylla* | | †*S. cordata;* probably also *S. syrticola* |
| *Salix myrtilloides* | | *S. pedicellaris* |

# APPENDIX: NOMENCLATURAL CHANGES

| ORIGINAL NOMENCLATURE | PAGE | CURRENT NOMENCLATURE |
|---|---|---|
| *Salix humilis* | | *S. humilis* var. *humilis* |
| *Salix tristis* | | *S. humilis* var. *microphylla* |
| *Salix sericea* | | †*S. subsericea* |
| *Salix petiolaris* | | *S. gracilis* (But still called *S. petiolaris* by many authorities.) |
| | | |
| EMPETRACEAE | 488 | EMPETRACEAE |
| *Empetrum nigrum* | | *E. nigrum;* and probably including other recently segregated species |
| | | |
| TAXACEAE | 493 | TAXACEAE |
| *Taxus baccata fastigiata* | | *T. baccata* var. *stricta* |
| *Taxus baccata adpressa* | | *T. baccata* var. *adpressa* (Not the same as the Japanese Yew, *Taxus japonica*.) |

# INDEX OF LATIN NAMES

529

# INDEX OF LATIN NAMES

# INDEX OF ENGLISH NAMES

# INDEX OF ENGLISH NAMES

## INDEX OF ENGLISH NAMES

A CATALOGUE OF SELECTED DOVER BOOKS
IN ALL FIELDS OF INTEREST

# A CATALOGUE OF SELECTED DOVER BOOKS
## IN ALL FIELDS OF INTEREST

WHAT IS SCIENCE?, *N. Campbell*
The role of experiment and measurement, the function of mathematics, the nature of scientific laws, the difference between laws and theories, the limitations of science, and many similarly provocative topics are treated clearly and without technicalities by an eminent scientist. "Still an excellent introduction to scientific philosophy," H. Margenau in *Physics Today*. "A first-rate primer . . . deserves a wide audience," *Scientific American*. 192pp. 5⅜ x 8.
S43     Paperbound $1.25

THE NATURE OF LIGHT AND COLOUR IN THE OPEN AIR, *M. Minnaert*
Why are shadows sometimes blue, sometimes green, or other colors depending on the light and surroundings? What causes mirages? Why do multiple suns and moons appear in the sky? Professor Minnaert explains these unusual phenomena and hundreds of others in simple, easy-to-understand terms based on optical laws and the properties of light and color. No mathematics is required but artists, scientists, students, and everyone fascinated by these "tricks" of nature will find thousands of useful and amazing pieces of information. Hundreds of observational experiments are suggested which require no special equipment. 200 illustrations; 42 photos. xvi + 362pp. 5⅜ x 8.
T196     Paperbound $2.00

THE STRANGE STORY OF THE QUANTUM, AN ACCOUNT FOR THE GENERAL READER OF THE GROWTH OF IDEAS UNDERLYING OUR PRESENT ATOMIC KNOWLEDGE, *B. Hoffmann*
Presents lucidly and expertly, with barest amount of mathematics, the problems and theories which led to modern quantum physics. Dr. Hoffmann begins with the closing years of the 19th century, when certain trifling discrepancies were noticed, and with illuminating analogies and examples takes you through the brilliant concepts of Planck, Einstein, Pauli, Broglie, Bohr, Schroedinger, Heisenberg, Dirac, Sommerfeld, Feynman, etc. This edition includes a new, long postscript carrying the story through 1958. "Of the books attempting an account of the history and contents of our modern atomic physics which have come to my attention, this is the best," H. Margenau, Yale University, in *American Journal of Physics*. 32 tables and line illustrations. Index. 275pp. 5⅜ x 8.
T518     Paperbound $2.00

GREAT IDEAS OF MODERN MATHEMATICS: THEIR NATURE AND USE, *Jagjit Singh*
Reader with only high school math will understand main mathematical ideas of modern physics, astronomy, genetics, psychology, evolution, etc. better than many who use them as tools, but comprehend little of their basic structure. Author uses his wide knowledge of non-mathematical fields in brilliant exposition of differential equations, matrices, group theory, logic, statistics, problems of mathematical foundations, imaginary numbers, vectors, etc. Original publication. 2 appendixes. 2 indexes. 65 ills. 322pp. 5⅜ x 8.
T587     Paperbound $2.25

THE MUSIC OF THE SPHERES: THE MATERIAL UNIVERSE — FROM ATOM TO QUASAR, SIMPLY EXPLAINED, *Guy Murchie*

Vast compendium of fact, modern concept and theory, observed and calculated data, historical background guides intelligent layman through the material universe. Brilliant exposition of earth's construction, explanations for moon's craters, atmospheric components of Venus and Mars (with data from recent fly-by's), sun spots, sequences of star birth and death, neighboring galaxies, contributions of Galileo, Tycho Brahe, Kepler, etc.; and (Vol. 2) construction of the atom (describing newly discovered sigma and xi subatomic particles), theories of sound, color and light, space and time, including relativity theory, quantum theory, wave theory, probability theory, work of Newton, Maxwell, Faraday, Einstein, de Broglie, etc. "Best presentation yet offered to the intelligent general reader," *Saturday Review*. Revised (1967). Index. 319 illustrations by the author. Total of xx + 644pp. 5⅜ x 8½.

T1809, T1810 Two volume set, paperbound $4.00

FOUR LECTURES ON RELATIVITY AND SPACE, *Charles Proteus Steinmetz*

Lecture series, given by great mathematician and electrical engineer, generally considered one of the best popular-level expositions of special and general relativity theories and related questions. Steinmetz translates complex mathematical reasoning into language accessible to laymen through analogy, example and comparison. Among topics covered are relativity of motion, location, time; of mass; acceleration; 4-dimensional time-space; geometry of the gravitational field; curvature and bending of space; non-Euclidean geometry. Index. 40 illustrations. x + 142pp. 5⅜ x 8½.            S1771   Paperbound $1.35

HOW TO KNOW THE WILD FLOWERS, *Mrs. William Starr Dana*

Classic nature book that has introduced thousands to wonders of American wild flowers. Color-season principle of organization is easy to use, even by those with no botanical training, and the genial, refreshing discussions of history, folklore, uses of over 1,000 native and escape flowers, foliage plants are informative as well as fun to read. Over 170 full-page plates, collected from several editions, may be colored in to make permanent records of finds. Revised to conform with 1950 edition of Gray's Manual of Botany. xlii + 438pp. 5⅜ x 8½.            T332   Paperbound $2.25

MANUAL OF THE TREES OF NORTH AMERICA, *Charles Sprague Sargent*

Still unsurpassed as most comprehensive, reliable study of North American tree characteristics, precise locations and distribution. By dean of American dendrologists. Every tree native to U.S., Canada, Alaska; 185 genera, 717 species, described in detail—leaves, flowers, fruit, winterbuds, bark, wood, growth habits, etc. plus discussion of varieties and local variants, immaturity variations. Over 100 keys, including unusual 11-page analytical key to genera, aid in identification. 783 clear illustrations of flowers, fruit, leaves. An unmatched permanent reference work for all nature lovers. Second enlarged (1926) edition. Synopsis of families. Analytical key to genera. Glossary of technical terms. Index. 783 illustrations, 1 map. Total of 982pp. 5⅜ x 8.

T277, T278 Two volume set, paperbound $6.00

IT'S FUN TO MAKE THINGS FROM SCRAP MATERIALS,
*Evelyn Glantz Hershoff*
What use are empty spools, tin cans, bottle tops? What can be made from
rubber bands, clothes pins, paper clips, and buttons? This book provides
simply worded instructions and large diagrams showing you how to make
cookie cutters, toy trucks, paper turkeys, Halloween masks, telephone sets,
aprons, linoleum block- and spatter prints — in all 399 projects! Many are easy
enough for young children to figure out for themselves; some challenging
enough to entertain adults; all are remarkably ingenious ways to make things
from materials that cost pennies or less! Formerly "Scrap Fun for Everyone."
Index. 214 illustrations. 373pp. 5⅜ x 8½.          T1251    Paperbound $1.75

SYMBOLIC LOGIC and THE GAME OF LOGIC, *Lewis Carroll*
"Symbolic Logic" is not concerned with modern symbolic logic, but is instead
a collection of over 380 problems posed with charm and imagination, using
the syllogism and a fascinating diagrammatic method of drawing conclusions.
In "The Game of Logic" Carroll's whimsical imagination devises a logical game
played with 2 diagrams and counters (included) to manipulate hundreds of
tricky syllogisms. The final section, "Hit or Miss" is a lagniappe of 101 additional puzzles in the delightful Carroll manner. Until this reprint edition,
both of these books were rarities costing up to $15 each. Symbolic Logic:
Index. xxxi + 199pp. The Game of Logic: 96pp. 2 vols. bound as one. 5⅜ x 8.
                                                  T492    Paperbound $2.00

MATHEMATICAL PUZZLES OF SAM LOYD, PART I
*selected and edited by M. Gardner*
Choice puzzles by the greatest American puzzle creator and innovator. Selected
from his famous collection, "Cyclopedia of Puzzles," they retain the unique
style and historical flavor of the originals. There are posers based on arithmetic,
algebra, probability, game theory, route tracing, topology, counter and sliding
block, operations research, geometrical dissection. Includes the famous "14-15"
puzzle which was a national craze, and his "Horse of a Different Color" which
sold millions of copies. 117 of his most ingenious puzzles in all. 120 line
drawings and diagrams. Solutions. Selected references. xx + 167pp. 5⅜ x 8.
                                                  T498    Paperbound $1.25

STRING FIGURES AND HOW TO MAKE THEM, *Caroline Furness Jayne*
107 string figures plus variations selected from the best primitive and modern
examples developed by Navajo, Apache, pygmies of Africa, Eskimo, in Europe,
Australia, China, etc. The most readily understandable, easy-to-follow book in
English on perennially popular recreation. Crystal-clear exposition; step-by-
step diagrams. Everyone from kindergarten children to adults looking for
unusual diversion will be endlessly amused. Index. Bibliography. Introduction
by A. C. Haddon. 17 full-page plates, 960 illustrations. xxiii + 401pp. 5⅜ x 8½.
                                                  T152    Paperbound $2.25

PAPER FOLDING FOR BEGINNERS, *W. D. Murray and F. J. Rigney*
A delightful introduction to the varied and entertaining Japanese art of
origami (paper folding), with a full, crystal-clear text that anticipates every
difficulty; over 275 clearly labeled diagrams of all important stages in creation.
You get results at each stage, since complex figures are logically developed
from simpler ones. 43 different pieces are explained: sailboats, frogs, roosters,
etc. 6 photographic plates. 279 diagrams. 95pp. 5⅝ x 8⅜.
                                                  T713    Paperbound $1.00

PRINCIPLES OF ART HISTORY,
  *H. Wölfflin*
Analyzing such terms as "baroque," "classic," "neoclassic," "primitive," "picturesque," and 164 different works by artists like Botticelli, van Cleve, Dürer, Hobbema, Holbein, Hals, Rembrandt, Titian, Brueghel, Vermeer, and many others, the author establishes the classifications of art history and style on a firm, concrete basis. This classic of art criticism shows what really occurred between the 14th-century primitives and the sophistication of the 18th century in terms of basic attitudes and philosophies. "A remarkable lesson in the art of seeing," *Sat. Rev. of Literature.* Translated from the 7th German edition. 150 illustrations. 254pp. 6⅛ x 9¼. T276 Paperbound $2.00

PRIMITIVE ART,
  *Franz Boas*
This authoritative and exhaustive work by a great American anthropologist covers the entire gamut of primitive art. Pottery, leatherwork, metal work, stone work, wood, basketry, are treated in detail. Theories of primitive art, historical depth in art history, technical virtuosity, unconscious levels of patterning, symbolism, styles, literature, music, dance, etc. A must book for the interested layman, the anthropologist, artist, handicrafter (hundreds of unusual motifs), and the historian. Over 900 illustrations (50 ceramic vessels, 12 totem poles, etc.). 376pp. 5⅜ x 8.          T25    Paperbound $2.50

THE GENTLEMAN AND CABINET MAKER'S DIRECTOR,
  *Thomas Chippendale*
A reprint of the 1762 catalogue of furniture designs that went on to influence generations of English and Colonial and Early Republic American furniture makers. The 200 plates, most of them full-page sized, show Chippendale's designs for French (Louis XV), Gothic, and Chinese-manner chairs, sofas, canopy and dome beds, cornices, chamber organs, cabinets, shaving tables, commodes, picture frames, frets, candle stands, chimney pieces, decorations, etc. The drawings are all elegant and highly detailed; many include construction diagrams and elevations. A supplement of 24 photographs shows surviving pieces of original and Chippendale-style pieces of furniture. Brief biography of Chippendale by N. I. Bienenstock, editor of *Furniture World.* Reproduced from the 1762 edition. 200 plates, plus 19 photographic plates. vi + 249pp. 9⅛ x 12¼.          T1601    Paperbound $3.50

AMERICAN ANTIQUE FURNITURE: A BOOK FOR AMATEURS,
  *Edgar G. Miller, Jr.*
Standard introduction and practical guide to identification of valuable American antique furniture. 2115 illustrations, mostly photographs taken by the author in 148 private homes, are arranged in chronological order in extensive chapters on chairs, sofas, chests, desks, bedsteads, mirrors, tables, clocks, and other articles. Focus is on furniture accessible to the collector, including simpler pieces and a larger than usual coverage of Empire style. Introductory chapters identify structural elements, characteristics of various styles, how to avoid fakes, etc. "We are frequently asked to name some book on American furniture that will meet the requirements of the novice collector, the beginning dealer, and . . . the general public. . . . We believe Mr. Miller's two volumes more completely satisfy this specification than any other work," *Antiques.* Appendix. Index. Total of vi + 1106pp. 7⅞ x 10¾.
          T1599, T1600    Two volume set, paperbound $7.50

THE BAD CHILD'S BOOK OF BEASTS, MORE BEASTS FOR WORSE CHILDREN, and A MORAL ALPHABET, *H. Belloc*
Hardly and anthology of humorous verse has appeared in the last 50 years without at least a couple of these famous nonsense verses. But one must see the entire volumes — with all the delightful original illustrations by Sir Basil Blackwood — to appreciate fully Belloc's charming and witty verses that play so subacidly on the platitudes of life and morals that beset his day — and ours. A great humor classic. Three books in one. Total of 157pp. 5⅜ x 8.
T749   Paperbound $1.00

THE DEVIL'S DICTIONARY, *Ambrose Bierce*
Sardonic and irreverent barbs puncturing the pomposities and absurdities of American politics, business, religion, literature, and arts, by the country's greatest satirist in the classic tradition. Epigrammatic as Shaw, piercing as Swift, American as Mark Twain, Will Rogers, and Fred Allen, Bierce will always remain the favorite of a small coterie of enthusiasts, and of writers and speakers whom he supplies with "some of the most gorgeous witticisms of the English language" (H. L. Mencken). Over 1000 entries in alphabetical order. 144pp. 5⅜ x 8.   T487   Paperbound $1.00

THE COMPLETE NONSENSE OF EDWARD LEAR.
This is the only complete edition of this master of gentle madness available at a popular price. *A Book of Nonsense, Nonsense Songs, More Nonsense Songs and Stories* in their entirety with all the old favorites that have delighted children and adults for years. The Dong With A Luminous Nose, The Jumblies, The Owl and the Pussycat, and hundreds of other bits of wonderful nonsense. 214 limericks, 3 sets of Nonsense Botany, 5 Nonsense Alphabets, 546 drawings by Lear himself, and much more. 320pp. 5⅜ x 8.   T167   Paperbound $1.75

THE WIT AND HUMOR OF OSCAR WILDE, *ed. by Alvin Redman*
Wilde at his most brilliant, in 1000 epigrams exposing weaknesses and hypocrisies of "civilized" society. Divided into 49 categories—sin, wealth, women, America, etc.—to aid writers, speakers. Includes excerpts from his trials, books, plays, criticism. Formerly "The Epigrams of Oscar Wilde." Introduction by Vyvyan Holland, Wilde's only living son. Introductory essay by editor. 260pp. 5⅜ x 8.   T602   Paperbound $1.50

A CHILD'S PRIMER OF NATURAL HISTORY, *Oliver Herford*
Scarcely an anthology of whimsy and humor has appeared in the last 50 years without a contribution from Oliver Herford. Yet the works from which these examples are drawn have been almost impossible to obtain! Here at last are Herford's improbable definitions of a menagerie of familiar and weird animals, each verse illustrated by the author's own drawings. 24 drawings in 2 colors; 24 additional drawings. vii + 95pp. 6½ x 6.   T1647   Paperbound $1.00

THE BROWNIES: THEIR BOOK, *Palmer Cox*
The book that made the Brownies a household word. Generations of readers have enjoyed the antics, predicaments and adventures of these jovial sprites, who emerge from the forest at night to play or to come to the aid of a deserving human. Delightful illustrations by the author decorate nearly every page. 24 short verse tales with 266 illustrations. 155pp. 6⅝ x 9¼.
T1265   Paperbound $1.50

The Principles of Psychology,
*William James*

The full long-course, unabridged, of one of the great classics of Western literature and science. Wonderfully lucid descriptions of human mental activity, the stream of thought, consciousness, time perception, memory, imagination, emotions, reason, abnormal phenomena, and similar topics. Original contributions are integrated with the work of such men as Berkeley, Binet, Mills, Darwin, Hume, Kant, Royce, Schopenhauer, Spinoza, Locke, Descartes, Galton, Wundt, Lotze, Herbart, Fechner, and scores of others. All contrasting interpretations of mental phenomena are examined in detail—introspective analysis, philosophical interpretation, and experimental research. "A classic," *Journal of Consulting Psychology.* "The main lines are as valid as ever," *Psychoanalytical Quarterly.* "Standard reading . . . a classic of interpretation," *Psychiatric Quarterly.* 94 illustrations. 1408pp. 5⅜ x 8.

T381, T382 Two volume set, paperbound $6.00

Visual Illusions: Their Causes, Characteristics and Applications,
*M. Luckiesh*

"Seeing is deceiving," asserts the author of this introduction to virtually every type of optical illusion known. The text both describes and explains the principles involved in color illusions, figure-ground, distance illusions, etc. 100 photographs, drawings and diagrams prove how easy it is to fool the sense: circles that aren't round, parallel lines that seem to bend, stationary figures that seem to move as you stare at them — illustration after illustration strains our credulity at what we see. Fascinating book from many points of view, from applications for artists, in camouflage, etc. to the psychology of vision. New introduction by William Ittleson, Dept. of Psychology, Queens College. Index. Bibliography. xxi + 252pp. 5⅜ x 8½.  T1530 Paperbound $1.50

Fads and Fallacies in the Name of Science,
*Martin Gardner*

This is the standard account of various cults, quack systems, and delusions which have masqueraded as science: hollow earth fanatics. Reich and orgone sex energy, dianetics, Atlantis, multiple moons, Forteanism, flying saucers, medical fallacies like iridiagnosis, zone therapy, etc. A new chapter has been added on Bridey Murphy, psionics, and other recent manifestations in this field. This is a fair, reasoned appraisal of eccentric theory which provides excellent inoculation against cleverly masked nonsense. "Should be read by everyone, scientist and non-scientist alike," R. T. Birge, Prof. Emeritus of Physics, Univ. of California; Former President, American Physical Society. Index. x + 365pp. 5⅜ x 8.  T394 Paperbound $2.00

Illusions and Delusions of the Supernatural and the Occult,
*D. H. Rawcliffe*

Holds up to rational examination hundreds of persistent delusions including crystal gazing, automatic writing, table turning, mediumistic trances, mental healing, stigmata, lycanthropy, live burial, the Indian Rope Trick, spiritualism, dowsing, telepathy, clairvoyance, ghosts, ESP, etc. The author explains and exposes the mental and physical deceptions involved, making this not only an exposé of supernatural phenomena, but a valuable exposition of characteristic types of abnormal psychology. Originally titled "The Psychology of the Occult." 14 illustrations. Index. 551pp. 5⅜ x 8. T503 Paperbound $2.75

FAIRY TALE COLLECTIONS, *edited by Andrew Lang*
Andrew Lang's fairy tale collections make up the richest shelf-full of traditional children's stories anywhere available. Lang supervised the translation of stories from all over the world—familiar European tales collected by Grimm, animal stories from Negro Africa, myths of primitive Australia, stories from Russia, Hungary, Iceland, Japan, and many other countries. Lang's selection of translations are unusually high; many authorities consider that the most familiar tales find their best versions in these volumes. All collections are richly decorated and illustrated by H. J. Ford and other artists.

THE BLUE FAIRY BOOK. 37 stories. 138 illustrations. ix + 390pp. 5⅜ x 8½.
T1437     Paperbound $1.95

THE GREEN FAIRY BOOK. 42 stories. 100 illustrations. xiii + 366pp. 5⅜ x 8½.
T1439     Paperbound $1.75

THE BROWN FAIRY BOOK. 32 stories. 50 illustrations, 8 in color. xii + 350pp. 5⅜ x 8½.
T1438     Paperbound $1.95

THE BEST TALES OF HOFFMANN, *edited by E. F. Bleiler*
10 stories by E. T. A. Hoffmann, one of the greatest of all writers of fantasy. The tales include "The Golden Flower Pot," "Automata," "A New Year's Eve Adventure," "Nutcracker and the King of Mice," "Sand-Man," and others. Vigorous characterizations of highly eccentric personalities, remarkably imaginative situations, and intensely fast pacing has made these tales popular all over the world for 150 years. Editor's introduction. 7 drawings by Hoffmann. xxxiii + 419pp. 5⅜ x 8½.     T1793     Paperbound $2.25

GHOST AND HORROR STORIES OF AMBROSE BIERCE,
*edited by E. F. Bleiler*
Morbid, eerie, horrifying tales of possessed poets, shabby aristocrats, revived corpses, and haunted malefactors. Widely acknowledged as the best of their kind between Poe and the moderns, reflecting their author's inner torment and bitter view of life. Includes "Damned Thing," "The Middle Toe of the Right Foot," "The Eyes of the Panther," "Visions of the Night," "Moxon's Master," and over a dozen others. Editor's introduction. xxii + 199pp. 5⅜ x 8½.     T767     Paperbound $1.50

THREE GOTHIC NOVELS, *edited by E. F. Bleiler*
Originators of the still popular Gothic novel form, influential in ushering in early 19th-century Romanticism. Horace Walpole's *Castle of Otranto*, William Beckford's *Vathek*, John Polidori's *The Vampyre*, and a *Fragment* by Lord Byron are enjoyable as exciting reading or as documents in the history of English literature. Editor's introduction. xi + 291pp. 5⅜ x 8½.
T1232     Paperbound $2.00

BEST GHOST STORIES OF LEFANU, *edited by E. F. Bleiler*
Though admired by such critics as V. S. Pritchett, Charles Dickens and Henry James, ghost stories by the Irish novelist Joseph Sheridan LeFanu have never become as widely known as his detective fiction. About half of the 16 stories in this collection have never before been available in America. Collection includes "Carmilla" (perhaps the best vampire story ever written), "The Haunted Baronet," "The Fortunes of Sir Robert Ardagh," and the classic "Green Tea." Editor's introduction. 7 contemporary illustrations. Portrait of LeFanu. xii + 467pp. 5⅜ x 8.     T415     Paperbound $2.50

EASY-TO-DO ENTERTAINMENTS AND DIVERSIONS WITH COINS, CARDS, STRING, PAPER AND MATCHES, *R. M. Abraham*
Over 300 tricks, games and puzzles will provide young readers with absorbing fun. Sections on card games; paper-folding; tricks with coins, matches and pieces of string; games for the agile; toy-making from common household objects; mathematical recreations; and 50 miscellaneous pastimes. Anyone in charge of groups of youngsters, including hard-pressed parents, and in need of suggestions on how to keep children sensibly amused and quietly content will find this book indispensable. Clear, simple text, copious number of delightful line drawings and illustrative diagrams. Originally titled "Winter Nights' Entertainments." Introduction by Lord Baden Powell. 329 illustrations. v + 186pp. 5⅜ x 8½. T921 Paperbound $1.00

AN INTRODUCTION TO CHESS MOVES AND TACTICS SIMPLY EXPLAINED, *Leonard Barden*
Beginner's introduction to the royal game. Names, possible moves of the pieces, definitions of essential terms, how games are won, etc. explained in 30-odd pages. With this background you'll be able to sit right down and play. Balance of book teaches strategy — openings, middle game, typical endgame play, and suggestions for improving your game. A sample game is fully analyzed. True middle-level introduction, teaching you all the essentials without oversimplifying or losing you in a maze of detail. 58 figures. 102pp. 5⅜ x 8½. T1210 Paperbound $1.25

LASKER'S MANUAL OF CHESS, *Dr. Emanuel Lasker*
Probably the greatest chess player of modern times, Dr. Emanuel Lasker held the world championship 28 years, independent of passing schools or fashions. This unmatched study of the game, chiefly for intermediate to skilled players, analyzes basic methods, combinations, position play, the aesthetics of chess, dozens of different openings, etc., with constant reference to great modern games. Contains a brilliant exposition of Steinitz's important theories. Introduction by Fred Reinfeld. Tables of Lasker's tournament record. 3 indices. 308 diagrams. 1 photograph. xxx + 349pp. 5⅜ x 8. T640 Paperbound $2.50

COMBINATIONS: THE HEART OF CHESS, *Irving Chernev*
Step-by-step from simple combinations to complex, this book, by a well-known chess writer, shows you the intricacies of pins, counter-pins, knight forks, and smothered mates. Other chapters show alternate lines of play to those taken in actual championship games; boomerang combinations; classic examples of brilliant combination play by Nimzovich, Rubinstein, Tarrasch, Botvinnik, Alekhine and Capablanca. Index. 356 diagrams. ix + 245pp. 5⅜ x 8½. T1744 Paperbound $2.00

HOW TO SOLVE CHESS PROBLEMS, *K. S. Howard*
Full of practical suggestions for the fan or the beginner — who knows only the moves of the chessmen. Contains preliminary section and 58 two-move, 46 three-move, and 8 four-move problems composed by 27 outstanding American problem creators in the last 30 years. Explanation of all terms and exhaustive index. "Just what is wanted for the student," Brian Harley. 112 problems, solutions. vi + 171pp. 5⅜ x 8. T748 Paperbound $1.35

SOCIAL THOUGHT FROM LORE TO SCIENCE,
*H. E. Barnes and H. Becker*
An immense survey of sociological thought and ways of viewing, studying, planning, and reforming society from earliest times to the present. Includes thought on society of preliterate peoples, ancient non-Western cultures, and every great movement in Europe, America, and modern Japan. Analyzes hundreds of great thinkers: Plato, Augustine, Bodin, Vico, Montesquieu, Herder, Comte, Marx, etc. Weighs the contributions of utopians, sophists, fascists and communists; economists, jurists, philosophers, ecclesiastics, and every 19th and 20th century school of scientific sociology, anthropology, and social psychology throughout the world. Combines topical, chronological, and regional approaches, treating the evolution of social thought as a process rather than as a series of mere topics. "Impressive accuracy, competence, and discrimination . . . easily the best single survey," *Nation*. Thoroughly revised, with new material up to 1960. 2 indexes. Over 2200 bibliographical notes. Three volume set. Total of 1586pp. 5⅜ x 8.

T901, T902, T903　　Three volume set, paperbound $9.00

A HISTORY OF HISTORICAL WRITING, *Harry Elmer Barnes*
Virtually the only adequate survey of the whole course of historical writing in a single volume. Surveys developments from the beginnings of historiography in the ancient Near East and the Classical World, up through the Cold War. Covers major historians in detail, shows interrelationship with cultural background, makes clear individual contributions, evaluates and estimates importance; also enormously rich upon minor authors and thinkers who are usually passed over. Packed with scholarship and learning, clear, easily written. Indispensable to every student of history. Revised and enlarged up to 1961. Index and bibliography. xv + 442pp. 5⅜ x 8½.

T104　　Paperbound $2.50

JOHANN SEBASTIAN BACH, *Philipp Spitta*
The complete and unabridged text of the definitive study of Bach. Written some 70 years ago, it is still unsurpassed for its coverage of nearly all aspects of Bach's life and work. There could hardly be a finer non-technical introduction to Bach's music than the detailed, lucid analyses which Spitta provides for hundreds of individual pieces. 26 solid pages are devoted to the B minor mass, for example, and 30 pages to the glorious St. Matthew Passion. This monumental set also includes a major analysis of the music of the 18th century: Buxtehude, Pachelbel, etc. "Unchallenged as the last word on one of the supreme geniuses of music," John Barkham, *Saturday Review Syndicate*. Total of 1819pp. Heavy cloth binding. 5⅜ x 8.

T252　　Two volume set, clothbound $15.00

BEETHOVEN AND HIS NINE SYMPHONIES, *George Grove*
In this modern middle-level classic of musicology Grove not only analyzes all nine of Beethoven's symphonies very thoroughly in terms of their musical structure, but also discusses the circumstances under which they were written, Beethoven's stylistic development, and much other background material. This is an extremely rich book, yet very easily followed; it is highly recommended to anyone seriously interested in music. Over 250 musical passages. Index. viii + 407pp. 5⅜ x 8.

T334　　Paperbound $2.25

THREE SCIENCE FICTION NOVELS,
*John Taine*
Acknowledged by many as the best SF writer of the 1920's, Taine (under the name Eric Temple Bell) was also a Professor of Mathematics of considerable renown. Reprinted here are *The Time Stream*, generally considered Taine's best, *The Greatest Game*, a biological-fiction novel, and *The Purple Sapphire*, involving a supercivilization of the past. Taine's stories tie fantastic narratives to frameworks of original and logical scientific concepts. Speculation is often profound on such questions as the nature of time, concept of entropy, cyclical universes, etc. 4 contemporary illustrations. v + 532pp. 5⅜ x 8⅜.
                                    T1180    Paperbound $2.00

SEVEN SCIENCE FICTION NOVELS,
*H. G. Wells*
Full unabridged texts of 7 science-fiction novels of the master. Ranging from biology, physics, chemistry, astronomy, to sociology and other studies, Mr. Wells extrapolates whole worlds of strange and intriguing character. "One will have to go far to match this for entertainment, excitement, and sheer pleasure . . ."*New York Times*. Contents: The Time Machine, The Island of Dr. Moreau, The First Men in the Moon, The Invisible Man, The War of the Worlds, The Food of the Gods, In The Days of the Comet. 1015pp. 5⅜ x 8.
                                    T264    Clothbound $5.00

28 SCIENCE FICTION STORIES OF H. G. WELLS.
Two full, unabridged novels, *Men Like Gods* and *Star Begotten*, plus 26 short stories by the master science-fiction writer of all time! Stories of space, time, invention, exploration, futuristic adventure. Partial contents: *The Country of the Blind, In the Abyss, The Crystal Egg, The Man Who Could Work Miracles, A Story of Days to Come, The Empire of the Ants, The Magic Shop, The Valley of the Spiders, A Story of the Stone Age, Under the Knife, Sea Raiders*, etc. An indispensable collection for the library of anyone interested in science fiction adventure. 928pp. 5⅜ x 8.        T265    Clothbound $5.00

THREE MARTIAN NOVELS,
*Edgar Rice Burroughs*
Complete, unabridged reprinting, in one volume, of Thuvia, Maid of Mars; Chessmen of Mars; The Master Mind of Mars. Hours of science-fiction adventure by a modern master storyteller. Reset in large clear type for easy reading. 16 illustrations by J. Allen St. John. vi + 490pp. 5⅜ x 8½.
                                    T39    Paperbound $2.50

AN INTELLECTUAL AND CULTURAL HISTORY OF THE WESTERN WORLD,
*Harry Elmer Barnes*
Monumental 3-volume survey of intellectual development of Europe from primitive cultures to the present day. Every significant product of human intellect traced through history: art, literature, mathematics, physical sciences, medicine, music, technology, social sciences, religions, jurisprudence, education, etc. Presentation is lucid and specific, analyzing in detail specific discoveries, theories, literary works, and so on. Revised (1965) by recognized scholars in specialized fields under the direction of Prof. Barnes. Revised bibliography. Indexes. 24 illustrations. Total of xxix + 1318pp.
          T1275, T1276, T1277    Three volume set, paperbound $7.50

HEAR ME TALKIN' TO YA, *edited by Nat Shapiro and Nat Hentoff*
In their own words, Louis Armstrong, King Oliver, Fletcher Henderson, Bunk Johnson, Bix Beiderbecke, Billy Holiday, Fats Waller, Jelly Roll Morton, Duke Ellington, and many others comment on the origins of jazz in New Orleans and its growth in Chicago's South Side, Kansas City's jam sessions, Depression Harlem, and the modernism of the West Coast schools. Taken from taped conversations, letters, magazine articles, other first-hand sources. Editors' introduction. xvi + 429pp. 5⅜ x 8½.        T1726    Paperbound $2.00

THE JOURNAL OF HENRY D. THOREAU
A 25-year record by the great American observer and critic, as complete a record of a great man's inner life as is anywhere available. Thoreau's Journals served him as raw material for his formal pieces, as a place where he could develop his ideas, as an outlet for his interests in wild life and plants, in writing as an art, in classics of literature, Walt Whitman and other contemporaries, in politics, slavery, individual's relation to the State, etc. The Journals present a portrait of a remarkable man, and are an observant social history. Unabridged republication of 1906 edition, Bradford Torrey and Francis H. Allen, editors. Illustrations. Total of 1888pp. 8⅜ x 12¼.
                    T312, T313    Two volume set, clothbound $25.00

A SHAKESPEARIAN GRAMMAR, *E. A. Abbott*
Basic reference to Shakespeare and his contemporaries, explaining through thousands of quotations from Shakespeare, Jonson, Beaumont and Fletcher, North's *Plutarch* and other sources the grammatical usage differing from the modern. First published in 1870 and written by a scholar who spent much of his life isolating principles of Elizabethan language, the book is unlikely ever to be superseded. Indexes. xxiv + 511pp. 5⅜ x 8½. T1582 Paperbound $2.75

FOLK-LORE OF SHAKESPEARE, *T. F. Thistelton Dyer*
Classic study, drawing from Shakespeare a large body of references to supernatural beliefs, terminology of falconry and hunting, games and sports, good luck charms, marriage customs, folk medicines, superstitions about plants, animals, birds, argot of the underworld, sexual slang of London, proverbs, drinking customs, weather lore, and much else. From full compilation comes a mirror of the 17th-century popular mind. Index. ix + 526pp. 5⅜ x 8½.
                    T1614    Paperbound $2.75

THE NEW VARIORUM SHAKESPEARE, *edited by H. H. Furness*
By far the richest editions of the plays ever produced in any country or language. Each volume contains complete text (usually First Folio) of the play, all variants in Quarto and other Folio texts, editorial changes by every major editor to Furness's own time (1900), footnotes to obscure references or language, extensive quotes from literature of Shakespearian criticism, essays on plot sources (often reprinting sources in full), and much more.

HAMLET, *edited by H. H. Furness*
Total of xxvi + 905pp. 5⅜ x 8½.
                    T1004, T1005    Two volume set, paperbound $5.25

TWELFTH NIGHT, *edited by H. H. Furness*
Index. xxii + 434pp. 5⅜ x 8½.                    T1189    Paperbound $2.75

LA BOHEME BY GIACOMO PUCCINI,
*translated and introduced by Ellen H. Bleiler*
Complete handbook for the operagoer, with everything needed for full enjoyment except the musical score itself. Complete Italian libretto, with new, modern English line-by-line translation—the only libretto printing all repeats; biography of Puccini; the librettists; background to the opera, Murger's La Boheme, etc.; circumstances of composition and performances; plot summary; and pictorial section of 73 illustrations showing Puccini, famous singers and performances, etc. Large clear type for easy reading. 124pp. 5⅜ x 8½.
T404    Paperbound $1.25

ANTONIO STRADIVARI: HIS LIFE AND WORK (1644-1737),
*W. Henry Hill, Arthur F. Hill, and Alfred E. Hill*
Still the only book that really delves into life and art of the incomparable Italian craftsman, maker of the finest musical instruments in the world today. The authors, expert violin-makers themselves, discuss Stradivari's ancestry, his construction and finishing techniques, distinguished characteristics of many of his instruments and their locations. Included, too, is story of introduction of his instruments into France, England, first revelation of their supreme merit, and information on his labels, number of instruments made, prices, mystery of ingredients of his varnish, tone of pre-1684 Stradivari violin and changes between 1684 and 1690. An extremely interesting, informative account for all music lovers, from craftsman to concert-goer. Republication of original (1902) edition. New introduction by Sydney Beck, Head of Rare Book and Manuscript Collections, Music Division, New York Public Library. Analytical index by Rembert Wurlitzer. Appendixes. 68 illustrations. 30 full-page plates. 4 in color. xxvi + 315pp. 5⅜ x 8½.    T425    Paperbound $2.25

MUSICAL AUTOGRAPHS FROM MONTEVERDI TO HINDEMITH,
*Emanuel Winternitz*
For beauty, for intrinsic interest, for perspective on the composer's personality, for subtleties of phrasing, shading, emphasis indicated in the autograph but suppressed in the printed score, the mss. of musical composition are fascinating documents which repay close study in many different ways. This 2-volume work reprints facsimiles of mss. by virtually every major composer, and many minor figures—196 examples in all. A full text points out what can be learned from mss., analyzes each sample. Index. Bibliography. 18 figures. 196 plates. Total of 170pp. of text. 7⅞ x 10¾.
T1312, T1313    Two volume set, paperbound $5.00

J. S. BACH,
*Albert Schweitzer*
One of the few great full-length studies of Bach's life and work, and the study upon which Schweitzer's renown as a musicologist rests. On first appearance (1911), revolutionized Bach performance. The only writer on Bach to be musicologist, performing musician, and student of history, theology and philosophy, Schweitzer contributes particularly full sections on history of German Protestant church music, theories on motivic pictorial representations in vocal music, and practical suggestions for performance. Translated by Ernest Newman. Indexes. 5 illustrations. 650 musical examples. Total of xix + 928pp. 5⅜ x 8½.    T1631, T1632    Two volume set, paperbound $4.50

THE METHODS OF ETHICS, *Henry Sidgwick*
Propounding no organized system of its own, study subjects every major
methodological approach to ethics to rigorous, objective analysis. Study discusses and relates ethical thought of Plato, Aristotle, Bentham, Clarke, Butler,
Hobbes, Hume, Mill, Spencer, Kant, and dozens of others. Sidgwick retains
conclusions from each system which follow from ethical premises, rejecting
the faulty. Considered by many in the field to be among the most important
treatises on ethical philosophy. Appendix. Index. xlvii + 528pp. 5⅜ x 8½.
                                                    T1608    Paperbound $2.50

TEUTONIC MYTHOLOGY, *Jakob Grimm*
A milestone in Western culture; the work which established on a modern
basis the study of history of religions and comparative religions. 4-volume
work assembles and interprets everything available on religious and folk-
loristic beliefs of Germanic people (including Scandinavians, Anglo-Saxons,
etc.). Assembling material from such sources as Tacitus, surviving Old Norse
and Icelandic texts, archeological remains, folktales, surviving superstitions,
comparative traditions, linguistic analysis, etc. Grimm explores pagan deities,
heroes, folklore of nature, religious practices, and every other area of pagan
German belief. To this day, the unrivaled, definitive, exhaustive study. Translated by J. S. Stallybrass from 4th (1883) German edition. Indexes. Total of
lxxvii + 1887pp. 5⅜ x 8½.
            T1602, T1603, T1604, T1605   Four volume set, paperbound $11.00

THE I CHING, *translated by James Legge*
Called "The Book of Changes" in English, this is one of the Five Classics
edited by Confucius, basic and central to Chinese thought. Explains perhaps
the most complex system of divination known, founded on the theory that all
things happening at any one time have characteristic features which can be
isolated and related. Significant in Oriental studies, in history of religions and
philosophy, and also to Jungian psychoanalysis and other areas of modern
European thought. Index. Appendixes. 6 plates. xxi + 448pp. 5⅜ x 8½.
                                                    T1062    Paperbound $2.75

HISTORY OF ANCIENT PHILOSOPHY, *W. Windelband*
One of the clearest, most accurate comprehensive surveys of Greek and Roman
philosophy. Discusses ancient philosophy in general, intellectual life in Greece
in the 7th and 6th centuries B.C., Thales, Anaximander, Anaximenes, Herac-
litus, the Eleatics, Empedocles, Anaxagoras, Leucippus, the Pythagoreans, the
Sophists, Socrates, Democritus (20 pages), Plato (50 pages), Aristotle (70 pages),
the Peripatetics, Stoics, Epicureans, Sceptics, Neo-platonists, Christian Apolo-
gists, etc. 2nd German edition translated by H. E. Cushman. xv + 393pp.
5⅜ x 8.                                           T357    Paperbound $2.25

THE PALACE OF PLEASURE, *William Painter*
Elizabethan versions of Italian and French novels from *The Decameron*,
Cinthio, Straparola, Queen Margaret of Navarre, and other continental sources
— the very work that provided Shakespeare and dozens of his contemporaries
with many of their plots and sub-plots and, therefore, justly considered one of
the most influential books in all English literature. It is also a book that any
reader will still enjoy. Total of cviii + 1,224pp.
            T1691, T1692, T1693   Three volume set, paperbound $6.75

THE WONDERFUL WIZARD OF OZ, *L. F. Baum*
All the original W. W. Denslow illustrations in full color—as much a part of
"The Wizard" as Tenniel's drawings are of "Alice in Wonderland." "The
Wizard" is still America's best-loved fairy tale, in which, as the author expresses
it, "The wonderment and joy are retained and the heartaches and nightmares
left out." Now today's young readers can enjoy every word and wonderful picture of the original book. New introduction by Martin Gardner. A Baum
bibliography. 23 full-page color plates. viii + 268pp. 5⅜ x 8.
T691     Paperbound $1.75

THE MARVELOUS LAND OF OZ, *L. F. Baum*
This is the equally enchanting sequel to the "Wizard," continuing the adventures of the Scarecrow and the Tin Woodman. The hero this time is a little
boy named Tip, and all the delightful Oz magic is still present. This is the
Oz book with the Animated Saw-Horse, the Woggle-Bug, and Jack Pumpkin-
head. All the original John R. Neill illustrations, 10 in full color. 287pp.
5⅜ x 8.                                      T692     Paperbound $1.75

ALICE'S ADVENTURES UNDER GROUND, *Lewis Carroll*
The original *Alice in Wonderland*, hand-lettered and illustrated by Carroll
himself, and originally presented as a Christmas gift to a child-friend. Adults
as well as children will enjoy this charming volume, reproduced faithfully
in this Dover edition. While the story is essentially the same, there are slight
changes, and Carroll's spritely drawings present an intriguing alternative to
the famous Tenniel illustrations. One of the most popular books in Dover's
catalogue. Introduction by Martin Gardner. 38 illustrations. 128pp. 5⅜ x 8½.
T1482     Paperbound $1.00

THE NURSERY "ALICE," *Lewis Carroll*
While most of us consider *Alice in Wonderland* a story for children of all
ages, Carroll himself felt it was beyond younger children. He therefore provided this simplified version, illustrated with the famous Tenniel drawings
enlarged and colored in delicate tints, for children aged "from Nought to
Five." Dover's edition of this now rare classic is a faithful copy of the 1889
printing, including 20 illustrations by Tenniel, and front and back covers
reproduced in full color. Introduction by Martin Gardner. xxiii + 67pp.
6⅛ x 9¼.                                     T1610     Paperbound $1.75

THE STORY OF KING ARTHUR AND HIS KNIGHTS, *Howard Pyle*
A fast-paced, exciting retelling of the best known Arthurian legends for young
readers by one of America's best story tellers and illustrators. The sword
Excalibur, wooing of Guinevere, Merlin and his downfall, adventures of Sir
Pellias and Gawaine, and others. The pen and ink illustrations are vividly
imagined and wonderfully drawn. 41 illustrations. xviii + 313pp. 6⅛ x 9¼.
T1445     Paperbound $1.75

*Prices subject to change without notice.*

Available at your book dealer or write for free catalogue to Dept. Adsci,
Dover Publications, Inc., 180 Varick St., N.Y., N.Y. 10014. Dover publishes more
than 150 books each year on science, elementary and advanced mathematics,
biology, music, art, literary history, social sciences and other areas.